VENEZUELA

VENEZUELA

Tarnished Democracy

Daniel C. Hellinger

Westview Press

BOULDER • SAN FRANCISCO • OXFORD

Westview Profiles/Nations of Contemporary Latin America

Published in 1991 in the United States of America by Westview Press, Inc., 5500 Central Avenue, Boulder, Colorado 80301, and in the United Kingdom by Westview Press, 36 Lonsdale Road, Summertown, Oxford OX2 7EW

Library of Congress Cataloging-in-Publication Data
Hellinger, Daniel.
    Venezuela : tarnished democracy / Daniel C. Hellinger.
       p.   cm. — (Westview profiles. Nations of contemporary Latin America)
    Includes bibliographical references and index.
    ISBN 0-8133-0700-7
    1. Venezuela—Politics and government—1935–   . 2. Venezuela—Economic conditions—1958–   . 3. Representative government and representation—Venezuela—History—20th century.   4. Political participation—Venezuela—History—20th century.   I. Title.
II. Series.
F2326.H36   1991
987.06′3—dc20   90-29009
                                                             CIP

Printed and bound in the United States of America

The paper used in this publication meets the requirements of the American National Standard for Permanence of Paper for Printed Library Materials Z39.48-1984.

10   9   8   7   6   5   4   3   2   1

Contents

Political Aftermath of the Riots, 193
Conclusion, 197

Tables and Illustrations

Foreword

When the subject is democratic political development in Latin America during the present generation, the country that comes most often to mind is Venezuela—by a wide margin. Drama is added by the fact that in this fifth most populous of South American countries democracy was scarcely known until the end of World War II. Then an all too brief three-year blooming was abruptly cut short under the shadow of the cold war, with a decade of authoritarian dictatorship ensuing. Yet since 1958 Simon Bolívar's homeland—long noted as the land of despotic caudillo dictators such as the legendary Juan Vicente Gómez (1908–1936)—has undergone a profound political transformation.

Time and again Latin America presents us with the oft perplexingly contradictory results stemming from application of either absolute or relative standards. From the first of these two perspectives, Venezuela is the only Latin American country to have institutionalized a stable and politically democratic system during a period in which most others passed through prolonged authoritarian experiences and encountered substantial turbulence. Moreover, it stands behind only much smaller Costa Rica and Uruguay in terms of democratic political processes at the present time. Still, when it comes to approximating an ideal model of a socially just nation, Venezuela leaves much to be desired.

From a comparative perspective the Venezuelan case affords a rich and fascinating contrast with the experience of each of the other major Latin American countries over the span of the past thirty-odd years. Since 1959, seven honest and highly competitive presidential elections have taken place in this part Andean, part Caribbean nation—with the opposition winning and smoothly assuming power four times. Clearly this contrasts dramatically with Cuba's single-party monopoly under Fidel Castro during the same period. Venezuela's vibrant electoral politics and active parliamentary life are also a far cry from the governing party's resort to force to hold onto power in Mexico, Argentina's alternation between military and civilian rule, and Brazil's prolonged gap between direct presidential elections (from 1960 to 1989). And although Venezuela has remained free from the manifold evils of narcopolitics that have plagued its neighbor Colombia—as well as Peru, Bolivia, and Panama— its failure to meet the needs of the base of the social pyramid have tarnished Venezuela's democratic reputation. Although its performance in this realm does not lag behind most other Latin American nations, Venezuela's stability and relative wealth justify higher expectations and the application of more rigorous standards.

Daniel Hellinger, who has devoted himself to the close study of Venezuela since the late 1970s, appropriately raises the fundamental question of whether Venezuela is currently moving in the direction of increased social justice rather than resting on its laurels as a dramatic example of political development. This focus involves him in a careful analysis of the Venezuelan model of political economy and examination of the democratic government's management of economic development. Because oil is at the center of this story, the author weaves it into his essentially chronological narrative. And as the petroleum question and oil policy have fundamentally international roots, Venezuela's foreign affairs are also built into the central exposition, not treated in a separate chapter. For internationally Venezuela's essential, indeed, almost exclusive, importance is as a major oil producer. OPEC was founded and to a considerable degree forged under Venezuelan leadership, and the country's influence in regional as well as global affairs rises and falls with the tide of uncertainty regarding the continuing availability of Middle East crude.

A sophisticated social scientist and thorough scholar, Professor Hellinger has dug deeply into the literature by both foreign and Venezuelan authors. His notes constitute an invaluable guide to this rich body of materials. His essential view is that the post-1958 model, although having accomplished much, has probably run out of steam and that new vehicles for participation will have to push much of the established party-dominated system aside if the legitimate demands of the Venezuelan masses are to be met. Although not specifically predicting the course of future events, the author does point out that the dominant forces of patronage populism face a challenge from both the neoliberals on the Right and the "New Left." His probing diagnosis of the present situation is particularly appropriate given the fact that the incumbent administration—once again under the baton of the 1974–1978 chief executive— is scheduled to run through 1993. Readers wishing to be equipped to understand all that may take place in Venezuelan national life to that point, or even beyond, will find their needs amply satisfied by *Venezuela:*

Tarnished Democracy. Those interested in knowing in what ways Venezuela is similar to and different from the other "Nations of Contemporary Latin America" will be equally rewarded.

Ronald Schneider
Queens College

Preface

Venezuela has received relatively little attention from North American social scientists and historians since the 1960s. We have been more preoccupied with the military regimes of the Southern Cone and Brazil, the gathering crisis in Mexico, and the outbreak of revolution in Central America. This is unfortunate because the opportunity created by the oil boom makes the Venezuelan democratic experience an important one for assessing whether electoral democracy can manage economic development under relatively favorable circumstances.

Venezuela is often compared by defenders of liberal democracy to Cuba, where the revolutionary overthrow of Batista came only one year after the Venezuelan people routed their last dictator in 1958. Cold warriors tend to overlook or excuse the painfully obvious deficiencies of Venezuelan democracy for fear of implying the superiority of the Cuban model. Likewise, defenders of the Cuban Revolution tend to treat Venezuelan democracy as little more than a sham, as though the post-1958 regimes have done little better in terms of human rights than the military dictatorships that overwhelmed democracy almost everywhere else in Latin America since 1958.

Both schools of thought forget that democracy is not something designed and implemented at one point in time but something to be developed and nurtured. The key question today in Venezuela is not "What if we had chosen the Cuban path?" but "How can the democratic gains of 1958 be defended, deepened, and expanded in the face of an economic crisis?" This question requires thoughtful reflection and historical study, not ideological polemics designed to reflect well or badly on another system that has its own faults and advantages.

I would like to thank those who have helped me think this question through, although of course I absolve them of any responsibility for errors or conclusions that seem foolhardy in this book. Among Venezuelans, I owe a special debt to José Arrieta, Luis Salomón Barrios,

Fernando Coronil, Carlos Eduardo Febres, Makram Haluani, Arturo Sosa A., and Edwin Zambrano Vidal. In particular, I would like to thank Dorothea Melcher and Bernard Mommer for their indispensable commentary on the history of oil in Venezuela. Among North American scholars, I especially thank Robert Kaufman, Jennifer McCoy, and Julie Skurski. Ron Schneider's close reading and constructive criticism served me well. Thomas Goodwin and Virginia Copeland of Page Crafters, Inc., generously provided help with tables and graphics, and Joann Eng-Hellinger gave useful editorial advice. I am grateful for the cooperation of many at Westview, in particular Barbara Ellington, Jane Raese, Mick Gusinde-Duffy, and Stephen Haenel. I must add a special word of thanks to Robert Alexander of Rutgers University, who encouraged me back in 1978 to tag along with him on one of his trips to Venezuela and introduced me to the Venezuelan people for whom we share such great affection.

I would like to dedicate this book to my mother and father, Elizabeth (Van Prooyen) Hellinger and Ernest Hellinger, especially for giving me the gift of education.

Daniel C. Hellinger

1

Introduction: The Venezuelan Model

The Spaniards who first viewed the native huts on stilts above Lake Maracaibo in 1499 called the area "Venezuela," after Venice. They noticed that the natives in the lake region used a black, sticky tar emanating from the waters to repair and caulk their canoes. The Spanish bottled some of the substance, called it "Devil's Excrement," and shipped it back to Europe for sale as a cure for gout. However, they quickly lost interest in its commercial possibilities.[1]

A little more than 400 years and one industrial revolution later, "Devil's Excrement" became the object of a worldwide search by Europeans and North Americans. The search intensified after World War I, which demonstrated that national power in the industrial era required access to oil. British, Dutch, German, and North American companies, backed by their governments, competed with one another for control of the "black gold." They sent their ships to Venezuela's shores carrying explorers—this time geologists—and warriors. Unlike the Spanish who perished seeking El Dorado in the upper reaches of the Orinoco, the modern conquistadors found what they sought.

Fifty years ago the oil derricks stood in enclaves isolated from the poverty-stricken, underpopulated, rural society around them. For 120 years of independence, Venezuelans had known almost solely civil war and dictatorships. Today huge petrochemical, steel, aluminum, and other industrial plants loom where once stood only isolated villages plagued by malaria and inhabited by machete-wielding campesinos or combative cowboys. A nation with no prior experience with stable, constitutional democratic government has experienced seven consecutive electoral transitions since 1958 and vigorously promotes itself, with the approval of the United States, as a model to be emulated elsewhere in the hemisphere.[2]

The Venezuelan experiment with democracy began in 1958 with the overthrow of General Marcos Pérez Jiménez in a military coup

1

supported by street fighting and a general strike. Following elections, President Rómulo Betancourt and his *Acción Democrática* (AD) political party survived both military uprisings and a leftist guerrilla insurrection. Many North American scholars saw in the Betancourt government the apotheosis of the type of reformism championed by the Kennedy administration's Alliance for Progress, an alternative to Cuban-style revolution. President José Napoleón Duarte, whom the United States promoted as a reformist option in El Salvador in the 1980s, once remarked, "We are following the Venezuelan example, and I am Rómulo Betancourt."[3]

On December 4, 1988, the Venezuelan electorate, for the seventh time since 1958, went to the polls to elect a president and a congress. Despite five years of austerity under President Jaime Lusinchi of AD, another *adeco* (member of AD), Carlos Andrés Pérez, won a landslide victory, the first time that the incumbent party had managed to retain control of the presidency since 1963. Pérez and his main opponent, Christian Democrat Eduardo Fernández, praised the Venezuelan people for the orderly and peaceful conduct of the election, citing it as evidence of the political maturity and stability of the system. The election seemed to demonstrate that democracy would survive the stresses of the new age of austerity that arrived with the collapse of world oil prices in the 1980s.

Ninety percent of Venezuela's exports and 75 percent of the government revenues are derived from the petroleum industry. Governments have tried to "sow the petroleum" in productive economic development with mixed success. State enterprises created by investments generated from petroleum exports were responsible for nearly 30 percent of the gross national product (GNP) in 1982.[4] However, even where the growth has been most dynamic—in petrochemical, steel, aluminum, and other metallurgical industries—the dependence on oil remains. For example, the Central Bank expected in 1985 that 90 percent of investment for expansion of the aluminum industry would come from the state, which continues to derive most of its revenues from oil exports.[5]

As repository and dispenser of oil export earnings and an active regulator of private sector employment, the state plays a key role in determining who benefits and loses in the Venezuelan economy. In 1982 approximately one-third of the work force was employed by the government, autonomous institutes of the government, and publicly owned enterprises. Ten percent of the workers outside of services and the petroleum sector are employed by companies controlled by the state. Politics greatly influences the distribution of income among social classes, but the overall direction of wages seems to be tied closely to the rise and fall of oil prices. Between 1968 and 1978, when income from oil exports rose 15.4 percent on an average annual basis, the average increase in real earning power of Venezuelan workers rose 4.2 percent. Between 1978 and 1984, when petroleum income fell by 5.4 percent on an annual basis, the real income of workers fell on an average by 5.1 percent.[6]

Although electoral abstention increased, little about the 1988 campaign or election suggested that the economic crisis was breeding political instability. Suddenly, on February 27, 1989, eleven days after Pérez announced a package of austerity measures demanded by the International Monetary Fund, the Venezuelan people launched a violent social explosion that shocked the bankers, the U.S. government, and their own political leaders. The government claimed that 300 died, but other estimates placed the number of fatalities between 800 and 1,000 after a week of violence in nineteen cities. Ten thousand troops were needed to suppress the revolt in Caracas, where one-third of all supermarkets had been looted. An estimated 2,900 businesses were damaged or destroyed nationwide, resulting in an estimated US$1.5 billion in losses for insured and uninsured businesses. Commented a reporter for the prestigious Caracas daily, *El Nacional*, "Yesterday, Caracas was Beirut."[7]

Venezuela, which had outlasted an epoch of military dictatorships and revolution elsewhere in the hemisphere, could no longer be deemed an exceptional case. It is clear that government can no longer rely on petroleum to lubricate the clashing gears of populist politics.

LAND AND PEOPLE

Above the oil, within an area approximately the size of Texas and Oklahoma (352,150 square miles), lives a population officially estimated in 1986 at nearly 18 million, but perhaps as large as 20 million once illegal immigrants (mostly Colombian) are counted. Four times each day, Venezuela's television stations are required to broadcast the national anthem. As they do so, Venezuelans are shown the majesty and diversity of their land, which includes imposing mountains and glaciers, glorious Caribbean beaches, spectacular tropical jungles (wherein lies Angel Falls, highest in the world), the metropolis of Caracas, the broad horizons of the central plains, and the massive waters of the Orinoco River, which drains 90 percent of the nation's territory.

Speculative estimates of Venezuela's pre-Columbian population place it at approximately 350,000 inhabitants. Nomadic peoples, whose economy was based on hunting, gathering, and fishing, inhabited parts of the tropical forests, the interior plains, and the lowland coastal areas around Lake Maracaibo. Sedentary tribes with more advanced methods of cultivation settled in the central highlands and northeast, but only in the Andes did the indigenous population develop a diversified ag-

Venezuela

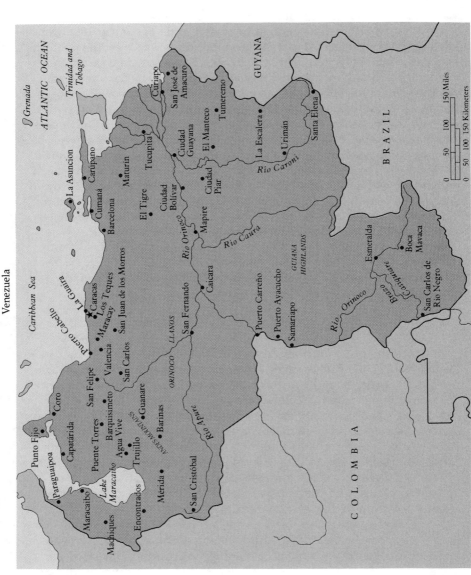

Source: Latin American Politics and Development, third edition, edited by Howard J. Wiarda and Harvey F. Cline (Westview Press, 1990), p. 284. Reprinted by permission.

Young peasant girl, state of Lara (photo by author)

economy with trade and small towns. Still, their cultural and technological accomplishments could not rival those of the Incas and other peoples further south on the continent.[8]

The first permanent Spanish settlements were along the eastern slopes of the Andes, in the western part of the country. Today most Venezuelans live in the valleys of the lower coastal range, which extends from Barquisimeto to Barcelona, including Caracas, in central Venezuela. Though dwarfed by Andean peaks near the Colombian border, the mountains still reach 9,000 feet. After its founding in 1567, Caracas quickly became the administrative center of the colonial society, which reached its apogee during the cacao boom of the eighteenth century. Approximately 4 million people live in the greater Caracas metropolitan area today, though many *Caraqueños*, from taxi drivers to radical Catholic missionaries in the poor barrios, say that the real count is closer to 6 million.

Caracas has always been at the center of political storms, but the route to power rarely has begun in the capital. As the basis of the export economy has shifted from cacao, to coffee, to oil, different regions have risen or fallen in importance. Regional identities were perhaps more important than *lo venezolano* until the turn of the century.

Slavery shaped the cultural and racial characteristics of Venezuela. African slaves were brought to the coastal lowlands, especially during the eighteenth century, to supply labor for the short-lived cacao boom. By 1810, there were 60,000 slaves in a population that probably totaled approximately 900,000.[9] The African influence is most pronounced in the region between Caracas and Barcelona, known as Barlovento, especially in its hybrid religious traditions—for example, in the percussion of the great *tambores* (drums made from hollowed tree trunks), which are sounded on the religious holidays of San Juan and Cruz de Mayo (St. John and Corpus Christi).[10] Although racism has far from disappeared, Venezuelans generally take pride in being a multiracial society.

The *llanos* are broad plains that stretch from the high Andes near Colombia (high *llanos*) eastward to the Guayana Highlands and southeastward toward the Orinoco Lowlands (low *llanos*). By modern standards they are sparsely populated, but in the nineteenth century, the *llanos* contained the most populous state, Guárico, center of the cattle industry. *Llanos* show the cultural and biological influence of all the races that have shaped Venezuelan history. Most *llaneros* are descended from the racially mixed settlers, *pardos*, whose labor was exploited on the great, traditional ranches (*hatos*). They produced beef and leather, which were major contributors to the colonial and nineteenth-century economies. However, it is more through the military prowess of its *caudillos* (military chiefs) that the *llanos* have left a lasting mark on Venezuelan history.

In the western region of Venezuela lies the spectacular mountain range, Sierra Nevada de Mérida, where four peaks reach over 16,000 feet in the three states bordering on Colombia. No sizable Indian communities remain in the Venezuelan Andes; however, the pre-Columbian influence is clearly visible in the faces, customs, and clothing of the mountain population, which is largely mestizo. Indigenous communities can still be found in the Guajira Peninsula, a lowland area along the western shores of Lake Maracaibo, and in the Amazonian Territory and Guayana, in the eastern region of Venezuela.

From the middle of the nineteenth century through the 1920s, exports of coffee dominated the Venezuelan economy, and the Andean region dominated production. To some extent, this accounts for the rise to the presidency of five military leaders from the Andean state of Táchira; they ruled Venezuela in varying degrees of autocracy for all but three years between 1890 and 1958. The most notable was Juan Vicente Gómez, whose tenure, from 1908 to 1935, provides a textbook case of individual autarchy.

Although the Maracaibo Basin in western Venezuela is part of the Caribbean lowlands, the state of Zulia has come to represent a separate pole of development, with Maracaibo, a city of approximately 1 million, at its center. This can largely be attributed to the spectacular growth of the oil industry after 1920. This development reinforced a sense of regional

El Molino, an Andean village, state of Mérida (photo by Alejandro González)

pride but also resentment that much of the wealth generated by Lake Maracaibo's petroleum reserves is controlled by Caracas. Zulia has struggled to capture a greater proportion of the revenue generated by its oil in order to diversify its own economy. However, Venezuelans have been more inclined to see their future in the eastern state of Guayana, where impressive natural resources are concentrated in abundance.

Guayana and the Amazonian Territory cover approximately 45 percent of the national territory. The Orinoco River flows through the region toward its delta on the Caribbean. One of its tributaries, the Caroní, is the site of the colossal Guri Dam, which provides electricity for the industries of Ciudad Guayana, a city of nearly 600,000 people where twenty-five years ago stood only a small town of 5,000 inhabitants. In Ciudad Guayana's industrial zone of Matanzas there have mushroomed, especially since the oil boom that followed the oil crisis of 1974, huge petrochemical, steel, and aluminum complexes and smaller, specialized, processing plants.

Although the interior regions of the country are increasingly linked to the center by roads and communications networks, in many areas the border with neighboring countries is ill-defined. Traditionally, mestizo communities have been linked by commercial, family, and cultural ties across an imprecise boundary between Colombia and the Andean states. Although Lake Maracaibo is recognized as completely within Venezuelan national territory, Colombia and Venezuela are bitterly at odds over control of the gulf waters north of the lake. In the east and south the border extends for 3,000 miles through territories that are sparsely populated but generously endowed with natural resources. As more remote regions have been opened to economic exploitation or militarily occupied, conflicts with neighbors have intensified. They are sharpest with the former British colony of Guyana in the east; they are relatively subdued, but nonetheless unresolved, with Brazil in the south.

Although one racial group might predominate more in one particular region or another, internal migration and immigration are eroding ethnic distinctions among regions. Andeans have migrated in great numbers to Caracas. *Caraqueños* vacation in Caribbean resorts and Andean mountain hostels. Laborers from all over Venezuela have flooded into Guayana. Since World War II a wave of immigrants, mostly from Southern Europe and other parts of South America, have changed the face of Caracas and other major cities. For 100 years after gaining its independence, Venezuelan governments unsuccessfully sought to attract European immigration. Venezuelan intellectuals, influenced by the European philosophy of positivism, argued in the nineteenth century that the country's backwardness resulted from racial or environmental inferiority. Progress depended, many thought, on attracting European stock, but few Europeans were interested in migrating to a land as violent and primitive as was Venezuela before oil.

With oil Venezuela was converted overnight from a peripheral, dreary outpost in the world's economic system to a land of opportunity for many immigrants. Beginning in the 1930s and dramatically accelerating after World War II, European emigrants began to shift their attention from Argentina to Venezuela. Many Latin Americans, especially Colombians, were attracted to Venezuela during the oil boom of the 1970s. As a result, at least one of every sixteen people living in Venezuela in the 1980s was not born in the country. Now, facing economic contraction, Venezuela must come to grips with competition between natives and immigrants for jobs. Venezuelans also must grapple with how their national culture is to be blended with those who have come from other nations.[11]

As with other consumer goods, earnings generated by the export boom have been used to import rather than to produce cultural products, and this presents another kind of challenge to Venezuelan identity. In 1976, only 17.8 percent of television programming originated in Venezuela, and only an additional 15.7 percent came from other Latin American countries. In 1980, half of all television programs shown were U.S.

imports. Only twenty-seven of ninety-five television programs broadcast during one typical week in July 1983 were produced within Venezuela. One critic commented that between 1958 and 1983, "cultural inflation was greater than economic inflation."[12]

Virtually every area of diversion and culture has been affected, even sports. While other South Americans follow soccer scores, Venezuelans focus on horseracing, boxing, and baseball. A young Venezuelan athlete is much more likely to dream of emulating Luis Aparicio, Tony Armas, or Andrés Galarraga and play major league baseball in North America than to dream of leading a national soccer team to victory in the World Cup.

The collapse of oil prices has not necessarily restored vigor to the cultural scene. In the economic crisis Venezuelan poets, musicians, actors, and athletes have found it difficult to earn a living practicing their art, while tastes for North American and European cultural products have not receded along with the tide of petrodollars. In 1985, Venezuelan bullfighters, dressed in full regalia, staged a hunger strike outside the main Caracas bullring to dramatize their unemployment, while Spanish matadors and picadors continued to head the weekly programs.

Venezuela is sometimes called the "least Catholic country" of Latin America, but Catholicism remains the religion of an estimated 92 percent of the population.[13] It is increasingly common to see protestant evangelical churches (Pentecostalists, Jehovah's Witnesses, and so on) in barrios (poorer neighborhoods) and in the frontier areas competing with the Catholic church for converts among indigenous tribes. A 1988 survey in several Caracas barrios found that only 65 percent of residents regarded themselves as practicing Catholics, and barely half had actually reported having participated in community religious activities. As late as 1970, 80 percent of priests were foreign born. In response, as elsewhere in Latin America, the church has become more actively concerned with human rights and social justice, and apparently more young Venezuelans are looking toward religious callings.[14] By far, the best magazine of social thought today is *Revista SIC*, published by the Jesuit think tank, *Centro Gumilla*.

THE PETROLEUM QUESTION

The petroleum age arrived in Venezuela in 1922 when a well called "*Los Barrosos No. 2*" exploded into a gusher, confirming the country's great subsoil resources. Since that time Venezuela has experienced a social and economic transformation more rapid and thorough than any other Latin American nation (possibly excepting Cuba) in this century. One of the poorest and most backward nations on the continent in 1936, by 1987 Venezuela could boast the highest per capita gross national product ($4,107) in South America—nearly $1,400 more than the next richest countries, Argentina and Uruguay.[15]

Underlying decades of change, however, is a basic continuity: The welfare of Venezuela's people has depended less upon the productive labor of its work force than upon revenue generated by oil exports. A high proportion of Venezuela's earnings from petroleum has historically taken the form of a rent which the developed capitalist countries have rendered in exchange for access to reserves below the surface. The price and profitability of Venezuela's oil exports have depended little upon the productiveness of labor used to extract petroleum, so perhaps it is understandable why so many Venezuelan politicians and intellectuals have regarded their mineral reserves as "natural wealth." However, there is very little "natural" about the value of a product almost worthless until the late nineteenth century, but subsequently called "black gold."

Extremely underdeveloped, dependent, and vulnerable to foreign pressures, Venezuela possessed little bargaining power when the companies arrived in force after 1920. Few of its ruling class understood how to maximize the price—what in classical political economy is called "ground rent"—that the companies would have to pay for access to the nation's subsoil wealth. However, even a small share of industry profits far exceeded what could be generated from other economic activities, including coffee exports, in the underdeveloped economy. The lucrativeness of oil extraction depends in part upon the natural productivity of reserves, and between 1922 and the end of World War II, Venezuelan fields were among the most productive in the world.[16]

By extracting rent from the lucrative oil industry, the Venezuelan ruling class was presented with an historic opportunity to develop rapidly one of the most backward, peripheral economies within the world system. However, oil rents also presented dangers of severe economic and social distortion. Oil income could be used not only for investment to modernize and develop domestic industry and agriculture, but it also provided ready foreign exchange for massive importation of consumer goods, basic and luxury items alike, that could smother unprotected, nascent industries. The historic dominance of the land oligarchy and of commercial and financial elites in Venezuelan politics ensured that the latter tendency prevailed in the early years. Part of the drama of the post-1958 democratic era revolves around the issue of how well the oil income has been sown in the economy under the populist guidance of the major political parties, in particular, of *Acción Democrática*.

Having achieved independence from Spain nearly a century before the petroleum boom, Venezuelans encountered the oil companies on different terms than did the peoples of Asia, Africa, and the Middle

East. As a result, through 1960 Venezuela played a key role in leading the oil-producing nations in their struggle to appropriate ground rent from the companies and industrial consuming countries.

The oil companies, unlike earlier imperialists from Europe and North America, had little interest in directly governing the land and people of Venezuela. Until World War II, multinational corporations showed little interest in investing in Venezuelan agriculture or manufacturing, and the domestic market was too small to attract their attention as a major export market. Foreign capitalists were much more interested in what lay below than above the land. Venezuelans of all social classes had little technological expertise or knowledge about the market value of petroleum or about the geological factors determining the value of deposits. The companies well understood from previous experience (e.g., in the United States) that their bargaining position was strongest while landowners were ignorant. They quite logically sought to lock in favorable concessions with long-term leases when the "dance of concessions" began in 1908.

This task was aided by political conditions in Venezuela. When the companies began to arrive in force, the country was controlled by a dictator, Juan Vicente Gómez, who shared much of the social and cultural outlook of the landowners and had consolidated his rule with help from the United States and European powers. He was predisposed to encourage foreign investment through tax incentives, which favored company interests. On the other hand, his own personal greed and his desire to limit the power of potential rivals influenced him not to give full discretion to landowners in the sale of concessions. Hence, landed elites tended to benefit from the boom only insofar as they were integrated into the system of corruption and patronage that constituted the backbone of *gomecismo*.[17]

Although there were some nationalistic stirrings within the Gómez regime itself, two conditions needed to be met before Venezuela could more effectively insist on appropriating more rent. One was a change in the international conjuncture, which was brought about by World War II. The other was for the emergence of social classes with an interest in a higher rate of appropriation of rent. The latter was set in motion almost immediately, despite Gómez's attempts to insulate the semifeudal social structure from the impact of the industry. Increased circulation of money encouraged the expansion of the service sector and penetration of wage labor in all areas of the country. The pressures of an overvalued bolívar and urban labor market accelerated the decline of traditional agriculture, which had never recovered from the world crisis of the 1890s.[18] As the power base shifted from the countryside to the city, new social and political actors emerged. A cohort of political leaders, known as the "Generation of 1928," defined for themselves the task of transforming Venezuela. Rómulo Betancourt was by far the most influential of these political elites.[19]

The social and economic history of twentieth-century Venezuela is inextricable from the history of Venezuela's political parties, foremost among them, *Acción Democrática* (Democratic Action, or AD). AD and the Christian Democratic party COPEI (Independent Political Organizing Committee), the only two parties to have controlled the presidency since 1958, remain the most staunch defenders of the present political system. Both were founded by members of the Generation of 1928, some of whom remain influential politically to this day. But since 1974, public confidence in the party system has been steadily eroded by corruption and by the evident failure of the two great parties to "sow" the massive influx of revenues that followed the world oil crisis of 1973 into an effective developmental project.

Betancourt's one-time private secretary, Carlos Andrés Pérez, assumed the presidency for the first time in early 1974 just as events in the Middle East set off a spectacular rise in oil prices. In response to the opportunity, Pérez promised in the Fifth National Plan to create "*Gran Venezuela*" by sowing the oil bonanza in ambitious projects of industrial expansion, especially in resource-rich Guayana. By 1989, as Andrés Pérez returned to the presidency, he would assume leadership not of *Gran Venezuela* but of a country burdened with a foreign debt absorbing 46 percent of export earnings (1988) and afflicted with massive corruption, a growing problem with drug trafficking, a rising rate of violent crime, and growing public cynicism about government. A national mood of unbounded confidence had given way to doubt and a sense of crisis, reflected in a wave of books with titles (translated) like *The Poverty of Populism, The Venezuelan Case: An Illusion of Harmony,* and *Where Is Venezuela Going?*[20]

Although the country has far from exhausted its oil reserves, Venezuelans often speak of the present era as "*la noche postpetrolera*" ("the postpetroleum night"). The sunset can be rather precisely dated: February 18, 1983. On that day, the government declared that the bolívar, the national currency, would no longer be fixed at 4.38 against the dollar. Venezuela, the only country in the hemisphere able to *increase* the value of its currency during the Great Depression, faced drastic devaluation (there had been a significant, but less traumatic devaluation in 1960) of its currency and a secular decline in its economy for the first time in sixty years. By June 1990, the bolívar stood at nearly 49 to the dollar. Some economists predict that it could reach 135:1 by 1992.[21] The sudden hike in oil prices (to US$40 per barrel at one point in October 1990) produced by Iraq's invasion of Kuwait in August 1990 brought some breathing space to the Pérez government, but it soon became clear that the new "bonanza" would do little more than arrest the downward spiral of the economy. President Pérez made it clear that his government would continue to implement policies, negotiated as conditions for new loans from the International Monetary Fund, of fiscal austerity, privatization, and opening of the economy to market forces.

So far, the economic crisis has produced little danger of a coup by the military, which has been relatively passive since several abortive coups in the early 1960s. Nor has a serious threat from the left emerged. Most guerrilla leaders of the 1960s have been integrated into the system through the small, traditional leftist parties which have been allocated a share in the spoils system. More pronounced criticism of the present political model comes from private business leaders and conservative intellectuals ("neoliberals") who want to reduce the role of the state in the economy and implement a more laissez faire system of government.

Another type of challenge to the party system is emerging from nascent grassroots movements, including neighborhood associations, environmental movements, Christian base communities, and dissident labor unions. They regard the party system as stifling not because it is too populist, but because the parties resist conceding autonomy to social movements and continue to dominate civil society through co-option and, when necessary, repression. The new social movements seek to preserve the democratic gains embodied in the Constitution of 1961, but also to move from populism to popular empowerment. For them, Venezuelan democracy can no longer be merely displayed every five years (the electoral cycle) like a shining trophy; the tarnish can be removed from the Venezuelan model only by extending democracy to more spheres of life. Whether they succeed will determine whether or not the "postpetroleum" era will also become known as the "postdemocratic" era.

2

Cradle of Stillborn Independence

History is usually taught, notes the Jesuit historian Arturo Sosa, "as if it were the religion of the country, with its gods, its saints, its passion-death-and-resurrection, its demons, and its temptations. We are taught a moral history, with good and evil, with patriots and traitors to the homeland, in black and white, with clearly distinct sides, without shadings nor internal problems."[1] This chapter presents Venezuelan history not merely as a pageant of historical villains and heroes, that is, as a morality play, but as a process involving cultural, social, and economic forces that shaped Venezuelan political culture and the country's response to the oil boom in the twentieth century.

CONQUEST AND COLONIZATION

The Spaniards first attempted to extract wealth from Venezuela around 1500 by forcing Indian divers to retrieve pearls from the waters near the Island of Margarita, off the northeast coast. Shortly afterward, conquistadors set off down the Orinoco River, lured by tales of a golden city—El Dorado. When the pearl beds were exhausted and after they despaired of finding El Dorado, most of the Spanish lost interest in the colony. Those who remained turned their attention to pacifying the local Indian population. As elsewhere in the New World, their success was ensured by superior military technology, Indian vulnerability to disease, and internal divisions among tribes. The Indian *cacique*, Chief Guaicaipuro, who led his Teques tribe in fierce resistance to Diego de Losada, founder of Caracas (in 1567), has been memorialized in a massive statue that stands along one of the major highway entrances to the city. However, efforts to have him honored in the National Pantheon, where Simón Bolívar and others considered heroes of democracy or resisters of Spanish

15

tyranny are enshrined, have generated little public enthusiasm and no official encouragement.[2]

Most of the region's estimated 350,000 Indians perished during the Spanish conquest. The survivors were often enslaved under harsh conditions or "entrusted" by the Crown to the missionaries in the interior. Nomadic peoples were forcibly concentrated into permanent communities, a practice continued today by the government and Protestant evangelical sects in remote areas in the Amazonian Territory as they are opened to ranching and mining or hydroelectric development. In the colonial era, more sedentary tribes were given over to conquistadors under the *encomienda*, a system of forced labor based on tribute. Indian rebels and resisters were exported to the Antilles as slaves upon capture.

Lacking precious metals and a great mass of exploitable native labor, the northern coast of South America quickly lapsed into the periphery of the Spanish Empire. In 1528, the Spanish Crown literally rented Venezuela to the German commercial banking firm of Welser, but by 1546 the Germans also abandoned hope of profit. The inhabitants turned to agricultural production, which was primitive and largely intended for consumption inside the colony. The consolidation of the colonial system dates from the founding of Tocuyo in the foothills of the Andes in 1545, but Caracas in the north central highlands would eventually become the political and administrative center of the colony.

The early economy was based upon the production of cattle on the southwestern *llanos*. Labor for the *hatos* (ranches) and agricultural activities was secured by use of the *encomienda*, which survived in Venezuela until the seventeenth century, more than 100 years after giving way to other systems of exploitation elsewhere in the empire. Sosa explains:

> In other colonies, the *encomienda* system was applied to wealthier activities to produce surplus and new capital. In general this was not the case in Venezuela due to its poverty. The little surplus was used to trade for consumer products from the metropolis or elsewhere in the empire. In Venezuela, only a few products like tobacco were able to generate profit. The principal accumulation of capital would come with cacao in the eighteenth century and with the labor of black slaves.[3]

Through 1650, the Spanish conquerors found it impossible to settle the central *llanos* and vast eastern territories. This aspect of the conquest was accomplished primarily through Catholic missionaries who founded more than 300 towns in these regions. While missionaries hastened the destruction of Indian culture and the subjugation of Indian communities to the conquerors, they also offered a spirited and often effective defense

TABLE 2.1 Price and Volume of Exports of Cacao in Bushels, Selected Years

Year	Destination				Price (reales) per bushel
	Mexico	Spain	Other destinations	Total	
1631	1073	50	74	1197	40-50
1706	7576	1275	1061	9912	50-70
1750	13385	17313	6047	36745	n.a.
1772	14008	30361	4134	48503	80

Source: Miguel Izard, Series estadísticas para la historia de Venezuela (Mérida: Universidad de los Andes, 1970), pp. 149-152, 187-190.

of Indian communities against the avarice of the creole elite. This established the basis for conflict with these elites, culminating in the relative subordination of church to state interests by the Liberals in the second half of the nineteenth century.[4]

In the mid-seventeenth century, Venezuela was part of Nueva Granada, which encompassed what are today the northern Andean republics and parts of the Caribbean and Mexico. Since Venezuela occupied a relatively peripheral place in the empire, the Crown left the colony with considerable political autonomy. This would change in the eighteenth century when exports of cacao, first cultivated around 1630, began to attract European attention (see Table 2.1). The Crown took an active interest in regulating commerce relatively late as part of an attempt to stem imperial decline. In 1728, when Mexico was still a larger market for Venezuelan exports than was Spain, the reformist Bourbon dynasty granted a complete commercial monopoly to a Basque consortium, the Compañía Guipuzcoana, which shifted the trading pattern toward Europe. In 1777, the Captaincy General of Venezuela, corresponding roughly to the present national territory, was created with Caracas as its capital.

Cacao for the first time promoted within Venezuela the emergence of a colonial ruling class. This ruling class, the creoles, came to be divided into factions: peninsulares, who were associated with Spanish colonial authority, and mantuanos, who increasingly chafed under Spanish rule and eventually revolted. The monopoly status and political power of the Compañía Guipuzcoana, severely limited the horizons of the mantuanos, who preferred to sell Venezuelan products directly to the English and other buyers. Many turned to Caribbean buccaneers for economic relief; they sought political refuge in the only colonial institutions under their control, the cabildos (town councils), which became experiments in self-rule. Some mantuanos, educated abroad, including Caracas-born Simón Bolívar, were attracted to Enlightenment political philosophy. Although the Compañía Guipuzcoana would be disbanded in 1781, the forces leading to the War for Independence had already been set in motion.[5]

The production of cacao required an expansion of the laboring classes at the base of the social pyramid. With little Indian labor available, the creoles turned to importation of African slaves. By the end of the colonial period, approximately 60,000 of the colony's total population of 800,000 to 1 million inhabitants were slaves. They were complemented by a large number of *pardos* who worked in virtual peonage and constituted 50 to 60 percent of the population. The Indians, largely unconquered or living in missionary communities, numbered approximately 50,000. At the other end of the social pyramid were the white and creole *peninsulares*, who constituted approximately 1.5 percent of the population; immediately below them were the *mantuanos*, many of very limited economic means, who constituted an estimated 20 percent.[6] Although chafing under Spanish rule, the *mantuanos* hesitated to break with colonial authorities whose power kept the *pardos* (racially mixed peons) and slaves subjugated. Several late eighteenth-century revolts (e.g., *Los Comuneros* in the Andes) failed when local elites, wary of slave and lower-class unrest, aborted uprisings. The liberal philosophies of the French and American revolutions were welcome insofar as they justified opposition to the arrogance and arbitrariness of the *peninsulares*, but few creoles took seriously the idea of equality among citizens.

The general decay of Spanish imperial and royal institutions favored the ambitions of those creoles, led by farsighted intellectuals like Bolívar, Mariscal Sucre, and Francisco Miranda, who sought independence. The imposition of a pretender on the Spanish throne by Napoleon and the ensuing war further weakened the monarchy between 1808 and 1810, leading to a declaration of independence by a creole congress in 1811. However, the movement hardly endorsed revolution; a new constitution retained slavery, made Catholicism the state religion, and excluded the propertyless *pardos* from rights as citizens. Even so, the church, which rightly understood that the liberal leaders of the independence movement intended to seize its land and "free" the Indians to serve in the labor force, backed the Crown. Religious authorities declared that an earthquake that devastated Caracas in 1812 was evidence of God's displeasure with the revolutionaries.

Many creoles were alarmed at the social unrest as slaves and *pardos* seemed more interested in freedom or land than in the grand political principles elaborated in proclamations and newspapers. The Indians had little to gain from a movement that sought to break up the religious haciendas, which afforded them some protection from the rapaciousness of the creole elites. The Spanish governor, José Tomás Boves, rallied many slaves and *pardos* against the independence movement, and taking full advantage of Miranda's military and political mistakes, ruthlessly crushed the independence movement. Boves's legendary cruelty and loyalty to the Crown have obscured the fact that he was Venezuela's first populist dictator.

Boves's victory proved only temporary. Pablo Murillo, who succeeded Boves as governor, instituted an oppressive military occupation that rekindled creole resentment of the centralized, colonial system of authority. Key *mantuano* leaders, like José Antonio Páez and his *llanos* horsemen, who had backed the Crown, swung behind the new struggle for independence led by one of Miranda's officers, Simón Bolívar. Bolívar understood better than Miranda the social bases of revolutions. He rallied lower-class support with a more egalitarian approach (more so than creoles later proved willing to tolerate), including, for example, promoting soldiers for merit regardless of their social background or color.

In early 1821, the Republic of Gran Colombia, embracing present-day Ecuador, Colombia, Panama, and Venezuela, was proclaimed after the defeat of Spanish forces in Maracaibo. Later that year, on June 24, a day celebrated today as Armed Forces Day in Venezuela, Bolívar sealed the defeat of Spanish forces in a last great battle of the war at Carabobo. More than 400 battles had been fought on Venezuelan soil, and one-third of the population had perished.

Venezuela had gained its national sovereignty but little else from the War for Independence. In the nineteenth century, Venezuelans suffered through periods of harsh dictatorships, mild dictatorships, and anarchy, punctuated by periodic but fleeting episodes of relative peace. By 1888, another 730 battles and 26 major insurrections would be fought on Venezuelan soil. The creole caste largely perished in the fratricidal bloodbath. Throughout the century, civil revolt remained a route to emancipation or property ownership for the rural masses. Regional strongmen capable of mobilizing peasant armies acted as power brokers. These *caudillos* (military chiefs), many of them semiliterate, dominated politics throughout the nineteenth century.

The Bolivarians stood for Pan-American unity and a strong central state, but the Constitution of Gran Colombia, written while Venezuela was still occupied by royalist forces, was designed to rally the creoles *against* central authority, i.e., the Crown. Although himself a slave owner, Bolívar decreed the abolition of slavery in 1823, but few of the Liberator's creole allies intended to keep their promises to the masses, and Bolívar had little leverage to force them to accept his decrees and his plans to build a centralized state and more egalitarian social order. Bolívar compounded his problems by governing in an inept, vacillating, and autocratic style. Gran Colombia disintegrated as regional military chieftains took advantage of discontent to seize power. In 1830, Páez, the able and imposing military leader of the *llanos*, declared Venezuela's independence from Gran Colombia. He would dominate politics for the first twenty years of the new republic.

From 1830 until 1869, what stability existed was provided by a system in which the principal *caudillo*—Páez for much of the time—presided over a network of regional strongmen who stood in a pyramidal relationship to *caudillos* at even lower levels. After another fratricidal war (1858–1863), a more centralized system emerged, but at the turn of the century this system collapsed in a whirlwind of economic crisis, renewed civil war, and gunboat intervention, which in turn led to the rule of the last and most successful of the *caudillos*, Juan Vicente Gómez, whose rule lasted until 1935.[7]

THE AGE OF THE *CAUDILLOS*

Robert Gilmore, in his influential study of *caudillismo* in Venezuela, defines *caudillismo* as "the union of personalism and violence for the conquest of power. It is a means for the selection and establishment of political leadership in the absence of a social structure and political groupings adequate to the functioning of representative government."[8] Gilmore argues that *caudillismo* should not be equated with military rule. The successful *caudillo* usually was a skilled fighter, a quality particularly encouraged by the "cowboy culture" of the *llanos*. The vast and wild plains afforded escaped slaves, fleeing debtors, and bandits a vast refuge beyond the reach of a weak central government hundreds of miles away. To survive, much less to lead, required skills more akin to those of a gangster than to those of a professional army officer.

Páez had built his army of 2,000 men from revolting slaves and the cowboy *pardos*; he provided Bolívar with an important rear guard during the independence struggle. Like Boves and Bolívar and many to follow him, he appealed to popular resentment of a primitive system of economic exploitation and social inequality. Individual followers of successful revolts sometimes reaped the spoils of war or advanced through the ranks through superior fighting skills, but invariably the masses benefited little from the wars that were always proclaimed to have great democratic goals.[9]

In the nineteenth century the Venezuelan ruling class consisted of the agricultural oligarchy, the financial and commercial elites in the ports and Caracas, and a small group of intellectuals and military leaders who unsuccessfully promoted the republican and Pan-American ideals of Bolívar. Just as under Spanish rule, the oligarchy sought to maintain its monopoly over land, to perpetuate a primitive system of exploitation of labor, and to repress social or political advancement by the *pardos*, who largely worked as artisans, day laborers, and small-scale cultivators.

Laws required all citizens to find employment for at least six months per year. Unemployed workers could be forced under vagrancy statutes to labor on the landed estates or on public works projects, like roads, that served the interests of the landowners. Workers were not allowed to leave haciendas at the end of the work day without permission of the landowner; a laborer could be arrested and detained for twenty-four hours if found in a city during working hours, and after three offenses he could be sentenced to forced labor. Indebted peons were required to carry books in which employers would certify the completion of work for which they had been advanced (inadequate) wages, often in specie. The laws provided for harsh penalties against those without their papers in proper order and against landowners who hired laborers with outstanding obligations, although they were rarely enforced in the latter case.[10]

The War for Independence left the landed oligarchy divided and insecure. According to historian John Lombardi:

> In the mature colonial society before the war, conflicts of interest at all levels were resolved through an elaborate, formal, and bureaucratized system. Disputes over land or authority, over precedence and honor, over concessions or profits—whatever the problem, a formal procedure existed to resolve it. . . . For all its failings and injustices, it did manage a complex society. With the wars of independence, this system disappeared during the clash of bandit armies and the confiscation and reallocation of property.[11]

Local military chieftains were not likely to investigate whether debts of a recruit were paid as they gathered cannon fodder for their internecine wars.

Political instability contributed to economic indolence. The economic infrastructure had been devastated, the national monetary system disappeared. For most of the century, regions of Venezuela would function as separate export enclaves—leather products from the *llanos*, cacao from the coast, and coffee from the central highlands and the Andes. They were linked with the international market through export houses, which, like the Compañía Guipuzcoana of the colonial era, became centers for accumulation of wealth and political influence. The political and economic weight of different regions shifted as the coffee industry expanded over the course of the century (see Figure 2.1). Caracas was the site for political intrigue among merchants, financiers, and representatives of the landed elite, but the central government had little command over the economy. It failed to establish a tax basis to pay the massive debt (especially to the British) accumulated during the war, which continued to grow throughout the chaotic nineteenth century.

22

Figure 2.1 Area of Influence of Principal Venezuelan Ports
During the 19th Century

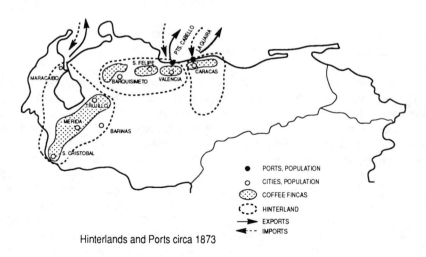

Hinterland and Ports Early 1800s

Hinterlands and Ports circa 1873

Source: Adapted from Eveling Bravo and Napoleon Franceschi, *Problemas de historia de Venezuela contemporánea* (Caracas: Vadell Hermanos, 1980), pp. 115-116

Ambitious *caudillos* in the interior would often seize upon discontent with bankers and merchants to challenge the central government, but ultimately they themselves would succumb to the influence of the Caracas elite and European creditors whose financing was crucial to the pursuit of power or ability to keep it. While scornful of urban intellectuals, *caudillos* turned to them to rationalize their rule and give their regimes a veneer of constitutional legitimacy as the inheritors of the ideals of the independence struggle. This rationalization was thereby transformed in popular memory into a morality play—into a mythical struggle for freedom spawned by the genius of Bolívar and a few heroic followers. Each rebellious movement would raise the cry of liberty and faithfulness to the Bolivarian ideal, but none addressed the colonial legacy of economic dependence and extreme social injustice. Bolivarian rhetoric masked the subordinate relationship of the ruling class to foreign banks and governments.

Bolívar was transformed into a secular saint, and he remains so today. That part of the Bolivarian legacy (particularly his later writings) that was critical of South America's social structure and the United States ("destined by Providence to plague Latin America with misery in the name of liberty") was forgotten. The Liberator became, in the words of Ali Primera, Venezuela's most prolific contributor to Latin America's New Song Movement, "merely a saint for whom one lights a candle." In Primera's "*Canción Bolivariana*" a Venezuelan boy holds an imaginary conversation with Bolívar, after whom the national currency is named, and informs him that Venezuelans are still not fully liberated.

> *Boy:* And what's worse is that my people are now without a Bolívar.
> *Bolívar:* They are without money? Terrible!
> *Boy:* Without consciousness, Liberator, without consciousness. The people have been fooled into believing the rich bourgeoisie who go to the National Pantheon to bring flowers on the anniversary of your death.
> *Bolívar:* Then why do they go, little patriot?
> *Boy:* To be sure that you are still dead, Liberator, truly dead.[12]

The Nineteenth-Century Civil Wars

For a period of about fifteen years after 1830, Páez was able to provide a modicum of social peace. His followers came to be known as Conservatives, or "*godos*." The opposition was composed of allies of Bolívar (who regarded Páez as a traitor to republican and Pan-American ideals), rival *caudillos*, and landowners who feared the economic power of the commercial and financial elite. Advocating a more decentralized state, expansion of suffrage, freedom of press, curbing of the church's power, and other reforms, they founded the Liberal party, the first organized political party in Venezuelan history. The "liberal" and "conservative" labels meant little. Páez, for example, deprived the church of much of its wealth and many privileges—to the delight of ambitious local *caudillos* eager to acquire church land and resources.

To induce merchants and money lenders to' return to Venezuela, Páez eliminated usury laws designed to protect indebted landowners, including many conservatives. Between 1830 and 1845, the economy recovered as production tripled in the principal export sectors, that is, cacao, coffee, and leather hides. But three factors limited the possibility of sustained economic development for Venezuela: the staggering external debt, the insecurity of land property, and competition from cheap manufactured imports, which smothered the artisan sector.

Public expenditure grew from 5 million bolívars (Bs.) to Bs. 18 million over these fifteen years, but inherited debts and lack of an effective tax system soon undermined the fiscal viability of the central government. By 1839, the external debt had swelled to ten times the value of exports; servicing it absorbed 40 percent of public expenditures. A National Bank of Venezuela (disbanded in 1850) was financed for a short while with foreign loans and customs receipts; however, the government only controlled 2,000 of its 10,000 shares, the rest being controlled by private Venezuelan citizens and foreigners, mostly British. Fifty percent of the state budget was used by Páez to keep unruly local *caudillos* in line.[13] Little of this money was spent on the central army, much to the consternation of Bolivarians. Local militias under control of the oligarchy, an inheritance of the late colonial era, were far more potent. An economic downturn or the departure of Páez from the political scene would severely test the stability of this system which so much depended upon the loyalty of local oligarchs and *caudillos* to the national *caudillo* in Caracas.[14]

In fact, the prosperity of the 1830s under Páez, which in any case never much benefited the low social classes, proved ephemeral. Classically dependent upon monoculture export (by region) and upon imports of European manufactured goods, the economy was highly vulnerable to the vicissitudes of the central economies. Contraction of the market for Venezuelan goods in Europe in the 1840s drove the peasants and landowners further into debt as they faced *monthly* interest rates of 15 percent. Avaricious merchants and financiers in the cities eagerly foreclosed on their property. The *godos* became increasingly unpopular, and the political fortunes of the Liberals began to rise. The landowners, many of whom often barely lived above the standard of living of the peasant masses, sought to defend their "property" the same way that many had gained it. They turned to violence with little exhortation.

After abortive rebellions in 1842 and 1847, the Liberals wrested control of the central government from Páez in 1849, but the countryside continued to seethe with unrest. In an effort to protect landowners and calm incipient revolts, the government granted legal protection against foreclosures. The result was the financial collapse of several banks and the arrival of British gunboats to force the government to compensate British creditors with state bonds. Domestic creditors demanded and received equal treatment. The government and financial system plunged further into crisis; the National Bank was dissolved in 1850.

The government sold public land to raise money, but the chief beneficiaries were not peasants but members of the government clique. The propertied classes, influenced by the philosophy of positivism, regarded the peasantry as culturally and racially inferior to Europeans; nor was it in their interest to raise the standard of living and education level of the rural masses. They looked instead to immigration as a means to settle and develop the vast, underpopulated interior. However, few Europeans found the violent and primitive conditions in Venezuela attractive. So while the ruling class vainly sought to populate the interior with foreigners, they denied land and property to the landless masses whose cheap labor was indispensable to the economy. Although slavery had become economically obsolete, it was only finally abolished in 1854 by the *godo* president José Gregorio Monagas, who feared that slaves would be recruited into the armies of his opponents.

Pressed financially, the landed classes intensified their exploitation of the *pardos* and former slaves. Provincial assemblies passed laws to intensify the already primitive system of exploitation. Local police were placed at the disposal of landowners to enforce the labor passbook laws, and flight from work was made punishable by imprisonment or forced military service. In most provinces, children were made eligible to contract debt at fourteen years—in some areas, ten years—of age and thereby forced into penury for life.[15] To a grotesquely exploited population, service rendered in the army of a *caudillo* remained one of the few ways of escaping penury.

Venezuela was a tinder box awaiting a match. It was provided by the worldwide economic crisis of 1857 and 1858. Prices of leather fell 30 percent, coffee 20 percent, and cacao 50 percent. In 1857, *llanero* discontent reached a fever pitch in response to an artificial crisis engineered by monopolistic, urban merchants who raised meat prices in the cities but drove down the price paid for cattle. Both Conservative and Liberal opponents took advantage of growing discontent to drive the ruling Monagas family (which had succeeded Páez) from power, but no new government emerged to fill the void.

Opponents of the central government gathered under the banner of "federalism" in 1858 and embarked upon a five-year war that profoundly marked Venezuelan society while solving few of its underlying problems. The Federal War produced a bloodbath in which 60,000 to 100,000 Venezuelans, approximately 5 percent of the population, perished. During the "long war," the country's total population fell from almost 1.9 million to less than 1.6 million (in 1864). The cattle industry was decimated as herds were reduced from 12 million to 1.8 million head. Where any semblance of government survived, it was only at the provincial level. The country was laid open to foreign intervention as outside powers financed their favorite faction in the war. *Caudillos* merely pocketed the money, paid off debts from old campaigns, or exhausted it on new ones. While the economy collapsed, foreign debt doubled between 1846 and 1865.[16]

In contemporary political mythology, the Federal War is viewed as an epic struggle for freedom and equality. This version is embodied in myths surrounding the populist *caudillo* General Ezequiel Zamora, who attracted followers to the cause of federalism with the promise, "There will be neither rich nor poor, neither slaves nor owners, neither powerful nor scorned, but brothers who disdaining leadership will treat each equally, face to face."[17] Indeed, the program offered by the Federalists included many progressive promises, for example, abolition of the death penalty, an end to restrictions on the movement of workers, complete freedom of speech, universal suffrage, even public assistance "in case of incapacity or general scarcity." However, the Federalists offered no comprehensive program of economic and social reform. Zamora himself remained committed to unconditional respect of property rights. Nonetheless, his egalitarian rhetoric infuriated not only his enemies but also many in the Federalist cause. Popular myth has it today that he fell not in battle (in 1860), but was shot in the back by his *caudillo* allies.[18] Thus fallen, Zamora entered the pantheon of popular heroes.

The Federal War ended in 1863, but intermittent violence persisted until the Federalist general Antonio Guzmán Blanco seized power in 1870 and asserted his personal hegemony over the warring political chieftains (*caciques*) and *caudillos*. Guzmán Blanco had fought under the Federalist banner for decentralized, liberal government, but he proceeded to transform the system of caudilloism from the localized variant to a more centralized one. To accomplish this, Blanco implemented a fiscal reform that transferred control of customs taxes, the main source of government revenue, from provincial and local governments to Caracas. Despite the victory of "federalism" in the civil war, provincial governments lost much of their fiscal independence; local *caudillos* became more dependent upon the central government than during the era of Páez.

Like his predecessors, Guzmán Blanco was corrupt and dictatorial, but he had a political project. In his address to Congress on March 1, 1873, the "Illustrious American" proclaimed:

In order that the Liberal Revolution, after 25 years of struggle, should be able to justify itself before posterity and history, it must consolidate a situation of eternal peace, of unquestionable liberty, of perfect order, and of material progress so general, so rapid, and so constantly reproductive that in four or five decades Venezuela may assume in the world scene a role similar to that which the United States has been playing for years.[19]

To achieve "eternal peace" Guzmán executed or imprisoned his opponents after defeating the last *godo* generals on the plains of Apure. He occupied the universities, strongholds of Conservative influence, in Mérida and Caracas. Destruction of the Conservative oligarchy and confiscation of their property provided a basis for enrichment and pacification of his unruly Liberal allies, approximately 150 generals and provincial power brokers. The dictator preferred to govern through rather than against them. When a particular regional *caudillo* would rise in revolt, he could rely on the others to suppress it.

Guzmán undertook an ambitious program of public works, although they grew grandiose and ill-conceived toward the end of his rule. He decreed free and obligatory primary education, through which he hoped to spread the gospel of European positivism. Such a system was never even nearly implemented, but it provided important legal precedents. He elaborated new civil, commercial, military, monetary, and penal codes, established civil matrimony, instituted the first national census, and completed the subordination of the church to the state.

These were important innovations, but like earlier *caudillos* Guzmán Blanco found it necessary to accommodate the financial and commercial elites who controlled the only dynamic part of the economy—exportation of agricultural products. The most important element of this accommodation was an agreement between the government and the *Compañía de Crédito,* a private bank founded and controlled by commercial interests. The *Compañía* functioned as the central bank and treasury of the nation. Revenues from customs taxes and from bonds sold in Europe and North America passed directly into the hands of the financial elite which controlled the institution, later called Banco Commercial.[20]

The bank financed and profited from many construction projects that have left their mark on modern Venezuela. Public buildings and private houses on the main streets of any sizable town were rehabilitated following French neoclassic styles admired by the dictator. Parks, theaters, and other public buildings mimicked European styles. Dedications of plazas and public holidays were occasions for impressive civic celebrations, all part of the plan by the Illustrious American, as the dictator styled himself, to modernize Venezuela. The figure of Bolívar on horseback became a fixture in the center of all main plazas. A national hymn was commissioned, written, and proclaimed, and the present Capitol building was constructed during the era of Guzmán Blanco.

Behind a nationalist facade the dictator looked to Europe to develop Venezuela's economy. Believing his own people inferior, he sought to attract European immigrants and successfully recruited several thousand from the Canary Islands. To induce investment, Guzmán gave foreign companies exclusive rights over natural resources. Foreign loans and contracts were arranged for construction of highways and transportation and to introduce electrification into the country. As an inducement, Guzmán Blanco guaranteed French, English, and German companies a minimum 7 percent profit, in response to which the companies grossly inflated costs.[21]

In 1888, Guzmán Blanco retired of his own volition and sailed off to Paris to live out the rest of his days. Despite all of his projects, in many respects Venezuela was less developed than when he had begun. Many immigrants returned, and few other Europeans proved willing to attempt to overcome the primitive economic infrastructure, dreadful health conditions, and so on. After eighteen years of expensive, foreign-financed projects, the national income from exports stood just where it had been at the start of his rule. By 1897–1898, foreign debt stood at Bs. 123.8 million, domestic debt at Bs. 74.2 million. Only 19 percent of the population was literate. "In very general terms," wrote Judith Ewell, "the Venezuelan population on the brink of the twentieth century was unhealthy, illiterate, unmarried, rural, concentrated on the coastal belt, and numbered just over 2 million. These demographic patterns had been produced by climate, geography, pestilence, civil war, and the demands of plantation agriculture, dotted with mining enclaves and urban commerce."[22]

Cultural Tendencies from the Colonial Period Until 1900

The conditions just described hardly were conducive to a flourishing of the arts, though there always have been worthy exceptions that have best reflected political and social trends. Very little of the pre-Columbian, indigenous heritage has been preserved. The most important archaeological site is located near Quibor, near Barquisimeto, where some accomplished ceramic pieces have been excavated. Sophisticated archaeological excavations have been rare; at a 1990 exhibit of Quibor artifacts in Barquisimeto, emphasis was placed more on educating the public about archaeology itself in order to discourage scavengers from destroying gravesites and other pre-Columbian ruins before they can be reclaimed for posterity.

The lack of internal unity makes it difficult to generalize about cultural tendencies of the colonial period.[23] The Caribbean region, with its African population, the Andes with its mestizo influence, and the *llanos* with its cowboy culture each developed very different types of traditions. The lack of wealth in the colony, for example, in the church, contributed to a simple, austere architecture, much in contrast with the grandeur of Mexico or Peru. When the cacao boom created more propitious conditions, the sentiments that were expressed reflected more *mantuano* resentment toward Spanish rule, particularly evident in the essays of Andrés Bello and in the educational philosophy of Simón Rodríguez, who exercised great influence over Bolívar, himself an important influence on culture as a writer and social critic. What all three have in common is a call, generally unheeded throughout Venezuelan history, for Venezuelans to build their own national culture, though drawing on European traditions and experiences. Among elites, the latter almost always smothered the former. One of the few to break this mold was Don Arístides Rojas, who expressed poetic and historical themes in stories with traditional themes and was greatly revered at the time of his death in 1894.

With independence came important innovations in journalism and the first attempts at historical investigation, but caudilloism and an extremely pessimistic positivism limited developments in both fields. For a brief period under the relative stability imposed by Guzmán Blanco, there was a flowering of nationalism in architecture and painting. Three painters and muralists—Martín Tovar y Tovar, Arturo Michelena, and Cristóbal Rojas—stressed nationalist themes, but with the exception of some impressive landscapes, much of the art depicted portraits and battle scenes from the Independence War. Though some of this work is of admirable quality, it also stands as an uncritical iconography that served to aid Guzmán Blanco's promotion of the cult of Bolívar. It did virtually nothing to awaken consciousness about the revolutionary content of Bolívar's republican and Pan-American ideals.

Had they looked within their own society, Venezuela's artistic elites might have found inspiration in a rich and variegated culture that produced dancing devils on the Caribbean coast, the story of an Indian girl (María Lionza) who became a protector of animals and nature (hardly to be admired by positivists) in rural Yarucuy, the rural fables about the wily rabbit (Tío Conejo) who always outsmarted the more powerful tiger, the spirited folk songs and dances (e.g., the *joropo*) in the *llanos*, and so on. But there was little meeting between city and countryside and little contact among folk traditions. Anyone who cares to dig below the surface of the crass commercialism that overlays modern Venezuelan society today can find many of these traditions still alive, though struggling, waiting to be rediscovered, diffused, and integrated with modern cultural tendencies.

THE ANDEANS TAKE POWER

As the century neared its end, the Venezuelan economy remained highly dependent and underdeveloped. The agricultural sector was divided between a dynamic export sector and an impoverished, underdeveloped sector producing for consumption or a limited domestic market. As late as 1920, 71.6 percent of the economically active population could be found in agriculture, and agricultural exports were still more than fifty-five times that of petroleum exports. The countryside was dominated by the *latifundista/minifundista* land tenure system. One study estimated that of a total of 26,085 property owners in 1891, nearly 20,000 were small holders struggling to survive on parcels of land averaging only 400 square meters each, while 1,184 great landowners controlled parcels averaging 19.4 square kilometers each.[24]

It would be an oversimplification to attribute all of the political changes about to engulf Venezuela around the turn of the century to changes in the pattern of economic dependence; however, the gradual displacement of cacao and leather by coffee as Venezuela's chief export certainly contributed to the shift of social and political power from the *llanos* and coastal plantations to the Andes. By the 1890s, coffee constituted approximately 80 percent of exports among these three principal commodities, with most of the production derived from the three Andean states. The new pattern left the country no less vulnerable, however, to economic crises in the metropolitan centers of capitalism. This revealed itself with disastrous consequences near the end of the century, as the price of Venezuelan coffee plunged from Bs. 5.47 per *quintal* (100 kilograms) in 1894/95 to Bs. 0.83 in 1898/99.[25] Tension among coffee producers, the financial-commercial elite, and the government generated unrest throughout the country. Once again *caudillos* found the situation ripe for political intrigue. The Andeans eventually triumphed, which led to their controlling the government for all but three years between 1899 and 1958. Fate had destined an Andean *caudillo* to occupy the presidential palace of Miraflores when the petroleum boom commenced.

In his report to Congress in February 1899,[26] President Ignacio Andrade's list of the country's afflictions included a plethora of political revolts, a raging viral epidemic, a fiscal crisis arising from the refusal of foreign creditors to authorize new loans, a drastic decline in imports and exports, a decline in the customs taxes (the main source of government revenues), and the collapse of coffee prices (see Table 2.2). Government income had fallen from Bs. 40.6 million to Bs. 27.3 million in only one year. The debt continued to climb (see Table 2.3). Neither Andrade nor any other *caudillo* could muster enough power to deal with the crisis. The only *caudillo* representing traditional liberalism and continuity with

TABLE 2.2 Quantity, Price, and Value of Coffee and Cacao Exports, Selected Years

Year	Product	Quantity[a] (No. of sacks)	Price (Bs. per sack)	Total value
1890	Coffee	847,143	106.14	89,915,758
	Cacao	122,226	88.54	10,821,890
1893	Coffee	959,525	88.34	84,764,438
	Cacao	122,537	78.76	9,651,014
1896	Coffee	789,535	83.58	65,989,335
	Cacao	147,791	62.57	9,247,283
1899	Coffee	803,327	43.24	34,735,859
	Cacao	84,693	76.82	6,506,116

[a]60 kilogram sacks
Source: Adapted, with totals corrected, from María Garbriela Troconis, *Venezuela republicana, siglo XIX* (Caracas: Centro Gumilla, Curso de Formación Sociopolítica 3, 1988), p. 44.

TABLE 2.3 Venezuelan Debt Between 1889 and 1898, in Bolívars (Bs. 5.20 = US $1.00)

Years	To domestic creditors	To international creditors	Total
1889-90	38,245,153	67,388,462	105,633,615
1893-94	104,877,970	72,125,424	177,013,394
1897-98	74,177,555	123,804,859	197,982,414

Source: Adapted from María Gabriela Troconis, *Venezuela republicana, siglo XIX* (Caracas: Centro Gumilla, Curso de Formación Sociopolítica 3, 1988), p. 44.

the Guzmán era, Juan Crespo, died in battle in 1898. Another formidable *caudillo*, José Manuel Hernández ("*El Mocho*," i.e., missing a hand), was unacceptable to the bankers and commercial houses because of his hostility to economic liberalism and suspicion of foreign capital. So in 1899, when General Cipriano Castro gathered a group of fifty-nine other disgruntled Andean comrades and began a march from his native Táchira toward Caracas, his prospects were better than they appeared. His force steadily grew and fought forty-two successful engagements costing 3,000 lives.

Castro's declared intention was to "restore" order and freedom along ideological lines laid down by the Federalist revolution. His second in command and most important financier was another Táchira native, Juan Vicente Gómez.[27] Castro seemed loyal to the traditional liberalism of Guzmán, and he carefully avoided taking sides in the internecine struggles among the other contenders for power. The Caracas elite, fearful of a new round of devastation and alarmed by the nationalistic Hernández, who had raised a formidable army, thought Castro a leader whom they could control. When Castro entered Caracas with only 507 officers and 1,460 troops in 1899 to assume the presidency, he was surrounded by a host of regional *caudillos* and elites who expected the Andeans'

"Restoration Revolution" to bring stability while they retained real power. With the support of the *caudillos* and the reluctant financial backing of Caracas bankers, Castro by May 1900 had subdued his main rival, Hernández, who had created Venezuela's first modern nationalist mass movement by orchestrating a public relations campaign with techniques he had learned in North America, particularly from the yellow press.

The elite and rival *caudillos* discovered that Castro, Gómez, and their compatriots had not marched on Caracas merely to restore the old system under which the president was little more than "first among equals" in an alliance of *caudillos*. They were determined to consolidate power by constructing a centrally controlled, effective national army. Before their advent to power, the army was little more than a fiction in the reports of the Ministry of War and Merchant Marine. Past presidents, including Páez and Guzmán Blanco, had relied more on regional militias and the private armies of allied *caudillos* to defeat internal revolts. Castro and Gómez implemented not a "restoration" of traditional ("yellow") liberalism, but a more modern centralized regime based on fiscal and military reform. The national army became a formidable institution—well equipped, systematically trained, and unified under Andean command.

Castro knew that to expand, train, and equip a professional army and to rule effectively it would be necessary to raise government revenues. He raised taxes on trade, reneged on paying some of the debt incurred by previous governments, and demanded that domestic bankers extend new credits. Extension of credit was especially needed to finance an army capable of defeating Hernández. The bankers had not counted on risking their own capital when they backed Castro, but the Andean, in an astonishing maneuver, jailed five of Caracas's leading financiers, including Manuel Antonio Matos, the single most powerful man in the capital, one of those who had accompanied Castro into Caracas only one year before. Awaiting transportation to a notorious military prison, the bankers reassessed their position and decided to extend the credits.[28]

The social composition and outlook of the Andeans differed from previous regional movements that had seized power since independence. Whereas earlier *caudillo* armies were composed mostly of masses of illiterate peasants seeking to escape penury, Castro's core following was small and included many educated urbanites who were denied opportunities for social advancement within the prevailing political and social structure, some of whom later looked to Gómez for leadership because Castro included non-Andeans in key government positions. Gómez, for example, was not a traditional farmer or landlord; he had made his early fortune as a feedlot operator. The Andean ranks included hacendados, shopkeepers, students, teachers—men whose ambitions and prosperity were threatened by perpetual anarchy and economic crisis. Their frustration had become evident in 1892 when they coalesced to fight for control of the Táchira state government; their march on Caracas was motivated by an attempt to put the national house in order in much the same fashion.

On the one hand, then, the Andean march to power marked a decisive step toward modernization of the central state—a development that preceded the petroleum boom. On the other hand, the Andean revolt was, like earlier uprisings, a regional one. Like earlier *caudillos*, Castro and Gómez had to cope with the reality of Venezuela's dependent economy and the power that the commercial and financial community could exercise as the crucial link to the metropolitan centers of the world economy.[29] Castro, by jailing the bankers, sought to govern *over* rather than *through* this commercial and financial elite. He angered foreign governments and private cartels by pursuing nationalist and Pan-Americanist objectives and by reneging on some foreign and domestic debts, some of which had been used to finance revolts against his own government. Castro also contested the validity of some contracts between the Venezuelan government and foreign companies. The economic situation remained dire as the debt continued to absorb export earnings, and things were to get worse. By 1910, the internal debt stood at Bs. 62 million and the foreign debt had skyrocketed to Bs. 197.5 million. Export earnings, which plunged to Bs. 39.7 million, had recovered in 1910 to only Bs. 96.9 million. With European markets contracting and new countries entering the international coffee market, the agricultural economy was in a grave situation.[30]

Despite the apparent violation of the Monroe Doctrine, the United States failed to support Venezuela in 1902 when England, France, Germany, and Italy blockaded and bombarded Venezuelan ports in an effort to force Castro to meet the demands of his creditors. The U.S. administration presented itself as a "mediator" and convinced Castro and the Europeans to submit the dispute to North American arbitration, despite the fact that U.S. companies were involved in the claims. The decision went heavily against Venezuela, but two years later, the International Court of Justice reduced European and U.S. claims drastically. Castro thus emerged with a significant, nationalistic triumph, infuriating his Yankee enemies, who asserted in the Roosevelt Corollary to the Monroe Doctrine in 1904 that henceforth only they, not the Europeans, would take responsibility for disciplining hemispheric renegades like Castro.

One foreign corporation with a special anger toward Castro was the New York and Bermudez Company, which resented the Venezuelan dictator's transference to another North American company of a concession it had received, but failed to develop, to extract tar from the Orinoco region. In 1892, the Bermudez Company decided to make common cause with Matos and a group of *caudillos* in organizing a revolt known as the "Liberation Revolution." The company provided Matos and a coalition of *caudillo* armies with $145,000 for arms.[31] A German-owned railroad and a French-owned cable company also provided aid because Castro was failing to honor the highly lucrative contracts that they signed with previous governments. Exploiting general discontent with the economic situation, Castro's enemies assembled the most formidable *caudillo* army Venezuela has ever seen. The old system of caudilloism was rallying one last time.

Matos and his allies readied 16,000 troops for an assault on the government's position in La Victoria. Castro rallied thousands of Venezuelans to his side, partly as a result of national revulsion against the European blockade and bombardment. The nationalist Hernández was released from prison and joined Castro's crusade. With Gómez in command, 8,000 government troops inflicted a devastating defeat on the *caudillos* at La Victoria, one of the most important battles ever fought on Venezuelan soil. (Hernández rose one more time in revolt, but he was defeated and sent into exile.)

The demise of the *caudillo* system was thereby sealed by the triumph of the Andean *caudillos* at La Victoria. The *caudillos'* way of war and politics had become obsolete. At La Victoria, the well-armed, numerically superior army assembled by Matos was crippled by the reluctance of each general to throw his followers into a decisive engagement. After all, the *caudillo* with the strongest military force would likely emerge as the next president. By contrast, the government troops were unified under Andean command and better trained and disciplined than any previous army put into the field by a Venezuelan government. After defeat, the *caudillos* scattered with their followers throughout the country. This afforded Gómez, commander of the army, the opportunity to defeat them one by one in their home regions. Altogether, 12,000 died in over 200 battles and skirmishes.

Castro, victorious over domestic and foreign foes alike, reached the epitome of his power. Blustering, corrupt, venal, greedy, and despotic, he nonetheless preached and practiced a fervent nationalism that evoked the enmity of the United States, which broke diplomatic relations with Venezuela in May 1908. Castro seemed secure in his power, but the same social and economic forces that left Venezuela dependent and underdeveloped at the turn of the century would shortly reassert themselves again and permit Castro's ambitious lieutenant, Juan Vicente Gómez, to seize and consolidate power.

Gómez Takes Command

Gómez seized power in 1908 after Castro, forced to seek treatment in Germany for an illness exacerbated by his libertine life style, left the government in his care. The new ruler's rise to power coincided with the emergence of U.S. military intervention and economic expansion into Latin America and the Caribbean. One of Gómez's first acts was to send word to the United States through the good offices of the Brazilian ambassador that he was prepared to negotiate settlements satisfactory to the United States on all outstanding matters, and he asked for help in consolidating power. By the time of the First World War (1914–1918), the United States was able to ensure that German influence, which had been growing in Venezuela, was thoroughly contained. As Rómulo Betancourt, who would launch his political career in the struggle to overthrow Gómez, once put it, "The unpredictable tyrant had been replaced by one who was submissive."[32]

The United States responded to Gómez's overtures in 1908 by sending a special commissioner to negotiate with the new government. Accompanying him were three U.S. battleships, ready in case the new ruler faced resistance from supporters of Castro. As Betancourt described it:

> Events now unfolded like a film script. In his first week of power, Gómez had various talks with the U.S. commissioner. The three great hulking warships of steel were at the La Guaira docks, their cannon shining in the sun, and their marines drilling on deck daily, with the steady crackle of small arms fire in the target practice area. They were a healthy warning to the natives.[33]

Three months later protocols were signed reversing or compromising economic victories achieved under Castro, including those won in the World Court. A grateful Washington coordinated a successful diplomatic and military blockade to prevent Castro from returning to Venezuela and fomenting a new revolt.

Gómez continued Castro's policy of modernizing the military. Service academies for commissioned and noncommissioned officers were opened. Modern arms and training were obtained from the United States, Europe, and other Latin American countries. A new Inspectorate General assured central control of the armed forces, and new roads and telegraph networks allowed Gómez to deploy and control the army as no Venezuelan dictator had ever done before. The military budget, which was only Bs. 3 million in 1900, rose to Bs. 7 million in 1910 and Bs. 10.9 million in 1913. In a country with 80 to 85 percent illiteracy, the army's budget was three times that allotted for education in 1920.[34]

Between 1908 and 1913, Gómez went about the process of consolidating power. The regional *caudillos* and *caciques* had supported the ouster of Castro in the hope of regaining their power, and Gómez did create a Federal Council on which they sat. However, by 1914 Gómez felt strong enough to abolish the council, signalling the end of the system of local autonomy that had heretofore characterized the *caudillo* system. Páez had ruled over a decentralized system of *caudillos* and *caciques*, Guzmán Blanco over a centralized one; Gómez constructed the first central state able to prevail over regional interests without having to play one *caudillo* off against another.

Like Guzmán and Páez, Gómez sought to utilize the mythology of Bolívar to legitimate his rule. He presented his new, powerful army as the instrument to realize, 100 years later, Bolívar's dream of building an authoritative, unified state. "Providence, inscrutable in its designs, has conceded me the very high honor of presiding over our country during the Centenary of our independence," he pronounced at Carabobo, site of an important battle of the war against Spain.[35] Gómez also sought to justify his autocratic measures and military expenditures by exaggerating the threat of a return of Castro, at least until the unfortunate "man without a country" died in 1924. Thereafter, anticommunism supplied a suitable replacement.

Gómez put state finances in order by appointing to his cabinet several technically capable ministers closely identified with the commercial elite and bankers. Fiscal reforms, enacted between 1914 and 1919, reduced the relative share of customs taxes among government revenues, much to the delight of importers, and increased collection of taxes on liquor, cigarettes, stamps, etc. A system of central vigilance over tax collection was installed, and a systematic, unified budget linking revenues to expenditures was created. As a result, total government debt rose but modestly from Bs. 210 million to Bs. 233 million between 1909 and 1923.[36]

The most articulate defense of Gómez came from Laureano Vallenilla Lanz. Though reviled today for his service to the dictator, Lanz transcended mere sycophancy. Like earlier Venezuelan positivists, Lanz denigrated the Venezuelan national character, but he avoided crude racism; his writings offer an insightful analysis of how nineteenth-century caudilloism, violence, and anarchy were rooted in the country's primitive social and economic structure. Lanz coined the phrase "Democratic Caesarism" to describe *gomecista* rule. Though not freely elected, he argued, Gómez's regime was democratic because it was embarked on a mission consistent with the national will.[37]

Of course, the rule of Gómez was anything but democratic. Dissidents found themselves condemned to primitive jails where one of the dictator's sons supervised tortures. Some prisoners were hung by their feet or genitals; some had straps tightened by a tourniquet around their head until their eyes nearly popped out. Prisoners customarily wore 100-pound leg irons around each ankle; one dissident editor languished for twenty years in this condition. Yet it is difficult to measure the actual degree of cruelty exercised by Venezuela's most notorious dictator. Just as his opponents had every interest in exaggerating his crimes while he was in power, his democratic successors find in his rule the mirror image of their idealized version of modern democracy. For example, opponents of Gómez claimed that in 1917 there were 100,000 exiles.[38] There is little doubt that many prominent Venezuelans were driven abroad, but since Venezuela barely counted 2,000,000 inhabitants at the time, this count seems exaggerated. As we shall see in the case of oil policy, the sins of unelected governments have usually been exaggerated and their accomplishments denigrated. The bromide that victors write history holds true for Venezuela.

Gómez relied upon an Andean clique to control the political and military apparatus. *Andinos* occupied ministries, presidencies of states, judgeships, congressional seats, municipal council seats, prefectures, diplomatic posts; they were appointed secretaries, archivists, telegraphists, justices of the peace. However, Andeans also endured more *gomecista* brutality than other Venezuelans, especially in Táchira, which suffered under the boot of the dictator's cousin, Eustaquio.

Gómez built a formidable overseas espionage network to complement a corps of petty officials who assiduously reported on opposition activities at home and who kept track of one another as well. Local judges were especially valued for their knowledge of local grievances and disputes; communications workers, in turn, reported on the activity of the judges and other local authorities. The historian Ramón Velásquez in his imaginary conversations with Gómez has the dictator explain, "I appoint telegraphists everywhere so that they respond to me, and I give the head telegraphist of each state the same confidence that I do the President of the state. Because the telegraphist communicates to me not only what the president chooses to send, but also sends me his own information, and then I can compare this information with other news."[39] This intelligence made it possible for Gómez to anticipate and diffuse challenges to his power from local and exiled *caudillos*. All five major revolts launched from outside Venezuela's borders were quickly snuffed out.

By 1910, Venezuela had a national political apparatus dominated not by a party, but by a regional clique headed by a single, autocratic

TABLE 2.4 Volume and Value of Coffee, Cacao, and Petroleum Exports, Selected Years

Years		Coffee	Cacao	Petroleum
1920-21	Amount[a]	622,464	288,339	100,970
	Value (Bs.)	45,357,205	17,657,058	5,261,443
1926-27	Amount	717,417	249,416	6,126,789
	Value (Bs.)	92,791,338	23,037,262	259,147,393
1935-36	Amount	969,663	268,944	22,618,474
	Value (Bs.)	32,077,280	8,320,420	676,769,078

[a]Coffee and cacao in metric tons, petroleum in barrels.
Source: Adapted from Eveling Bravo and Napoleon Franceschi, *Problemas de la historia contemporánea* (Valencia: Vadell Hermanos, 1980), pp. 217-218.

caudillo. The cradle of South American independence descended into another twenty-five years of despotism. It would not end until Gómez died in bed in 1935.

GÓMEZ STRIKES OIL

Even before the arrival of the oil industry, it was clear that the Gómez era represented a watershed in Venezuelan history. The subordination of regional and local *caudillos,* fiscal and administrative reforms, and the professionalization of the military were all accomplished *before* the influx of oil revenues began in earnest. In 1921, earnings from coffee exports were nearly nine times greater than petroleum exports. Between 1921 and 1925 petroleum exports rose from Bs. 5.26 million to Bs. 259.15 million. In 1936, oil earnings were Bs. 676.77 million, more than twenty-one times coffee earnings (see Table 2.4).[40] From the mid-1920s through World War II, Venezuela was the world's second-largest producer (after the United States) of petroleum and was its largest exporter.

Unlike coffee, oil was not produced primarily by Venezuelan labor or capital. Most of what the nation retained depended upon what the state could capture through a combination of taxes and royalties. In the early era, the bulk of company wages went to foreign employees—to technical, managerial, and skilled employees from Europe and North America and to semiskilled and unskilled laborers imported from the Caribbean. The oil industry thus was implanted as an enclave, a source of economic accumulation and investment with few direct forward or backward linkages to the rest of the domestic economy.

This was perfectly consonant with political philosophy and style of *gomecista* rule. In a 1911 interview, the dictator avowed, "Far from wanting, like Castro, to isolate Venezuela, my desire is to open her to foreign labor in more favorable conditions and with guarantees of peace, security, and stable property." Thirty months later he proclaimed to

Congress that he had "put an end to war and opened for my compatriots the stockade of riches of the true Republic." The nation lacked, Gómez argued, "capital, labor, science, and experience for our industrial development; and as we do not have such indispensable factors, it is necessary to obtain them from the foreigner who offers us good will." He went on to promise that Venezuela would be financially responsible so that it might "enjoy the broad benefit of happiness under the protection of that perfect peace [that comes to] governments which comply with their duties."[41]

Self-educated, a teetotaler, unmarried but sexually promiscuous, Gómez, who had acquired a modest personal fortune as a cattle feedlot operator in his native Táchira, did not hesitate to exploit the "stockade of riches" himself. He acquired and developed an immense personal fortune in ranching, feedlots, slaughterhouses, and a dairy industry in the city of Maracay, approximately 100 miles west of Caracas, which he made his personal headquarters and the most important military base in the country. His relatives and close friends followed suit. When the companies began in earnest to acquire rights to explore and extract oil, Gómez used state ownership of subsoil resources to allocate concessions first to his relatives and friends, who subsequently sold them to the companies. His personal fortune has been estimated by his enemies to have reached $300 million in 1927, perhaps as much as $400 million by his death.[42] This may be an exaggeration, but there is little doubt that he was the largest landowner and wealthiest individual in Venezuela upon his death.

The governing circles were composed of family and close friends. In 1925 close relatives of Gómez occupied the presidencies of five states. Gómez shared with the landed oligarchy a determination to minimize the impact of the industry on the traditional, semifeudal, rural society and economy, but the oil boom only compounded the crisis of the agricultural export sector, including Andean coffee producers. As Venezuelan society was becoming more complex (see Table 2.5), the political structure was actually becoming more rigid. Although the dictator and his clique kept their grip on power for twenty-five years, the system of rule created by Gómez was ultimately inconsistent with the social consequences of the oil boom.

This contradiction made itself felt in the military. As Castro and the other *caudillos* receded as a real threat, the Gómez clique found other ways to use the armed forces. As the public works budget expanded, *gomecista* army officers and local political chiefs put troops to work to complete highly lucrative contracts. This practice gave rise to the term "highway Colonels," officers who completed projects with little technical expertise but large profit margins. More professional officers resented

TABLE 2.5   Distribution of the Work Force in Venezuela, 1920 and 1936

Sector	1920 Number of persons	Percent	1936 Number of persons	Percent
Petroleum	2,000	0.3	13,800	1.2
Industry	20,000	3.1	51,000	4.7
Artisans	35,600	5.6	96,600	9.0
Commerce	51,100	8.0	64,300	6.0
Construction	8,000	1.3	4,400	0.6
Transportation	16,000	2.5	25,000	2.3
Public Services	13,400	2.1	56,200	4.0
Domestic Service	35,000	5.5	108,300	10.0
Agriculture	457,000	71.6	625,000	57.9

Source: Adapted from Eveling Bravo and Napoleon Franceschi, *Problemas de la historia Venezuela contemporánea* (Valencia: Vadell Hermanos, 1980), p. 218.   Bravo and Franceschi's figures for 1936 differ from Central Bank data presented in Table 4.1; however, the latter is not based on comparable categories used for data available for 1920.

such practices, but if they criticized the system they found their own careers cut short. Many found their advancement limited by political favoritism, and the higher ranks were filled with incapable *gomecistas*. The situation worsened after some officers rebelled in solidarity with a student uprising in 1928. Gómez abolished the Inspectorate General and placed its functions under control of his son, whom he had made vice-president. Thus were sown the seeds of the coup of 1945, when some officers would ally themselves with civilian modernizers to inaugurate Venezuela's first experiment with electoral democracy.

Rented Nation

The political change that rapidly engulfed Venezuela after the death of Gómez cannot be understood apart from an appreciation of how the arrival of the oil industry transformed Venezuela and its role in the world economy, and also how the relationship between the Venezuelan state and the oil companies logically encouraged a heightened sense of Venezuelan nationalism. The relationship between the Venezuelan state, as owner of the nation's subsoil resources, and the companies assumed that of a landlord-tenant relationship. As tenants, the companies sought to secure concessions of long duration and stable terms, with minimal obligations, for example, to maintain the level of investment toward the end of the lease, and (of course) with a rent fixed as low as possible. Other potential areas of negotiation included conservation, tax incentives, technology transfer, training and employment, and the crucial issue of how the price on which the royalty would be calculated was to be determined.

From the time of Gómez until the founding of the Organization of Petroleum Exporting Countries (OPEC) in 1960, Venezuela and other host countries had little control over pricing, but the high and expanding demand for oil in the industrial countries ensured that even without this power the profits to be divided between the companies (renters) and the state (landlord) would be extraordinary compared to other industries. The key issue, then, until 1960 was what percentage of these extraordinary profits would accrue to the landlord state. Although in most agrarian societies the property owner had more power than the tenant, this was not the case with oil in the Third World. With little technological or scientific expertise of its own and virtually no economic infrastructure, Venezuela's initial bargaining position was weak.[43]

On the other hand, Venezuela held one significant advantage over most other Third World countries with oil, including those in the Middle East: It was politically sovereign. It had the juridical right to tax its citizens—corporate and real, private and foreign. This right to tax is not subject, in theory, to limitation; it is the absolute right of a sovereign nation. Hence, regardless of limits on royalty payments embodied in formal contracts, the state might potentially use its powers of taxation to increase its share of profits, that is, to increase rents. The companies, as tenants, were determined to limit this power.

Thus, the Venezuelan state has presented two faces to the companies—that of landlord and that of sovereign. Whether or not the government would assert its sovereign powers of taxation to raise rents depended not only upon the international conjuncture but also upon the character of the state itself. Gómez shared the social outlook of Venezuela's landed oligarchy, but the main goal seemed to be to convert as much of the country as he could into his personal hacienda. While the agricultural crisis persisted, landowners found opportunities to enrich themselves through land speculation, subsidies, commissions, leases, and so on.

Although Venezuela was sovereign, it was dependent and weak. Few Venezuelans had any familiarity with the oil industry, and the companies had little interest in raising their knowledge. (Of course, they themselves were not fully aware of the extent and natural productivity of the country's reserves.) Early relations with the companies and legislation reflected the weakness of the host country and the hegemony of landed property within the political system. In conformity with Hispanic and colonial traditions, which themselves reflected feudal relations of property, ownership of mines was vested in the state. When a new Law of Mines was passed in 1909, it granted private landowners the right to sell concessions to the companies and mandated that these landowners should receive one-third of the profits realized from exploitation. Until 1976, Royal Dutch Shell extracted the majority of its production in Venezuela from concessions obtained originally under this law, but it did not long have to abide the high royalties. With the support of the government, which (correctly) saw this provision as an obstacle to attracting foreign capital, the Supreme Court ruled the royalty provision void and returned ownership of subsoil resources to the state.

With the first successful wells and the experience of World War I, Venezuela's elites began to awaken to the potential value of oil on the world market. Gumersindo Torres, Gomez's minister of investment, represented the views of the landed oligarchy, a social class that well understood the concept of rent and regarded it as an inalienable property right. He suspended concessions in 1917 and, based on a study of practices in the United States and Mexico, advocated that a 5 percent royalty on production and additional fees be collected. These were not to go to the state but to private landowners. The state should be content with a low enough tax not to discourage foreign capitalists from seeking such concessions. In contrast, the banker Vicente Lecuna presented a different view: Because Venezuela, unlike the United States, did not consume the oil it produced, it was more important for the state to maintain ownership of the oil, forego royalties, and instead rely on taxes to extract a portion of oil profits equivalent to 15.5 percent (what Lecuna believed to be the royalty extracted on federal lands in the United States) and put them to work for the nation (i.e., capitalists like Lecuna).

This latter position was naturally opposed by the companies who preferred to deal with multiple landlords and have a contractually fixed rent (royalty), rather than deal with a single landlord (the state) with the option of increasing its share of oil profits by raising taxes. A decline in oil prices at the time helped their case. A 1920 law more favorable to Lecuna's position was revised under pressure from the companies and landlords, resulting in the compromise law of 1922. This law provided for royalties (not taxes) somewhere between the U.S. level and the 5 percent advocated by Torres. Companies were given the expanded right to retain control over proven reserves, an incentive for them to increase production despite falling prices. State ownership was reaffirmed, but landowners were given preferential rights in the competition for concessions—that is, to establish themselves as intermediaries between the state and companies.[44]

Virtually all concessions granted after 1918 came to be covered under the 1922 law, which with minor modifications governed company-state relations until the major reform of 1943. With the important exception of the Shell concessions, the most important Venezuelan fields were brought into production under the provisions of the 1922 law. By the time the dance of concessions was over, Standard Oil (Creole, in Venezuela) was the largest company. These two companies and Gulf

Oil Corporation together came to control 99 percent of production by the end of the 1930s.

Company profits on Venezuelan operations were fantastic. In 1927, Venezuelan Shell paid its shareholders a 55.5 percent dividend on investment, gaining $3.8 million on only $10 million invested. The Standard Oil of Indiana subsidiary, Lago Petroleum, earned $8 million on an investment of only $3.5 million. At the end of the Gómez period, the companies were paying royalties amounting to only 10 percent, well below standards elsewhere in the world. Although never articulated precisely in these terms, the Venezuelan state was unable by terms of the lease it had signed to raise the "rent" on its wealthy tenants because it had granted generous tax exemptions, and the long-term leases (concessions) prohibited it from raising taxes.

The importance of the tax exoneration was not lost on Torres. After returning to his cabinet post in 1929, he reported that in the previous seven years the Venezuelan state had received Bs. 187 million from the companies. However, as a result of the exoneration from customs taxes on business-related imports, a provision liberally interpreted by the oil companies, the state had forgone Bs. 219 million. "From the comparison of these figures," asserted Torres, "comes the distressing calculation that it would have been preferable not to have collected any tax on exploitation in favor of the payment of exonerated customs taxes."[45]

CONCLUSION

Even without the revenue foregone through tax concessions, the influx of dollars for rents, investments, and wages constituted a dramatic economic windfall for a small, technologically backward country just emerging from a century of near anarchy and economic crisis. During the 1920s, a number of Venezuelan thinkers began to examine the issues raised by the boom. One, Alberto Adriani, who would briefly serve before his untimely death in the cabinet of Gómez's successor, called the oil industry "a foreign, provincial enclave within the national economy," one that "exercises a relatively insignificant influence over the prosperity of our people." Looking about at the rest of the continent, Adriani warned:

> In general, the Latin American, upon acquiring more or less considerable capital, is preoccupied only in transforming it into luxury goods and in diversions and other non-economic employment. The person that accumulates capital, or in any case his offspring, retreats from his people to Paris or to the capital, and deserts production.[46]

Oil well in eastern fields, state of Anzoátegui (photo courtesy of Petroleos de Venezuela S.A.)

As the oil-based economy collapsed in the 1980s, Venezuelans might easily mistake Adriani's analysis for a contemporary critique.

Other intellectuals and some Venezuelan businessmen began to look beyond the narrow horizons of the financial-commercial elites of Caracas, the circle of Andeans around Gómez, and the traditional landed elite, but they lacked a political strategy to implement an alternative economic future. Several families with immigrant roots, most notably the English Boultons, the German Vollmers, and the Basque Zuloagas, had growing and diversified economic interests, but they lacked the political will to challenge the system. However, from the ranks of the growing middle class and working class, especially from university students, there emerged political leaders with a new perspective on Gómez, oil, and Venezuela's place in the world. They began to demand that Venezuela, in the words of intellectual Arturo Uslar Pietri, "sow the petroleum" before it ran out.[47]

One group of students, inspired by the Russian Revolution, was drawn early to communism. As early as 1921, two of them, Salvador de la Plaza and Gustavo Machado, went into exile after participating in antiregime protests. In exile, Machado would become an ally of the Salvadoran Communist Faribundo Martí and head of the hemispheric solidarity committee, "Hands Off Nicaragua," which organized support for the Nicaraguan patriot Agusto César Sandino fighting to expel the U.S. Marines from his country. Other young Communists, like Juan Bautista Fuenmayor, Rodolfo Quintero, and Pio Tamayo, began organizing petroleum workers in the western fields and camps. These were the roots of the Venezuelan Communist Party, which issued its first manifesto in 1931 and officially constituted itself as a formal party in 1937.

The young Communists abroad were later joined in exile by another large group of Venezuelan students who had organized a demonstration against Gómez in April 1928. Some of these students also studied Marxism, but they were also influenced by the Mexican Revolution and by the radical student movement, APRA, which had emerged in the sister republic of Peru under the leadership of Víctor Raúl Haya de la Torre. In January 1932, a young student of this "Generation of 1928" issued his first major theoretical work, "With Whom and Against Whom We Stand." He wrote:

> For those of us who have analyzed the history and the present situation of the country from a materialist point of view, there is no room for vacillation in affirming that in Venezuela exists a tyranny—sharply defined as the dictatorship—of a class, and not of one man or of one region. . . . In Venezuela exists the tyranny of the landlord, merchant, industrial class—in one word, capitalist—exercised over the great productive masses

of the nation with the collaboration of Gómez and his coterie of petty thieves and relatives.[48]

Rómulo Betancourt, who would dominate Venezuelan politics for the next fifty years, had begun to define a political project that would culminate in the founding of *Acción Democrática*, the dominant party in Venezuelan politics since 1941 and the ultimate arbiter of how Venezuela would "sow" its petroleum.

3

Acción Democrática, *Vanguard of the Venezuelan Bourgeoisie*

On December 17, 1935, General Juan Vicente Gómez, dictator of Venezuela for a quarter century, died of natural causes. Following the extant constitution, the cabinet met and chose General Eleazar López Contreras, another Andean, as president. Aware that close relatives and associates of Gómez mistrusted him, López Contreras sought to rally popular support by announcing the release of political prisoners and the return of exiles. Four days later, Eustoquio Gómez, hated governor of both Táchira and the important central state of Lara, tried to seize power. The army remained loyal to López; Eustoquio died in the revolt. Neither the army nor the Venezuelan people had much stomach for a continuation of *gomecista* rule. A wave of violence washed over those most closely identified with the dictator in the countryside.

Gómez was dead, his closest collaborators liquidated, but important aspects of *gomecismo* lingered. In three whirlwind months Venezuela passed from a feverish, revolutionary atmosphere to a new political equilibrium managed by López Contreras and his successor, General Isaías Medina Angarita. The violence failed to overturn the semifeudal, social structure in the countryside. By limiting suffrage, the oligarchy continued to dominate local and state politics; indirect elections allowed them to retain a majority in Congress and great influence over the courts and the president. Many *gomecista* generals remained in the top ranks of the military, to the consternation of many professionally trained officers. Against these forces, López and Medina balanced the demands of the Communists and reformists.

However, the forces of change were ineluctable. In 1945, Medina was overthrown by military officers who had committed themselves to direct, popular elections. This led to a three-year period, the *trienio*,

47

during which Betancourt's Democratic Action (AD) party totally dominated the government. After three years, AD was overthrown, and
Venezuela slipped under the heel of yet another Andean general, Marcos
Pérez Jiménez. Nonetheless, the future of Venezuela, history would prove,
lay more with Betancourt and his civilian contemporaries than with the
military.

How did Betancourt, once editor of a Communist newspaper in
Costa Rica and a virulent critic of U.S. imperialism, evolve into a
reformist, anticommunist leader, sympathetic toward the United States?
How did the Democratic Action party wrest hegemony over the working
class from the Venezuelan Communist Party (PCV)? Why and how did
the military snuff out an overwhelmingly popular government in 1948
with hardly any resistance? The answers lie in understanding the relationship between the political parties and the social and economic
forces generated by the oil boom.

RÓMULO BETANCOURT AND
THE DEMOCRATIC ACTION PARTY

Rómulo Betancourt was born in Guatire, a small commercial town
in the state of Miranda, twenty-five miles east of Caracas, a two-and-
one-half-hour journey by automobile. His father was an accountant and
the manager of a retail store. Fortunately for Betancourt, his parents
moved to the capital and enrolled young Rómulo in a prestigious
secondary school. He entered the Central University of Venezuela (UCV)
in 1926 to study law. At the UCV he developed associations with a
group of students who would become the protagonists of twentieth-
century Venezuelan history, the Generation of 1928. Among them were
Jóvito Villalba, a fiery orator who founded an influential political party,
Democratic Republican Union (URD); Raul Leoni, a cofounder of *Acción
Democrática* and president of Venezuela from 1963–1968; and Juan Bautista
Fuenmayor, a founder of the PCV.[1]

The Federation of Venezuelan Students (FEV), successor to an
organization dissolved by Gómez in 1921, had called for a week of
celebrations beginning February 6, 1928, to commemorate its reconsti-
tution. The original plans called for a nonpolitical event, but the organizers
found it impossible to suppress their discontent with the dictatorship.
After the "queen" of the festival laid a wreath on the tomb of Bolívar
in the *Panteón* (where Venezuela's national heroes are buried), Villalba
addressed the crowd with a cryptic prayer. "Our Father, Simón Bolívar;
our father, Liberator," he implored, "Speak, oh father! Before the university, where the fatherland was forged years ago. Your rebel voice of
San Jacinto can be heard again at this place, where Beatriz I of Venezuela

has offered you the fresh sweetness of these flowers. Give us the secret of three hundred [sic] years ago."[2]

The students accused Gómez of imprisoning liberty within the *Panteón;* the dictator wasted little time in imprisoning the students. What was unexpected was the massive popular response to his action. Twenty years of frustration and repression exploded in a storm of protests and strikes, confronting Gómez with something quite unlike the *caudillo* revolts he had so skillfully and easily suppressed. He released the students after only eleven days.

In April, Betancourt and some of the other students supported an unsuccessful coup by lower-ranking officers frustrated with the incompetency and dominance of the Andean military clique, a harbinger of the civilian-military conspiracy of 1945 that brought AD to power. López Contreras, minister of defense, respected for his professionalism yet loyal to Gómez, suppressed the revolt but managed to moderate the punishment meted out to the conspirators. Thus, the future successor to Gómez acquired a reputation for moderation and respect from those who wanted change, even as he proved his loyalty to *gomecista* rule.

Betancourt and other students joined a coterie of exiled political opponents, mostly old *caudillos* and radicals affiliated with the Communist Venezuelan Revolutionary Party (PRV), founded in 1926 in Mexico. The PRV (nicknamed *"perros rabiosos,"* or "mad dogs") derided Betancourt and his allies for their naivete and their lack of a class analysis of the dictatorship. Later, Betancourt would admit that cooperation with an ill-fated *caudillo* revolt in 1929 was action for action's sake—*"garibaldismo."*[3] In fact, some of the young Communists were drawn to similar conspiracies. Nonetheless, the criticism and countercriticism was often vitriolic, contributing to a lifelong enmity between Betancourt and most Venezuelan Communists.

Betancourt liked to describe the period between 1929 and 1935 as part of his political "prehistory." Describing his own participation in the Costa Rican Communist party as a youthful flirtation, he claimed:

> As was common among most American youth of the 1930s, most of the exiled students—with the fervor of neophytes—delved deeply into the classics of socialism. For a brief time, at least, we believed that Russia was developing a social system that would have universal application. We even dreamed of a Bolshevik-type revolution with our czar of Maracay [Gómez] being shot at dawn. However, none of us who later founded the Acción Democrática political party . . . ever became active members of political groups subordinate to the Third International. . . . We began to understand that this political party was under foreign influence, was deaf

and blind to the vital needs of our peoples, and was only a cult of worship
which gave blind obeisance to the imperious orders of the Comintern.[4]

Betancourt certainly never joined any Venezuelan Communist group,
and he may have never "subordinated" himself to the Third International.
However, his participation in the Costa Rican Communist party cannot
be written-off as merely a youthful dalliance. Betancourt rose to the
ranks of leadership in the Costa Rican party and was entrusted with
the sensitive task of editing its newspaper, *Trabajo*. The party acknowledged the leadership of the Comintern's Caribbean Bureau, embraced
Marxist class analysis and Lenin's theories on imperialism, and constituted
itself internally along democratic centralist lines.[5] Betancourt applied the
principles of class analysis and the organizational lessons he absorbed
in Costa Rica to a reformist project once he returned to Venezuela.

Over time, any suggestion that Marxism or communism had contributed to the *adeco* (AD party) formula for political success became a
heresy within AD. In 1958, Betancourt deliberately excluded the Communists from the political pact formed to ease a transition to democracy,
which contributed to the outbreak of guerrilla warfare in the 1960s.
Fidel Castro and Cuba both became anathema to Betancourt. Upon
Betancourt's death in 1981, obituaries in the daily newspapers, ignoring
his editorial work at *Trabajo*, suggested that he had regarded Marxism
and nationalism as antithetical all of his life. To affirm that the "father
of Venezuelan democracy" was for almost five years in Costa Rica one
of the principal leaders of a Communist party had become too controversial for public acknowledgment.[6]

In fact, Betancourt's progression from the naive collaborator in the
caudillo revolts of 1928 and 1929 to the extraordinarily successful leader
of Venezuela during a period of intense social and economic transformation owes much to Marxism and to Leninism, which unmistakably
influenced his analysis of the Gómez regime and his conception of how
a political party should be organized. In 1931, Betancourt wrote to a
fellow exile that his experience and studies in Costa Rica were preparing
him "to approach this new type of politics less pre-occupied with intrigue
and more in possession of the scientific keys for solving problems."[7]
Shortly afterward, there appeared the *Plan of Barranquilla*, issued by
Betancourt and other young exiles who had formed the Revolutionary
Group of the Left (ARDI). When the exiles returned to Venezuela after
the death of Gómez, they formed a broader group, the Organization for
Venezuela (ORVE), with a similar perspective.

In the *Plan* and then in "The Minimal Plan of ARDI," Betancourt
and his colleagues advocated a reformist program designed to appeal
not only to the Venezuelan working class, which, they argued, was

minuscule and incapable of forming the social base for a socialist revolution, but also to the middle class, petty bourgeoisie, and the peasantry. The *Plan* asserted that Venezuela lacked not only a working class, but also lacked a capitalist class capable of leading national development. This void could be filled only by the state, but the existing state, dominated by the domestic oligarchy and imperialists (the oil companies), could not be expected to take initiatives to modernize Venezuela. Therefore, Betancourt asserted:

> We aspire to the formation of a provisional united front with the exploited sectors of the city and the countryside, semi-proletarians, poor peasants, schoolteachers, commercial employees working for starvation wages, etc., to oppose . . . the reactionary front which will result from the collaboration between imperialist finance capital and the international bourgeois-*caudillo* bloc.[8]

The PRV initially derided ARDI's program and multiclass strategy, which to them smacked of social democracy, then under attack by the Comintern dominated by Stalin, as a type of fascism. Following the line of the Comintern and disregarding the agrarian, semifeudal social structure of *gomecista* Venezuela, the PRV insisted that a working class and peasant alliance could bring about an immediate socialist revolution. However, in 1935, faced with the growing strength of fascism, the Comintern shifted and stressed the importance of building popular fronts. This paved the way for the creation of the Democratic Nationalist Party (PDN) which joined together the PRV, ORVE, and other Communist and reformist groups, notably those in Maracaibo and the nearby oil fields.

Politics After the Death of Gómez

The alliance of ORVE and the Communists under the umbrella of a single party would last only until 1938, but these were critical years for the future of Venezuela. The death of the dictator and the coup attempt by Eustoquio had unleashed a wave of mass revulsion against Gómez's family and cronies, threatening to ignite a full-scale popular uprising. Mobs sacked *gomecista* homes in Maracaibo and Caracas. Strikes broke out among bus drivers, longshoremen, textile workers, and other workers in Venezuela's small industrial sector. Riots broke out in the oil town of Cabimas and in several camps.

In rural areas, peasants marched on the homes of landowners and local government officials closely associated with the hated regime. One newspaper account described a Christmas Eve confrontation between the wife of a landowner and an angry mob of campesinos:

Señora Muños Rueda asked them what they wanted, and [the leader] responded that they had come by order of the government to kill, burn, and exact justice for seven years of tyranny. The *señora* demanded that he show the papers authorizing such horrors, and he responded that he did not have to show her any paper, shouting: "Long live the liberty of the Poor, down with the Rich!" . . . They hurled themselves through the portico that separated the house from the crowd, destroying it, and they began to spread kerosene, . . . smashing the furniture and other belongings to pieces with their machetes.[9]

The Caracas press continued to report unrest throughout January 1936. The government suspended constitutional rights, but this only provoked more demonstrations. On February 14 troops opened fire on an unarmed crowd in front of the municipal building in Caracas. Massive protests erupted throughout the city. In response, López Contreras removed the governor of the Federal District (Caracas) and restored constitutional guarantees. The new president adroitly moved to distance himself from the old regime and to gain the support of the new urban forces in politics by announcing—in the nation's first political address carried by radio—his "February Program," the first social and economic program of government in Venezuelan history. It included a constitutional legality, measures to promote the health, education, and welfare of citizens, labor rights, reform of taxation and banking laws, investment in communications and transportation, and other promises that marked a distinct break with the philosophy of *gomecismo*.

The *gomecistas* were hardly in a position to challenge López Contreras, given the explosive political conditions. The Communist and noncommunist left feared, however, that *gomecista* elements would take advantage of the violence and near anarchy to impose a new dictatorship. In April 1936, ORVE and PRV jointly announced that they would find it acceptable for the *gomecista* Congress to meet to confirm López Contreras as the legitimate constitutional president for a full term (1936–1941) of office. According to their plan Congress would amend the constitution to permit direct elections and then resign. Indeed, Congress met and confirmed López Contreras as president, but that was all it did.

Although failing to achieve direct elections, the left organized actively and confidently throughout 1936. In the Maracaibo area, other leftist groups were organizing workers in the crucial petroleum sector. In December 1936, they launched a historic strike for higher wages, improved working conditions, more jobs for Venezuelans, recognition of unions, and other demands. The strike became a national crusade, evoking acts of solidarity throughout the country. For example, the children of oil workers were brought to Caracas for care to relieve the financial burden on their parents. However, the strike came during the Depression, an era of slack demand for petroleum. Although middle-class groups offered solidarity, white collar employees refused to strike themselves. López Contreras, no nationalist firebrand and alarmed that the leadership of the oil workers was preponderantly Communist, imposed a settlement that raised wages modestly but failed to satisfy the key demand, recognition of the union and a negotiated contract with the companies.

The strike proved a political watershed. The president reversed his field politically. The *gomecista*-controlled Congress had passed an anticommunist law (*Ley Lara*), and López seized upon it to declare all existing leftist parties and organizations illegal. Most Communist and leftist leaders were forced once again into exile. A few, including Betancourt, evaded capture and organized clandestinely for several years. In 1939, Betancourt was captured and sent into his second exile in Chile, returning in 1941.

By quelling popular agitation and refusing to permit direct elections, López Contreras had removed a major deterrent to foreign intervention and a bargaining chip to use in negotiating with the oil companies. The companies helped to publish a book, the notorious *Libro Rojo* (*Red Book*), filled with materials "proving" that many ORVE members, including Betancourt, were Communists. The Dutch government stationed a gunboat capable of entering Lake Maracaibo just off shore during the petroleum workers strike, a reminder to the new president that Shell regarded its arrangements with the former dictator as sacrosanct. It was widely rumored, and taken seriously by the U.S. embassy, that the oil companies were encouraging a *gomecista* general to foment a secessionist revolt in the Maracaibo area. The embassy, following Roosevelt's Good Neighbor Policy, kept an arms length from such tactics, but it also did nothing to encourage a reasonable attitude on the part of the companies.[10]

Despite the growing threat from the government, relations between most of the Communists and Betancourt's followers remained tense. Each continued to publish its own newspaper even after merging into the PDN. In 1938 the Communists left the PDN to form the Communist Party of Venezuela (PCV). The PDN was decimated, but Betancourt threw himself into clandestine organizing. He combed the country, eluding police, developing a network of grassroots supporters and organizers in a wide range of social sectors. The Communists were stronger among the petroleum workers, dock workers, and other blue collar sectors, but the PDN was expanding among teachers and public employees. Unlike most other reformist parties of the time, the PDN under Betancourt's leadership recruited peasant organizers. This became a crucial resource for its successor, AD, providing the party with the social base for its three landslide electoral victories between 1945 and 1948 and its majority in 1958.[11]

BETANCOURT'S ECONOMIC AND POLITICAL PROGRAM

While the *Plan of Barranquilla* provided a political map to power, Betancourt's economic ideas were still in development when he returned to Venezuela in 1936. Through their mutual acquaintance with the Venezuelan historian Mariano Picon Salas, Betancourt received a minor post in 1936 under Alberto Adriani, a cofounder of ORVE, who as minister of agriculture and finance greatly influenced the February Program. Betancourt and Adriani parted ways after ORVE aligned with the PRV, but the idea that the oil wealth would not indefinitely guarantee prosperity is unmistakable in the regular columns that Betancourt anonymously wrote for *Ahora*, a daily newspaper reflecting the viewpoint of ORVE between 1936 and October 1939.[12]

Over these three years, Betancourt developed a reformist agenda for "sowing the oil," a phrase coined to describe the February Program by the intellectual Arturo Uslar Pietri in 1936. A brief exile between 1939 and 1941 in Chile, where a Popular Front government sought to sow copper revenues, reinforced his views on activist government. His philosophy, which would become the program of AD after 1941, can be summarized as follows.

Political democracy. Betancourt called for universal mass suffrage, direct elections, and other liberal democratic reforms. The main problem with the February Program of 1936, he believed, was not its content but the lack of a political organization, will, and base to carry it out. Electoral democracy was crucial to creating a state capable of carrying out economic and social reform, and it assumed priority over all other commitments.[13]

Higher taxes on the petroleum industry; insistence on the oil companies' acceptance of the sovereignty of the state, especially in the area of labor law; and state sponsorship of a parallel, national, oil industry. Betancourt admired the successful struggle undertaken by the Cárdenas government in Mexico, where the revolutionary government nationalized the oil industry in 1938 after the latter refused to comply with Mexican labor laws. However, he argued that Venezuela was technologically unprepared to run its own oil industry, so he advocated creation of a state company to begin to acquire expertise needed to allow Venezuela to produce and market its own petroleum products sometime in the indefinite future.[14]

Opposition to fascism at home and abroad, but exploitation of Great Power rivalries to advance Venezuela's economic interest. The First World

War had demonstrated the strategic importance of petroleum. Anticipating the failure of the Munich Pact, and aware that the Civil War in Spain (covered daily on the front page of *Ahora*) was merely a dress rehearsal, Betancourt correctly predicted the onset of a terrible, highly mechanized world war in which access to oil would be critical. He advocated that Venezuela prepare to redress grievances with the oil companies during the conjuncture, a position summarized later in the slogan "Venezuela First."[15]

Industrialization based on import substitution in areas where domestic raw materials and agricultural goods could serve as inputs, and active use of state revenues derived from oil to promote agricultural and industrial development. Early articles by Betancourt in *Ahora* reflected a position closer to that of Adriani, that is, that Venezuela's proper place in the world economy was as a producer of agricultural goods. However, Betancourt, influenced by the examples of Colombia, Chile, and Mexico and aware that shortages of manufactured imports were experienced during World War I, came to advocate that Venezuela develop some manufacturing capacity, particularly where inputs of domestic raw materials could be utilized.[16] He viewed industries tied to the export sector, especially petroleum refining, as the key to Venezuela's industrial future. However, Betancourt's enthusiasm for industrialization was tempered by the weakness of Venezuela's bourgeoisie, which he viewed as parasitic— more interested in speculation, real estate, and commerce than in productive investment.[17] As a result, AD did not embrace import substitution industrialization as completely as other nationalist, populist movements in Latin America.

Agrarian reform. Betancourt called for the expropriation and parcelization of *gomecista* properties and other *latifundia*, colonization of the interior, enforcement of the right of peasants to cultivate municipal properties (*ejidos*), and provision of credit to farms willing to cooperate in modernizing projects.[18] Of course, this was vigorously opposed by the agrarian oligarchy, but the collapse of the agricultural export sector had weakened conservatives, and the potential impact of land reform on landlords was eased by the opportunities for real estate speculation in urban areas, the availablity of funds (from oil rents) for compensation, and the large number of oligarchs who were already drawing massive rents from the early petroleum concessions. Hence, conditions were propitious for including peasants in the popular alliance built by Betancourt and AD.

Modernization of education, massive health programs, and other investments in human capital. Each day, *Ahora* carried a photo-essay and commentary on poverty in some region of the country, emphasizing not only human suffering, but the lost potential for economic development.

Betancourt advocated social spending not simply as welfare, but as a necessary investment to improve the quality of the work force. Thus, populism was wedded to modernization, and until the collapse of oil prices and devaluation of the bolívar in 1983 it was consistent with the bourgeoisie's project for extracting and distributing oil rents.

Enforcement of the new labor law (passed in 1936 as part of the February Program) and its associated regulations (decreed in 1938), especially of provisions facilitating organization of unions and protection of labor rights. Far from advocating a workers' state, Betancourt believed that most working-class goals could be achieved if only the state enforced the 1936 law. Betancourt's views prevailed over those of labor leaders who opposed the law because it inhibited formation of single unions by enterprise or industry and granted the Labor Ministry broad powers to regulate internal union affairs. Long before coming to power in 1945, Betancourt had adopted a perspective in which social peace took a higher priority than class struggle. But he was not alone. Virtually the entire organized left had opted to support López Contreras in the tumultuous months after the death of Gómez.[19]

Betancourt, Rockefeller, and the United States

Betancourt had evolved from a revolutionary to a reformist already by 1936, but one critical area of further evolution between 1936 and 1945 involved his attitude toward the United States government and the oil companies. His attitude toward the United States warmed as his relationship with the Venezuelan Communists deteriorated. His personal contempt for veterans of the PRV (although not for other Communists, like Juan Bautista Fuenmayor) was reinforced by the uncritical adherence of the PCV to the political line of the Comintern, particularly after it came under the hegemony of Stalin and after the signing of the 1938 nonaggression pact between the Soviet Union and Nazi Germany. The antiimperialist thrust of his writings gave way to a more accommodating attitude about the role of foreign capital within Venezuela.

Betancourt's attitude shifted from suspicion to admiration for Franklin Roosevelt, particularly after the North American president refused to intervene in the dispute between the Mexican government and the oil companies in 1938. Early in 1938, Betancourt was still expressing skepticism about the Good Neighbor Policy, but in August he admitted that Roosevelt's advisers on Latin America seemed more respectful and knowledgeable on Latin America than their predecessors. In December, he effusively praised Roosevelt for his handling of a dispute between U.S.-owned utility companies and the Venezuelan government. Betancourt was also impressed with Roosevelt's domestic agenda, describing the

New Deal as a philosophy of state involvement in the economy consistent with his own plans for Venezuela.[20]

Still, Betancourt remained highly suspicious, if not hostile, toward North American capitalists, particularly the oil companies. This attitude was hardened in 1939 by Standard Oil's victory in the Venezuelan courts, still dominated by *gomecistas*, invalidating a government move to limit the company's exonerations from import taxes. Angry about the decision, Betancourt remarked during a visit by Nelson Rockefeller to Venezuela that the Standard Oil scion was no more than an "evangelical huckster," a "Johnny Ten Cents," whose visits to several orphanages supported by Creole "moves one to tears." Although the "colonialists of 1939" might consider him a fool, he wrote, "the moment is coming when Venezuela will see the exploiters of our country in all of their hypocrisy."[21] Yet by the end of 1947, in the midst of the *trienio*, Betancourt struck up a personal friendship with Rockefeller, one that mirrored in many ways the future direction of the relationship between North American capital and the Venezuelan economy.

Growing hostility between the *adecos* and the PCV undoubtedly contributed toward Betancourt's shift in attitude toward foreign capital, but his desultory attitude toward the Venezuelan bourgeoisie was probably just as important. North American businesses were willing and able to join in the kinds of collaborative ventures that failed to interest Venezuela's domestic capitalists, whom Betancourt described in his *Ahora* column (May 21, 1939) as "larvae" that "exhibit indisputable feudal tendencies." As first elaborated in the *Plan of Barranquilla*, Betancourt continued to believe that the state would have to take the initiative in modernizing both the agricultural and industrial economy. Such a project of modernization was highly compatible with the outlook of the ascendant, internationalist-oriented business elite, whose hegemony became unquestioned in the United States during World War II. Their most prominent spokesperson was the visionary Rockefeller, who had served as coordinator of Latin American affairs for the State Department during World War II.

This confluence of interests would result during the *trienio* in the signing of an agreement in 1947 between the Venezuelan Investment Corporation, founded by the *adeco* government, and Rockefeller's International Basic Economy Corporation (IBEC) to create the Venezuelan Basic Economic Corporation, comprising four food processing industries. Though a modest experiment, the IBEC set a pattern that would characterize Venezuelan industrialization from that time forward—the association of foreign capital and domestic (private and public) capital. Also, during the *trienio*, the oil companies wisely abandoned the uncompromising attitude struck in the age of *gomecismo* and reached an accommodation with Venezuela's modernizing elites.

This pattern of association distinguishes the development process in Venezuela from that in other Latin American countries (Brazil, Argentina, Chile, Mexico, etc.) where a populist, nationalist alliance confronted foreign capital and relied on a strategy of import substitution to industrialize. From the start Venezuelan economic development was more in the "associated dependent" pattern that emerged elsewhere after the import substitution was exhausted and the populist era superseded by military dictatorship.[22]

THE *TRIENIO:* AD IN POWER

The regimes of Generals Eleazar López Contreras (1936–1941) and Isaías Medina Angarita (1941–1945) were transitional ones in which elements of the past and future coexisted uneasily. Some of Venezuela's most reform-minded ministers (e.g., Uslar Pietri, Adriani, and Manuel Engaña) served in their cabinets, but Congress, the courts, and the military continued to be controlled by conservatives. But the Venezuelan social structure had become too complex to continue to exclude the middle and working classes from electoral politics. By 1945 military and civilian reformers felt strong enough to move against Medina and inaugurate Venezuela's first experiment with electoral democracy, the *trienio*, referring to the three years of *adeco*-dominated government, which was terminated by another military coup in 1948.

Besides AD and the Communists, two other political parties emerged from the tumult of the 1930s. The URD (Democratic Republican Union), led by the charismatic Villalba, presented a centrist alternative attractive to parts of the middle class and (after 1945) supporters of deposed President Medina. In 1952, with AD illegal, the URD was deprived of an apparent electoral victory by fraud. However, the party never offered a program as coherent and attractive to the working class and peasantry as that elaborated by AD. After 1958, the URD became over time little more than a vehicle for advancing Villalba's personal ambitions.

The other major party founded during this period, the Independent Electoral Political Organizing Committee (COPEI), would grow from modest beginnings to become the only serious electoral competitor to AD after 1958. COPEI emerged from the Catholic student movement, formed in the 1930s to compete with the leftist Venezuelan Student Federation founded by Betancourt and Villalba. Its ideology was influenced by the social reform doctrines of the Vatican, although it no longer presents itself as a confessional party today. COPEI's leader was Rafael Caldera, who would be elected president of Venezuela in 1968, and who stands second only to Betancourt in stature as a founder of the contemporary political system. (Caldera remains active in politics today.)

Early in his career, Caldera earned a reputation as a strident anticommunist and critic of the left in general, but he was not compromised by the Gómez regime. This considerably enhanced his stature as a credible opposition voice to the *adecos*, most of whom readily adopted the anticlerical attitudes of the nineteenth-century Liberals. Over time, COPEI would lose its confessional character, but in the 1940s it was the church's vehicle for opposing secular reform of education, the cherished goal of students and teachers, two key constituencies among the *adecos*. COPEI's most important mass base during the *trienio* was in the Andean states, a bastion of traditional Catholicism.[23]

Medina permitted those exiled by López Contreras to return. He exercised toleration toward all political tendencies, and in the new political space both the Communists and AD expanded their mass base. After the 1941 German invasion of the Soviet Union, Medina enjoyed the support of the Communists, who followed the "United Front" line of supporting governments, democratic or not, allied in the fight against fascism. Communist unions, the majority in the petroleum sector, muted their conflict with the companies; Medina reciprocated by permitting the Communists to organize unions and participate in elections behind legal fronts.

With Medina and the Communists tacitly allied, AD, which was registered as the legal successor to the PDN in 1941, seized the initiative on the popular issue of direct election of the president and Congress by universal suffrage. Restricted suffrage and indirect elections were vital to the political survival of conservatives and remaining *gomecistas*, and they began to look toward a return of López Contreras to stem the advance of the left. At the end of his term, AD pressured Medina to hold free elections, or at least to nominate a successor who would be pledged to a rapid transition to democracy. An agreement on the latter nearly was completed, but the compromise candidate to carry out the transition suffered a mental collapse. Medina, under pressure from conservatives, now temporized and named as his successor an Andean civilian, effectively offering a break with military rule, but without a clear promise of free elections.

Unknown to Medina during his negotiations with AD, a group of military officers, including a colonel of Andean origins, Marcos Pérez Jiménez, frustrated by the dominance of unprofessional *gomecista* officers, had already approached AD with a proposal for a coup. If successful they would hand control of government over to AD, with the understanding that free elections would be held, control of the military would be depoliticized, and professional criteria would be used in promotions, assignments, and other military affairs. After Medina named his successor, the *adecos* accepted.

On October 18, 1945, Medina was overthrown. The day after the 1945 coup, AD created the Council (*Junta*) for Civil and Administrative Culpability, which vigorously prosecuted previous government officials for corruption. This was followed by a law calling for public revelation of the private economic assets of government officials. The junta targeted not only *gomecistas* but moderates (like Uslar Pietri) who had served in the López and Medina cabinets as well. This generated considerable bitterness from opponents who charged that the junta was a thinly disguised instrument to harass and oppress the opposition. Even today COPEI, the Communists, and other critics argue that the *trienio* regime was sectarian and that by cooperating with the coup AD violated its long-standing commitment to electoral democracy. This, they say, cast a shadow of illegitimacy over the subsequent regime, thereby contributing to the coup of November 24, 1948, which ultimately led to the brutal dictatorship of Pérez Jiménez.

In defense of their decision to support the 1945 coup, the *adecos* point out that among the first decrees were those establishing universal suffrage and direct, secret voting for a Constituent Assembly. Whereas only 5 percent of the population voted in 1941, 36 percent voted in the October 27, 1946, elections. *Acción Democrática* garnered nearly 1.1 million votes (70.8 percent) to only 185,347 for COPEI, 50,879 for the URD, and 50,837 for the PCV. In December 1947, AD won control of the new Congress and elected novelist Rómulo Gallegos to the presidency with 70 percent of the vote. The *adecos* repeated this performance in the 1948 municipal elections. These impressive victories demonstrated that in ten years AD had been transformed from a small coterie of middle-class reformers inspired by Betancourt to the dominant mass institution in the country. Other parties had important social or institutional bases, but none could match the national scope and diversity of the base built by Betancourt's party. The political strategy first elaborated by Betancourt in the *Plan of Barranquilla* had been realized. Now AD set out to use this power to implement a program of social and economic modernization.

The Character of AD Rule During the Trienio

During the three years ("*trienio*") of *adeco* rule, the government was a decree-making machine. In the area of oil the regime faced an immediate problem that the state share of industry profits was in danger of falling below 50 percent, a level that had been achieved two years earlier under the oil reform of 1943. The regime's response was to install a temporary levy designed to ensure a 50 percent share for the state, a principle made permanent, after negotiations with the oil companies, in 1948, at which time it became known as the "fifty/fifty" policy. Even though the oil minister, Juan Pablo Pérez Alfonzo, was an advocate of conservation, production was expanded. State income from oil rose from Bs. 865 million in 1945 to Bs. 1.776 billion in 1948. The government forced the companies to comply with an agreement, reached under Medina, to build three refineries. It laid plans for the state to undertake its own exploration, extraction, and refining, as well as to acquire its own national tanker fleet.[24]

Land reform proceeded slowly as 6,000 peasants received 73,770 hectares expropriated from the Gómez family and another 1,130 families were settled on 29,350 hectares of newly colonized land. Agricultural credits rose 81 percent, and (in contrast to the post-1958 reform) peasants were major beneficiaries. More impressive was the growth of the peasant union movement, spurred by AD organizers and supported by a friendly government. From a mere 53 organizations with 3,959 members in 1945, the number of peasant unions grew to 515 with 43,302 members by November 1948. A similar process took place in the urban sphere, as the number of unions rose from 215 with 24,336 members in 1945 to 1,047 with 137,316 members in November 1948. Over that period of time, the average daily wage rose from Bs. 7.42 to Bs. 15.11.[25]

The budget of the Ministry of Health was increased from Bs. 28 million to Bs. 110 million, and malaria was virtually eradicated through extensive spraying of DDT. Major expenditures on hospitals, sewerage systems, rural water supply, and other health-related projects were undertaken. The housing bank's capital was raised from Bs. 20 million to Bs. 90 miliion. Expenditures for education skyrocketed from Bs. 38 million to Bs. 119 million, and the number of students in primary schools rose from 131,000 to 500,000.[26] The Venezuelan Investment Corporation was formed to channel funds into new industrial development. Government expenditures and investment substantially increased the role of the state in the economy (see Figure 3.1).

Despite these impressive accomplishments, one should not exaggerate the revolutionary character of the *trienio*. For example, the land reform program exclusively affected former Gómez properties; only publicly owned vacant lands were utilized in colonization schemes. Expropriations of major *latifundia* were deferred, at least until studies had been completed. Betancourt himself would insist during the 1950s that the goal during the *trienio* was not to revolutionize the social and economic structure, but to modernize it in a way compatible with the interests of capitalist investors. Pointing to increased profits for business, Betancourt asserted that confidence in the *trienio* government "was

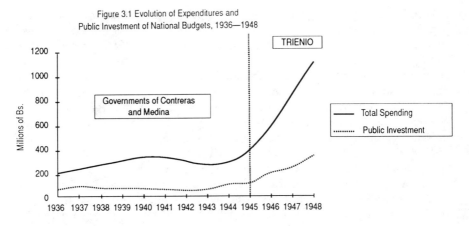

Figure 3.1 Evolution of Expenditures and
Public Investment of National Budgets, 1936—1948

Source: Pedro España, Venezuela y su petroleo
(Caracas: Centro Gumilla, 1988)

reflected in foreign investment circles which now understood that while the democratic government of Venezuela no longer accepted colonial treatment, it was led by serious men aware of their responsibilities."[27]

Key to such confidence, Betancourt believed, was the policy of "social peace." No sector was more crucial in this respect than petroleum. With the war over and Medina out of power, the Communists were once again pursuing a more radical labor agenda. The companies had historically rejected unions or attempted to organize their own company unions. Now with unions widely accepted in North America, and facing the prospect of Communist unions as the alternative, the companies decided that it would be better to deal with AD's "serious men aware of their responsibilities." Negotiations were difficult; the Ministry of Labor was intent on winning an attractive contract that AD could use to consolidate its control and squeeze the Communists out of the labor movement. The agreement reached in February 1948 resulted in the first legally negotiated collective bargaining contract in the petroleum sector.

The *adeco* labor project was a modernizing, not a revolutionary one. As one labor historian puts it:

> The collective bargaining contract was an instrument designed to satisfy the masses within the limits imposed by capital, to pacify entrepreneurs, to stimulate investment and accumulation and to bring about a climate of confidence and social peace that would stabilize the regime. The strategic area for the Venezuelan economy and foreign investment was controlled and pacified for 19 months.[28]

The government's policies often evoked consternation from *adeco* labor leaders who pressed for more aggressive prolabor policies and active commitment to the "socialist thesis" in official party doctrine. More radical leaders would lead defections from AD during the tumultuous 1960s, but during the *trienio* the labor leadership acquiesced to the leadership of Betancourt and his policy of social peace.[29] There was a reciprocal benefit for *adeco* labor leaders—the support of Ministry of Labor. The ministry had been endowed since 1936 with the right to participate in the bargaining process, to determine the legality of strikes, to certify internal elections, to audit internal finances, to distribute financial benefits, and to approve and enforce collective bargaining agreements. Support of the ministry therefore was crucial to *adeco* unionists not only in their confrontation with employers but also in retaining control of their own unions.

The oil companies generally appreciated the labor policies of the government. Just two months before the overthrow of the Gallegos government in 1948, the New York *Journal of Commerce* waxed enthusiastically:

> Another important development was the expulsion last week of communist members from the executive council of the powerful oil workers federation, which is controlled by the Government Democratic Action Party. In negotiations over the new collective wage contract with Creole Petroleum Corp . . . the communists tried to hold out for certain managerial rights such as tripartite hiring and firing boards. They were expelled by the union for trying to "sabotage" the negotiations, and a new three-year contract was promptly signed with Creole. Similar contracts are now being negotiated with other oil companies.
>
> This, more than any other single event, has served to clear away suspicions in oil circles as to the government's intentions.[30]

The cooperative relationship between the government, union organizers, and the companies is evident in the text of a cable sent by the U.S. Ambassador to the State Department on September 14, 1948:

> President manifested keen interest in my statements and said he would instruct army to remove dangerous Communist elements from strategic points in case emergency and he would instruct AD labor leaders visit interior at once and maintain regular contacts with AD labor syndicates. He asked me give him in strict confidence some data I collected on Communist activities remarking that he intended to get to work on this problem at once. I consider meeting most satisfactory and am inclined believe that from now on government and army will be on alert against Communism in oil fields and at other strategic points in Venezuela.[31]

The all-too-real threat to the elected government came not from the Communists, but from the army. In the waning days of the *trienio* the government became daily preoccupied with its relationship to the military, which was being encouraged by all sectors in the opposition to intervene. Labor leaders asked for weapons and tried to win cooperation of Betancourt and Gallegos in preparing a general strike to respond to a coup attempt. Instead, the two leaders refused even to acknowledge publicly the military threat. They redoubled their efforts to promote "social peace" and discouraged any contingency planning by workers to organize resistance.[32]

One particularly thorny issue for AD that was skillfully exploited by its opponents was education policy. For AD, control over the curriculum was envisioned as essential to ensure that the schools would generate a more technically capable and skilled labor force and a citizenry prepared to embrace liberal democracy. As developed and articulated by the most famous teacher of the Generation of 1928, Luis Beltrán Prieto Figueroa (who would split from AD to found another party in the 1960s), the *adeco* educational philosophy envisioned an "*Estado Docente*," "a teaching state," stressing "democratic humanism" in the curriculum.[33] This was anathema to the church, which enjoyed virtually a monopoly upon middle-level education and rejected "democratic humanism." Religious leaders viewed the secular and Marxist roots of *adeco* ideology with alarm and regarded the government's policies as an attack upon the institutional autonomy of the church.

Many *copeyanos* (members of COPEI) regarded AD as the party of militant, atheistic Marxism; many *adecos* saw the church as a bastion of *gomecismo*. Relations between government and opposition were especially tense in the Andes, where *adeco* and *copeyano* militants sometimes clashed violently. A crisis was reached after May 30, 1946, when the government issued a sweeping decree law on education designed by Prieto Figueroa, the minister of education. It included a requirement that students in private schools pass examinations prepared and administered by the state. The church fought back, bringing parents, students, and parochial teachers into the streets. The conservative opposition correctly surmised the dilemma facing the government, that is, that it could retreat only with difficulty from a position fervently supported by AD's youth, teachers, and intellectuals. The government, eager to preserve social peace, rescinded the decree and implemented a less far-reaching reform.[34]

The Fall of the Trienio Government

The conflict with the church encouraged a process of polarization that characterized *trienio* politics almost from the start. An early indication of difficulties came in April 1946, when Caldera, then procurator general, resigned after a violent clash between *adeco* and *copeyano* cadres in San Cristobal, an Andean stronghold of COPEI. Tensions remained high for the next two years. In May 1948, Caldera claimed that he was deliberately teargassed by the police, and on November 9, COPEI complained that its leaders were stoned by *adeco* militants after leaving a meeting in the port city of Puerto Cabello. In fact, *adeco* political rallies and facilities were also subject to violent attack. Betancourt and other party leaders discouraged violence, but many young *adecos* did not share their conciliatory attitude, and the opposition was more inclined to exploit than to defuse conflicts.[35] Luis Herrera Campins, a prominent *copeyano* (president from 1979 to 1984), just days before the coup, declared to the press that discontented military officers "have two alternatives. If the officer is dissatisfied with the sectarian line of the regime, he has the obligation to resign his commission; if he stays, it means the approval of the arbitrary policies of the government. These officers . . . must some day respond to the deviation of the revolution."[36]

The immediate motive for the military's coup of November 24, 1948, is not entirely clear. The successful conspirators claimed that AD was recruiting younger officers into party ranks and arming its own cadre, both of which would have represented a threat to the corporate interests of the armed forces. However, AD's overtures to officers were calculated more to advance the goal of professionalization than to recruit them to party membership. Betancourt and Gallegos consistently refused to sanction any arming of *adeco* cadre.[37] In retrospect, it is plausible that the most important conspirator, Pérez Jiménez, was motivated more by ambition than anything else. In the interregnum between 1948 and 1952, he maneuvered with adroitness and brutality to marry his ambitions to U.S. anticommunism and the greed of the Venezuelan bourgeoisie.

The Cold War chill that descended after World War II certainly did not help the *trienio* government even though Betancourt and Gallegos cooperated with the new anticommunist offensive launched by Washington. Reactionary political sectors ascendant in the United States were deeply suspicious of a government headed by a man whose past included membership in a Communist party. U.S. support or tolerance for a wave of military coups throughout the hemisphere did little to discourage Venezuelan conspiracy theorists. After being overthrown, Gallegos cited the presence of a U.S. military adviser in the Caracas garrison during the coup, accused the U.S. embassy and the oil companies of complicity in his overthrow. However, there has never emerged any evidence linking the officer, nor any other North American, directly to the plot. The State Department understood the difference between AD and the Communists.[38]

If the *adeco* government fought communism, sought to provide a more capable labor force, and pursued labor peace, why did the Venezuelan bourgeoisie fail to defend the regime in 1948? As Betancourt had concluded during his days as a clandestine political organizer, but as he seemed to disregard once in power, the business sector in Venezuela was more interested in commerce, speculation, and corruption than in modernization of the economy. They were unaccustomed and unwilling to deal with unions; to many, AD's roots and reformism still smacked of communism. Most preferred a regime that would maintain the flow of subsidies with fewer restraints on opportunities for corruption, high profits, and speculation. Many profited handsomely from the free-spending policies and corruption of Pérez Jiménez.[39]

THE LANDLORD STATE AND
THE OIL COMPANIES, 1941–1948

A common political myth in Venezuela is that AD support for unions, the "fifty/fifty" policy, and the government's policies of "no more concessions" brought the wrath of the companies down on the government, a claim sometimes echoed in North American scholarship.[40] The Venezuelan state's share of profits from the oil industry was derived from two sources: royalty payments, in crude oil or in dollars, which in practice was established as a fraction of the wellhead price of crude; and tax payments, principally from customs revenues and income taxes. Royalties were fixed by contract, and the companies insisted that tax payments were also covered, a position supported by the Venezuelan Supreme Court.

Venezuelan nationalists did not consciously conceive of the oil income as ground rent. Most, like Uslar Pietri, Pérez Alfonzo, and Betancourt, considered oil a depletable treasure of "natural wealth," a kind of capital in danger of being exhausted without lasting benefit unless the state acted to ensure that the Venezuelan nation captured a larger share and reinvested ("sowed") it. Some, including Betancourt, called on the government to abrogate contracts with the companies on the grounds that their agreements with Gómez were illegal, that they had failed to comply with conditions (e.g., to put fields into production) in the contracts, and that they had practiced fraud, for example, by underreporting production. The *adecos* blamed the court decision to uphold the company's position on taxation on its *gomecista* composition, but the law as written did seem to favor the company position. Ultimately, however, revision of the relationship between the companies and the state depended less upon legal arguments than upon international developments and political change within Venezuela.[41]

By 1935, the Venezuelan middle class and the working class were too large and influential to be ignored. They provided a social base for a nationalist, populist movement similar to those emerging in other Latin American countries where an alliance of the nationalist bourgeoisie, the middle class, and the working class sought to wrest power from mercantile and landed interests in order to pursue import substitution.[42] However, unlike populist alliances elsewhere in South America, such as those led by Perón in Argentina, Vargas in Brazil, and the Popular Front in Chile, the populist alliance constructed by *Acción Democrática* also included the peasantry, and it placed less stress on industrialization through import substitution.[43]

The nature of Venezuelan populism was also influenced by the weakness of the agrarian oligarchy, which had never really recovered from the depressed coffee markets of the 1890s and the impact of competition from Brazil and Colombia. Petroleum earnings slumped mildly during the Great Depression, falling from Bs. 634 million in 1930 to Bs. 531 million in 1932, but thereafter resumed their upward climb. In contrast, a 35 percent increase in the volume of coffee exports between 1926 and 1935 was accompanied not by an increase in earnings, but a decrease of 65 percent. The bolívar fell modestly between 1929 and 1932 from Bs. 5.22 to Bs. 6.77 against the dollar, but after the devaluation of the dollar in 1933, it climbed again, reaching Bs. 3.19 by 1938.[44] The strong bolívar further devastated the traditional export sector. Banking and commercial interests in Caracas favored a strong bolívar, and Gómez, a fiscal conservative, found little reason to wrest control over monetary affairs from their hands. Venezuela was the last major country of South America to create a central bank, in 1938.

Gómez and López did increase agricultural subsidies and credits, but much was merely siphoned off by the oligarchy to provide money for speculative and commercial endeavors in the cities. The peasantry received no benefit from these policies. As late as 1939, the paltry Bs. 7 daily wage of laborers in the miserable oil camps was attractive to peasants barely able to earn Bs. 3 in the countryside.[45] The structural roots of the crisis were thus left unresolved, and despite discouragement on the part of the government, the flow of peasants from the countryside to the cities and oil camps continued.

The February Program of López Contreras included no plans to revise Venezuela's relationship with the oil companies. Indeed, the worldwide Great Depression, although it affected Venezuela less than any other Latin American country, proved an unfavorable international context for change, and Lopez's anticommunist mentality limited his ability to mobilize domestic pressure against the companies, as his handling of the Great Petroleum Strike made clear. In the late 1930s,

TABLE 3.1 Production of Petroleum, State Income, Profits, Rate of
Profit on Investment, and Distribution of Rent Between the Venezuelan
State and the Oil Companies, Selected Years, 1926-1950

Year	Production in 1000 barrels	State income from oil exports Bs. 1000	Company profits Bs. million	Company profits as percent of net investment	State: company share of rent
1926	35,654	17,879	111.4	27.7	31:69
1930	135,246	47,332	362.5	35.5	18:82
1932	116,737	45,145	298.5	27.6	15:85
1938	188,040	118,612	413.7	28.2	21:79
1943	179,000	133,000	99.0	6.7	57:43
1944	257,000	263,000	260	15.6	43:57
1945	323,000	411,000	275	13.8	60:40
1946	388,000	457,000	442	17.7	51:49
1947	435,000	726,000	745	21.2	49:51
1948	490,000	1,201,000	1,060	24.1	53:47
1949	482,000	943,000	704	13.2	57:43
1950	547,000	947,000	970	16.5	49:51

Source: Adapted from Angel Márquez, *El imperialismo petrolero II y la revolución venezolana: Las ganancias extraordinarias y la soberanía nacional* (Caracas: Editorial Ruptura, 1977), pp. 66-67, 142-143, with corrections and calculations of shares of rent courtesy of Dr. Bernard Mommer, Universidad Central de Venezuela. Rent was estimated as total oil export revenues, less costs of production, and less profits calculated according to the average rate of profit for the global oil industry.

the government's share of oil profits remained at only 20 percent (see Table 3.1). However, both domestic and international political conditions would soon shift in Venezuela's favor.

Medina Angarita came to power in 1941 with World War II fully underway. The wartime demand for oil provided an opportunity that the new president, less afflicted by irrational anticommunism, did not fail to exploit. In 1943, the government negotiated a new arrangement and consolidated it in a petroleum law that would define (with some modification) basic company-state relations until the nationalization of the oil industry in 1976. Under the 1943 law, the royalty was raised to 16⅔ percent, equivalent to the higher standard prevailing in some parts of the United States; imports for the oil industry were made subject to customs taxes; the companies were required for the first time to develop refining capacity in Venezuela; provisions were made to guard against decapitalization when concessions reverted to the state. But more important than anything else, *profits were subjected to the state's general taxation powers.* Medina had prepared the ground for this development by introducing an income tax law under which, by virtue of the system of income brackets used, the highest rate (12 percent) fell only on the oil companies and those Venezuelans who were receiving royalties by virtue of having been landowners or intermediaries between the state and companies when the original concessions under Gómez were granted.

Medina, a former minister of defense and an Andean, had been chosen president through the indirect system of elections, but he understood the need for popular support. He formed a tacit alliance with the Communists, who were the strongest party among the oil workers. During negotiations he toured the country, visiting the oil fields to drum up support in classical populist style. At one point, Medina declared the North American president of Creole persona non grata and forced Standard Oil to replace the offending executive. The U.S. embassy made it clear to the companies that it regarded good relations with a major supplier of oil as a top priority and warned the companies that they could expect little support if they remained obstinate about renegotiating state-company relations.[46]

Not all of the cards were held by the government during the negotiations. The commitment to aid the Allies against the fascist powers had to be weighed against Venezuela's immediate opportunity. *Gomecistas* still held considerable influence within the government. In exchange for accepting the new arrangement, the companies were offered an extension of their concessions under the new terms for another forty years and were relieved of claims against them for fraudulent and illegal practices in the past. This prompted AD to accuse Medina Angarita of having sold out Venezuelan interests by granting a new round of concessions and by renouncing the nation's right to recover disputed revenues from past years. Since 1948 *adecos* have maintained that their "fifty/fifty" policy, enacted during the *trienio,* was a nationalistic corrective to Medina's compromise.[47]

This critique fails to appreciate, aside from the limits upon the government's bargaining strength, the full significance of Medina's victory in asserting the state's sovereign right to subject companies to the general laws of taxation. The royalty itself was to remain contractually fixed, but Venezuela now had the authority to increase its share of the profits unilaterally, that is, to appropriate a larger share of ground rent by raising taxes. Under the terms of Medina's agreement, Venezuela's share (rent and taxes) of oil company profits reached *60 percent* in 1944, a level that the *trienio* regime failed to maintain despite the legal tool then at its disposal. In fact, this was actually the percentage of profits that Medina had intended to capture; the preamble to the 1943 law specified that its intent was that the royalty and other "taxes" that fell specifically on petroleum should equate to 50 percent of industry profits *before* the application of the general tax rate. With the latter, the total share of profits accruing to the state was anticipated to be 60 percent, a level effectively achieved in 1943. Because oil prices rose after 1943 while the rate of taxation and the royalty remained the same, the state's share of oil profits fell back below 50 percent (although in absolute terms oil income continued to rise). To remedy this, Medina began to prepare new tax legislation; however, the coup of 1945 intervened.[48]

Instead of pursuing this path, the new government declared an extraordinary profits tax for one year. Then in 1948 it decreed that henceforth the oil companies would be required to pay whatever amount would be necessary to raise the state's share of profits to 50 percent— the "fifty/fifty" policy. This 50 percent share was to include general taxes, a clear retreat from the goals of Medina. Furthermore, although the adecos have decried the 1943 law and touted their version of "fifty/ fifty" as a breakthrough, the 1943 reform was actually a precondition to their own policies insofar as it had removed the contractual limitation on the state's sovereign powers of taxation. Although Betancourt had denounced Medina's compromise with the companies, the adecos consulted industry representatives before proceeding with their 1948 policy. The resulting agreement to fix the division of profits at fifty/fifty (including general taxes) only came to light when companies complained in December 1958, that a unilateral raising of their taxes by the provisional government of the time violated the accord reached in 1948.[49]

The companies could hardly be dissatisfied with a policy that seemed to have restored a contractual limit on the state's ability to extract rent through taxation. The agreed-upon level also equated to the amount that they could recover as tax credits in the United States; in effect, Venezuela was merely recapturing for its own coffers a portion of the rent syphoned by the U.S. government as taxes. For this reason, the companies agreed to make retroactive payments to bring the state's share of their profits to fifty percent for 1946 and 1947. The U.S. companies touted the policy to Middle Eastern countries where they were competing with the Europeans for concessions and where they preferred that the "fifty/fifty" version of the adecos would take hold before the concept championed by Medina (i.e., fifty/fifty before general taxes) could take hold. Fortune Magazine hailed the new arrangement as "Mr. Proudfit's Fifty," referring to the president of Creole.[50]

AD has also insisted that its policy of "no new concessions" was a major irritant to the companies. However, it is not clear that the Big Three (Standard, Gulf, and Shell) were interested in any new concessions after the round that followed the 1943 agreement. By 1945, they already controlled enough reserves to meet anticipated demand for many years. New concessions meant the possibility of competition from independent companies, and indeed many concessions granted under the profligate Pérez Jiménez regime went to their competitors. Pérez Alfonzo, minister of mines and hydrocarbons during the trienio, did speculate about concentrating production in the hands of a single state company that would subcontract production to the foreign companies. While this raised the spectre of nationalization, the minister's immediate goal was to concentrate production in the hands of the largest companies, which, he correctly understood, were the most technologically efficient in terms of conservation and profitability, both beneficial to the landlord state. In any event, the idea never went beyond speculation.[51]

Sowing Petroleum or Flooding the Economy?

The *trienio* era was too short to measure adequately the success or failure of *adeco* policies for "sowing the petroleum," but by 1948 some Venezuelan intellectuals were beginning to worry that the nation's "natural wealth" might be squandered. There were many signs that instead of development, the boom was producing greater economic dependence. In 1948, petroleum exports were 96 percent of export earnings and 58 percent of state revenues in a country whose most important export only twenty-three years earlier had been coffee. The figures would rise to 98 percent and 64 percent, respectively, in the next decade.[52] In 1949, Uslar Pietri warned:

> The Venezuela through which is flowing the destructive flood of uncontrolled wealth has but two extreme alternatives: To use this oil wealth to finance its transformation into a modern, prosperous, and politically stable nation—both economically and socially, or to stand, when petroleum is finished, like the abandoned Potosí of the Spanish Conquest, or like Cubagua, where the pearls were, but where now not even the sea gulls stop, like those sites over which wealth flows without soaking in, leaving more poverty and sadness than before.[53]

The experience of the *trienio* and the growth of rampant consumerism and corruption led Pérez Alfonzo, the dean of *adeco* theorists on oil, to draw conclusions not unlike those of Uslar Pietri. He began to view oil as a nonrenewable resource that should be conserved for future generations rather than as a source of capital for immediate development. Pérez Alfonzo calculated in 1968 that Venezuela was capable of absorbing only 50 percent of oil export earnings as new, productive capital, and that the rest served as a basis only for waste and corruption. He called for a gradual reduction of exports to a level equal to capital investment, implying that half or more of the oil export earnings were not being used productively. In fact, the oil has kept on flowing from Venezuela's soil, and for another thirty-five years it would exceed the country's effectiveness in "sowing" it. A second generation *adeco*, Carlos Andrés Pérez, would, in fact, have an extraordinary challenge in this regard after 1974.[54]

AD, THE COMMUNISTS, AND THEIR DISPUTE FOR POPULAR HEGEMONY

Between 1928 and 1968, the Venezuelan Communist Party exerted an influence over Venezuelan history second only to AD among the parties. Its founders were members of the PRV, founded in the 1920s, and labor organizers in the western oil fields. The PCV explicitly constituted itself as a party when the Communists left the PDN in 1938. The PCV adopted democratic centralism and insisted on subordinating organizations of civil society (e.g., unions, student associations, women's groups, etc.) to the control of the party, always considered the vanguard of social progress—but in this respect they did not differ from AD. Both parties developed internal structures rooted in the experience that their founders had with democratic centralism while in exile, and this was reinforced by periods of clandestineness that both experienced between 1937 and 1941 and between 1948 and 1958. Through 1945, the PCV was the only party that could seriously contest AD for popular hegemony over labor.

In the uncertainty that followed the death of Gómez, the Communists proved just as cautious as Betancourt. As spontaneous, mass protest erupted against *gomecistas*, the Communist PRV joined ORVE in issuing a plea for social peace and then calling in April for Congress to meet and legitimate the succession of López Contreras. Like Betancourt, the Communists generally hailed the Labor Law of July 1936 as progressive, despite the objections of labor leaders that it seriously compromised the independence of their movement.[55] In fact, the law encouraged the subordination of the labor movement to the parties, setting the stage for fifty years of partisan struggle for control over the union movement, a persistent and ongoing feature of Venezuelan political reality today.

Labor leaders initially strove to create single unions in each branch and enterprise, but both ORVE and the Communists' political leadership virtually ignored this demand and supported the approach embodied in labor legislation passed in 1936 as part of the February Program, which permitted plural unions and federations within different branches of industry and enterprises. The result was to encourage parallel unions, a device by which the political parties have continued to compete for control of labor to this day. Any split within the ranks of a party with a labor constituency has reverberated within the labor movement. Linkages between the fledgling unions and political organizations were originally weak, but the experience of the great petroleum strike, which began in December 1936, drove the labor and political leadership closer. Divisions between reformists and Communists within the PDN had already manifested themselves, and the political fragmentation of labor increased once the Communists departed and the PCV began to compete with the PDN, led by Betancourt, for control of labor.[56]

From 1941 to 1945, the Communists relied heavily on a tacit alliance with President Medina in their competition with AD for control of labor; through 1943, they were probably the majority party. Certainly, they were within the petroleum sector. However, not all Communists agreed with the party's decision to mute class struggle in deference to the united front policy. The dissidents were also in disagreement with the leadership's call for the PCV to dissolve itself into a larger, non-Leninist, multiclass party in the interest of building a broad united front among antifascists ("Browderism"). This induced a debilitating split within Communist ranks. Among those who left in 1944 to form the *Partido Comunista Unido* were its most militant and important labor leaders.

In 1946, some of the dissident Communists returned to the PCV fold, but others remained outside forming a separate party that became known as the "Black Communists" because of the color it was allocated for electoral purposes. Apparently, this faction was tolerated by the Pérez Jiménez regime, which hoped thereby to weaken *adeco* influence in the unions. Eventually, the Black Communists returned to the fold in the mid-1950s, as the PCV assumed a leading role in organizing opposition to the dictatorship. However, during the 1960s, the PCV would suffer further defections and schisms as a result of disagreements over the party's role in the guerrilla war of that period. In the zigs and zags of a quarter century, the PCV seemed to exhibit a central flaw originally diagnosed by Betancourt: It too closely tied itself to Moscow and pursued strategies not adequately attuned to Venezuelan reality.

AD missed few opportunities to exploit the vulnerability of the PCV on this score. Between 1941 and 1945, Betancourt and the *adecos* appealed for worker support with the slogan, "Venezuela First," which advocated loyalty to the Allied cause in World War II, but stepped-up pressure to wrest a new deal for workers and the nation with the oil companies. AD exploited anticommunist sentiments by deliberately forcing Medina, who still had to deal with *gomecistas* entrenched in the military and Congress, to move against his tacit allies. The decisive moment came in 1944 when *adeco* labor leaders, under instructions from Betancourt, maneuvered to expose the Communist affiliation of the majority of delegates attending a labor congress called, ironically, to create a single labor confederation. Medina, forced to choose between his conservative allies and the PCV, dissolved the Communist unions. Although many were quickly reconstituted, AD jumped into the breach and seized the initiative. Control of the Labor Ministry after 1945 enabled AD to consolidate its dominance of the labor movement and of the reconstituted Confederation of Venezuelan Workers (CTV), but it is clear that *adeco* hegemony over labor cannot be attributed solely to the *trienio*. The PCV had failed to develop a strategy that reconciled its loyalty to the Comintern with an effective strategy to compete with AD for leadership of the Venezuelan working class.[57]

Although reformist, AD was internally organized along Leninist principles that Betancourt had experienced during his first exile in Costa Rica. Democratic centralism and subordination of unions to party control permitted the party leaders to discipline labor leaders during the *trienio* as Betancourt and Gallegos strove to provide "labor peace" in a futile effort to maintain the confidence of Venezuelan capitalists. Although AD never fully installed a single-party system, AD was able to cement an alliance among labor, the middle class, and the peasantry for a project of social and economic modernization under the umbrella of a highly centralized, bureaucratic party structure.

Legacy of the AD's Rise to Hegemony

Generally, the *trienio* is viewed as a period of political adolescence as Venezuelan politicians learned the importance of sharing power, compromise, and avoiding sectarianism, lessons applied after 1958. Certainly, there is some truth in this observation, but political elites were not the only ones to demonstrate immaturity. When AD came to power in 1945, the economy and society were still dominated by the commercial and financial bourgeoisie. Neither the *"godo"* Páez, the Federalist Guzmán Blanco, nor the Andino generals had been able to consolidate a government without placating these sectors; the petroleum boom initially strengthened their grip as petrodollars filled bank coffers and generated foreign exchange for imports and the conservative Gómez showed no inclination to modernize. The Venezuelan bourgeoisie was so weak that it did not even form its own national interest group association until the founding of the Federation of Chambers of Commerce and Industry (FEDECAMARAS) in 1940.

Venezuelan capitalists were not prepared to modernize if this meant accepting collective bargaining and an activist role for a state not subject to their direct control. Betancourt and the *adecos* had to look elsewhere for support for economic modernization. Between 1935 and 1945, their populist and nationalist strategy viewed foreign capital as part of the enemy alliance, as Betancourt articulated in the 1930s. As we have seen, Betancourt's views evolved in the post-1935 era, and so did the attitude of the oil companies. The nationalist rhetoric remained, and so did the notion that the state would have to take the lead role in developing the economy, but after 1945 AD's strategy to modernize Venezuela shifted in favor of a model that relied on an alliance between the state and foreign capital—an associated dependent model of development.[58]

Unlike any other political party of the period AD presented the best and brightest of Venezuelan society a vehicle to shape Venezuela's development and its place in the international economic order. In this sense it filled a role much like that envisioned in Antonio Gramsci's *The Modern Prince*. "In the political party," wrote Gramsci, "the elements of an economic social group get beyond that moment of their historical development and become agents of more general activities of a national and international character."[59] Yet, in some respects, the dominance of AD in Venezuelan political life since 1945 has continuities with the past. As Arturo Sosa stated:

> The nineteenth century *caudillo* was simultaneously a political and military leader, and a *"patrón"* to his followers. With the appearance of mass parties this relationship is modernized. Personal adhesion to a chief rather than to a doctrine is maintained, but the chief is not the immediate *"patrón,"* even though he represents "the cause" or power. He is personalized in the State and the possibilities of participating in the overall process of modernization that is underway at all levels in Venezuelan society.[60]

FROM ONE VENEZUELA TO ANOTHER

Nothing more vividly illustrates the socioeconomic transformation wrought in Venezuela between 1935 and 1958 than the growth of the urban sector. Between 1935 and 1961, the urban population swelled from 29 percent to 69.5 percent; by 1988 it would rise to 85 percent.[61] In 1930, only Caracas and Maracaibo could claim more than 50,000 inhabitants. Caracas remained a charming city of red roofs set in a relatively unspoiled valley, with a perpetual spring. By 1958, the valley's haciendas and vacant lands (except for the slopes of Mount Avila, which has been preserved as parkland) were covered with middle-class neighborhoods (*urbanizaciones*), the luxury homes (*quintas*) of the affluent, shopping centers and office buildings, high-rise housing projects, and the modest homes and shanties (*ranchos*) of poor and working-class barrios.

The total population of Venezuela in 1936 was counted at only 3,364,347. The average life span was only 38 years. In 1935, malaria killed 1,431 of every 100,000 Venezuelans each year. By 1954 that rate had fallen to one per 100,000. By 1960, men could expect to live until age 55, women until 65; by 1980, the average life span was 65 and 71 years, respectively. In 1941, 53 percent of the work force was still employed in agriculture and mining; by 1961, only 38 percent of Venezuelans were employed in these sectors. The largest increase in employment occurred in the service sector as Venezuelans found employment in the state bureaucracy, domestic service, and commerce.[62]

In 1930, there were only sixty teachers with pedagogical degrees in the entire country; there were no rural schools, only eighteen secondary schools, and only two universities (the Central University in Caracas and the University of the Andes in Mérida) with a total of 532 students. Illiteracy was estimated to be 65 percent. By 1940 (before the *trienio* expansion), the numbers of teachers had already doubled, the number of secondary institutions had risen to twenty-eight; there were 2,600 university students. Still, in 1944, it was possible for all secondary students to take their final exams together at the pedagogical school, something that became impossible thanks to the rapid expansion of education during the *trienio*.

Venezuela's population expanded much faster than its infrastructure or capacity to generate productive employment. Land speculation drove housing prices beyond the reach of 35 percent of the urban population, and by 1950 Venezuela's cities, especially Caracas, were facing for the first time the problem of widespread marginality. Pérez Jiménez attempted to solve the problem with enormous, ill-conceived housing projects lacking adequate services such as electricity, elevators, and running water. Nonetheless, they attracted migrants from the countryside, drawn in part by employment in construction and services.

Physical reminders of the past were bulldozed off the face of the landscape. There hardly exists in Caracas today a building over 50 years old, except in one or two neighborhoods struggling to preserve their character against the pressures of land speculation and urban sprawl. As one of Betancourt's high school friends commented in 1976:

> Those of us born in the second decade of this century and aware from our youth of the decadence of agrarian Venezuela are able only with difficulty to reconcile our memories with the present image of a society predominantly urban and sinking into the depths of what seems to be inexhaustible consumerism. As we reached adulthood in 1936, we saw an abrupt change in a country that we thought we knew, and we suddenly became foreign, just as we were reaching maturity.[63]

Nearly all the colonial and traditional architecture of Caracas and other areas was destroyed to make way for commercial and residential development, and the ecological quality of the valley deteriorated. Smog from industry and automobile emissions began to choke the air; streams were clogged with inadequately treated or untreated industrial effluent and human waste.

The oil boom did create new economic opportunities for long-oppressed sectors of the population. For example, the growth of the middle class and demand for labor led to a cultural insurgency by women. The political parties established women's branches. Each week, *Ahora* devoted an entire page exclusively to women's issues. By 1950, 6 percent of women had entered the labor market; by 1967, this figure had risen to 19 percent.[64] However, women were also specially targeted for the corrosive forces of mass advertising and commercial culture that threaten to submerge the traditional folk culture. In 1948, one North American advertising executive waxed enthusiastically that "the lack of exchange restrictions in Venezuela makes it one of the few countries in the world where the exporter and importer have almost complete freedom of action," and he advised his colleagues:

> American businessmen find a ready response to the same type of advertising practiced at home. Wherever one goes in that energetic country just north of the equator, one sees the ads and billboards, the neon signs and the show-cards of "Singer," "Coca-Cola," "Orange Crush," "Ford," "Bayer's," "Wearever," "Caterpillar," "Lucky Strike," and "Palmolive." These products are being bought and they are being used.

Already, mass media was shaping the culture, he observed.

> Radio fills the advertising gaps. There are more than 50 stations in Venezuela, merrily singing commercials and plugging products with the same cash register success that one finds up north. And television too, has made a start—the first station is to be opened in Maracaibo.[65]

Thanks to the oil industry, Venezuela was converted into a consumer bazaar where the motto, "So cheap—I'll take two!" became a popular slogan. Mass advertising saturated the media with North American cultural norms, including the feminine mystique of fashion and beauty. Nothing illustrates this better than Venezuela's phenomenal "success" in international beauty pageants, which have become an institutionalized method for women to enter into the entertainment industry and the television news booth as anchor persons.[66]

The material benefits of petroleum revenues are evident in the statistics on improvement in health and education, but, as the intellectual Mario Briceño Iragorri puts it, the country suffers from the "absence of an honest and useful historical sense of *venezolanidad*" because petroleum revenues were used mostly "to satisfy our baser, orgiastic instincts, instead of dedicating ourselves to assuring the permanent fertility of what is Venezuelan."[67]

Cultural Tendencies

The involvement of intellectuals in the struggle for political democracy did generate some lasting cultural achievements. Some important literary figures, notably novelist Miguel Otero y Silva, were attracted to communism, but more filled the ranks of AD. Among the leading intellectuals attracted to AD were the popular poet, Andrés Eloy Blanco, who as president of the Constituent Assembly during the *trienio* greatly influenced the 1947 Constitution.

Foremost in the *adeco* ranks was the acclaimed novelist and educator, Rómulo Gallegos (1884–1969), who had already developed an international reputation when López Contreras appointed him minister of education in 1936. When López swung right, Gallegos was purged and became a sympathizer, though not a member, of the PDN. He was later elected president of the Caracas Municipal Council and ran as the PDN's symbolic candidate for president in the 1941 elections. In 1948, he became the first democratically elected Venezuelan president. (Betancourt, however, as leader of AD, remained the dominant figure of the regime.)

Gallegos's literary output reflects a preoccupation with modernization. He was for traditional Venezuela "the synthesis and bridge to modernity."[68] Like the nineteenth-century Venezuelan positivists, Gallegos believed in the demonstration effect of foreign immigration, but he also promoted moral and civic renovation of Venezuelan society through education and democracy. Early on, his work reflected an admiration for rural Venezuela, but less so his masterwork, *Doña Barbara*, published in 1929, which won him international recognition and stature. The principal character of the novel is an absentee landowner from the civilized city, the protagonist against the barbaric tendencies of an indolent rural population easily swayed by *caudillos*. Still, Gallegos eschewed the despairing conclusion of earlier positivists that nothing good could come from the tropical environment.

The main thrust of Gallegos's work is consistent with AD's emergence as a middle-class, reformist party. His protagonists are characterized by a sense of mission and destiny. Many encounter the modern through contact with Europeans or North Americans, and then commit themselves to the transformation of Venezuela with a sense of civic duty typical of the values stressed by Gallegos, the educator, and Betancourt, the politician. They represent a bridge, says Carmelo Vilda, between the nineteenth-century caudilloism and the increasing influence of bourgeois individualism, discipline, and achievement. Gallegos presents a great portrayal of Venezuela's struggle to modernize, "but unfortunately," argues Vilda, "his work and person represent order, control, the *godo* cultural perspective that had governed Venezuela after independence.

These were the values that the bourgeoisie needed to inculcate discipline and to impose their power definitively."[69]

Venezuelans were out of step with much of the rest of the continent, which had already encountered modernism and was now looking again for its roots. Venezuela was literally bulldozing its past and replacing it with North American mass culture—baseball, pizza, hamburger, commercials, skyscrapers, movies, and other cultural imports. After Gallegos, the most impressive cultural accomplishments came mostly from those who separated themselves from the deluge or who maintained a firm connection with traditional and popular life styles. Representative of those who turned back to popular themes were the novelists Enrique Bernardo Nuñez (1895–1964), whose stories take place in historical settings, and Guillermo Meneses (1911–1977), who depicted the darker side of modernization—poverty, alcoholism, prostitution—social ills that separated the city from the countryside in a way not adequately treated by Gallegos.

Representative of isolation is artist Armando Reverón (1889–1954), who gave birth to Venezuelan expressionism through daring use of color. Reverón rejected all social pretense and custom, isolating himself in a small *rancho* in the seaside resort of Macuto. Despite his isolation, Reverón inspired a new generation of artists to experiment in similar techniques. As one admirer put it, "Reverón is alone in Venezuelan art, painting as we want to be alone in life. His retirement in Macuto brought him thousands of kilometers from his companions, thousands of kilometers expressed on his canvas."[70]

With the exception of world famous guitarist Alirio Díaz, musical achievement also depended upon a reexploration of the past and the traditional rather than embracing European and North American themes. One exception to this tendency was the work of artist Jesús Soto, who has inspired a school of kinetic artists, perhaps reflecting the sense of movement and change that has characterized Venezuela for the past five decades. Venezuela's national symphony was largely composed of foreigners, but there was a vigorous reassertion of traditional themes in the work of folk artists like Luis Mariano Rivera and Simón Díaz, of salsa artist Oscar DeLeón, and of Juan Vicente Torrealba, who popularized the *llanera* harp.[71] After 1960, Ali Primera, Soledad Bravo, and Lilia Vera have been among those who injected Venezuelan folk themes and instrumental styles into the hemispheric New Song Movement. However, since the collapse of oil prices and the onset of economic depression in 1983, Venezuela's folk artists have found few opportunities to record or to make a living through performance.

Caracas is the site every two years for the Latin American Theater Festival; the experimental Rajatabla Ensemble has received international praise for its productions. Playwright José Ignacio Cabrujas has achieved international recognition for plays like *"El día que me quieras,"* ("The Day That You Would Love Me"), a comedy that compares Venezuela's love affair in the 1930s with the Argentinian tango singer Carlos Gardel to the infatuation of some at that time with Bolshevism. But for a city of 4 million, Caracas offers limited options for a theatergoer; its best playwrights survive by writing formula plots for *telenovelas.*

Without denigrating the notable exceptions, what is striking about Venezuelan cultural achievements are the opportunities missed, not the accomplishments. No Venezuelan has contributed to the postwar boom of Latin American literature in a seminal way. A promising start in cinema was overwhelmed by foreign competition. Salsa survives as a marketable commodity, but foreign music is less assimilated than it is imported. Perhaps the most stunning failure is in architecture, which almost totally ignored climate, landscape, tradition, history, and aesthetics in favor of crude functionality and profit. The fine facades, balconies and patios of Caracas disappeared under skyscrapers and housing projects. Most of the skyscrapers belong to the post-1958 era, but the pattern was set in motion during the great transformation of 1935 to 1958.

CONCLUSION

If ever the economic and cultural changes of a given time and place were epiphenomenal to world market forces, that has been true for Venezuela since 1920. The first warnings against the destructiveness of petroleum export earnings were sounded by Adriani in 1936 and Uslar Pietri in 1949. The warning would subsequently be taken up by an *adeco,* Pérez Alfonzo, but in general AD would subscribe to the positivist, modernizing clarion call of Betancourt and Gallegos. Even though the first *adeco* experiment failed to survive the political immaturity of the bourgeoisie, the *trienio* proved to be a precursor of the political future. After 1958, COPEI would emerge a major partner in the *adeco* political project, but the design of the project itself was largely the work of Betancourt and AD.

During the *trienio* AD had not gotten too far in advance of the Venezuelan people; its overwhelming electoral victories proved its popularity. However, it had gotten too far in advance of the Venezuelan bourgeoisie, and in 1948 foreign capital was not so wedded to Venezuela's primitive industrial economy to rescue it from its domestic opponents. By 1958, the situation had changed considerably. Ten years of rapid economic expansion nourished a larger sector of the bourgeoisie interested in profit from production, not just from commerce, services, and finance.

Ten years of corruption and brutality under another Andean dictator eventually threatened the economy with collapse. And ten years later, across the Caribbean, a radical revolutionary experiment in Cuba would induce a new U.S. administration to give higher priority to supporting reformist projects of the sort championed by Betancourt.

4

Institutionalization of the Party System, 1948–1974

Between 1948 and 1958, Venezuela slipped back into the shadows of dictatorial rule. By 1952, another Andean strongman, General Marcos Pérez Jiménez, had consolidated a regime of fear, corruption, and greed reminiscent of the Gómez era. His downfall resulted from a united national struggle that returned the military to the barracks but left the future very problematic. One year after the fall of Pérez Jiménez came the fall of Batista in Cuba. These events ushered in a period of great expectations throughout the hemisphere—expectations of democratic, electoral rule combined with profound socioeconomic transformation. The Venezuelan revolution proved much less radical than its Cuban counterpart, much to the frustration of many *adeco* and Communist youths who viewed the policies of Betancourt, winner of the December 1958 presidential election, as a betrayal of the antidictatorial struggle.

The United States and the Kennedy administration viewed the Betancourt government as an experiment for the proposition that reformism combined with effective counterinsurgency training could fend off communism and revolution. A test of this theory came between 1962 and 1969 when a guerrilla movement with both urban and rural fronts undertook armed struggle against the regime. The defeat of this insurgency was a blow from which the left in Venezuela has never recovered.

On the eve of the extraordinary oil boom that commenced in 1974, the major features of the contemporary Venezuelan political system were firmly established. Venezuelans call this system *"partidocracia,"* a reference to the pervasive influence that political parties, especially COPEI and AD, exercise in virtually every area of Venezuelan society. While conceding some political space to smaller political parties, AD and COPEI compete for control of government and society like two heavyweight wrestlers locked in fierce competition but able to combine when necessary to expel any other serious contender from the ring. Together, they share the credit and the blame for the record of Venezuelan democracy since 1958.

DICTATORSHIP, POPULAR RESISTANCE, AND CRISIS

Virtually all the opposition to the Gallegos government welcomed the November 24, 1948, coup that ended the *trienio* and installed in power a junta composed of three colonels—Marcos Pérez Jiménez, Carlos Delgado Chalbaud (minister of defense during the *trienio*) and Felipe Llovera Páez. The opposition parties expected the junta to organize new elections quickly. They had bitterly charged the *adecos* with using control of government for sectarian ends and hoped to gain from AD's loss of incumbency. AD was proscribed immediately after the coup, but many expected nothing worse than a temporary return to the kind of autocracy with a liberal face that characterized the Medina presidency. Some of the Communists anticipated that the new regime would favor them in the competition for control of the labor movement, but after the military intervened to end a legal strike in the oil fields in May 1950, the petroleum workers union and Venezuelan Communist Party (PCV) were outlawed.[1]

Delgado Chalbaud became head of government while Pérez Jiménez became minister of defense, a base from which he consolidated control over the military, now the key arbiter of power. Under this arrangement, the repression was relatively mild, but on November 13, 1950, Delgado Chalbaud became the first Venezuelan chief of state assassinated in office. Circumstantial evidence pointed, though not conclusively, toward Pérez Jiménez as the author of the crime.[2] For two more years Pérez Jiménez remained content to rule behind the facade of two appointed civilian presidents. This second period ended after he manipulated the outcome of an election called to choose a National Constituent Assembly on November 30, 1952. The assembly was in turn to choose a president. Pérez Jiménez expected his supporters to defeat the remaining legal opposition parties easily—not an unrealistic proposition since AD was proscribed.

The climate of terror intensified before the election when Leonardo Ruíz Pineda, the underground leader of AD, was assassinated by police on a crowded Caracas street. The major political parties began to reassess the costs of continuing to compete with one another. The entire legal opposition, except for the rump faction of the Communists (the "Blacks"), agreed to unite behind the URD and its leader, Jóvito Villalba. AD continued to urge its supporters to abstain from voting but at the last moment threw its support behind the URD.

Early returns on November 30 showed URD winning. On December 1, Pérez Jiménez suspended the vote count and transmission of news. The next day, with the support of the six chiefs of the branches of the armed forces, he declared himself provisional president. Shortly afterward Col. Llovera Páez, the remaining member of the 1948 junta, and the civilians who had served in government between 1948 and 1952 were sent into exile. Next, Pérez Jiménez handpicked a new assembly that declared him the constitutionally elected president for the period 1953–1958. From this point onward, Pérez Jiménez, aided by his chief ideologue Laureano Vallenilla Lanz, Jr., the less talented son of Gómez's intellectual apologist, and by Pedro Estrada, the brutal chief of the National Security Police, exercised absolute control.

Between 1953 and 1956, the dictatorship was stable. The clandestine apparatus of AD was thrown into disarray by the assassination of Ruíz Pineda and the deaths of both of his successors. Communist leaders survived but were limited by the operations of Estrada's police. Official censorship prevailed where self-censorship was not enough. Venezuela was a country without effectively operating political parties, much to the delight of Vallenilla Lanz, who offered the country the philosophy of "*el nuevo ideal nacional*."

> The present government of the Republic considers that the solution to a majority of our problems lies in engineering. Housing, water, communications are challenges that can be solved through the techniques of analysis. The new national ideal is grounded in the mystique of rationally directed work. This is based upon a technocracy whose required philosophy is St. Simon and Stuart Chase.[3]

Of course Pérez Jiménez was no technocrat; he was a brutal dictator with little use for efficiency or rationality and even less for democracy.

No independent estimate of the number of political prisoners or exiles exists. In January 1954, the regime admitted after releasing 400 political prisoners that it still held at least 300 more. Betancourt claimed that 30,000 people were imprisoned extrajudicially in the first five years and that there were "thousands" of actual political prisoners in 1953. Nine hundred prisoners were sent to a notorious labor camp, Guasina, in the Amazonian interior. Throughout the dictatorship, sadistic tortures and assassination were commonly practiced.[4]

This repression was no doubt a major factor in inducing the parties after 1958 to set aside the sectarianism that weakened the *trienio* regime.[5] Just as important, however, is the evolution of the bourgeoisie and its experience with the economic crisis induced by the dictatorship's corruption and inefficiency. The changing attitudes among political and economic elites were articulated in a series of pacts. The most important was the Pact of Punto Fijo, signed in October 1958, ten months after the fall of Pérez Jiménez, under which AD, COPEI, and the URD agreed to form a government of national unity regardless of which won the December elections.[6]

The Dictatorship and the Politics of Social Change

Between 1940 and 1960, Venezuela was transformed from a rural to an urban society. Even though the number of people living in rural areas rose slightly from 2.33 to 2.45 million, the urban sector exploded from 1.5 to 5.1 million, nearly 63 percent of the population. In 1945, Caracas was still a sleepy, traditional capital of 693,900. By 1961, its population surpassed 1.3 million. Although other cities, like Maracaibo, experienced growth, the capital's share of the population jumped from 7.7 percent in 1936 to 13.7 percent in 1950 and 17 percent in 1961. By 1970, Caracas would be the residence of one in every five of Venezuela's approximately 10 million people.[7]

The face of Venezuela was being transformed by foreign immigration as well. The 1941 census found 55,654 foreign-born residents in Venezuela's total population of 3.9 million; the 1961 census found 541,563 foreign-born residents among a total of 7.5 million people. Hundreds of thousands of Colombians and other Latin Americans entered the country, but for the first time Europeans came in large numbers as well. Between 1946 and 1959, an average of 30,000 Europeans per year entered Venezuela for an extended stay, and many became permanent residents. Italians, Spanish, and Portuguese came and left their mark on Caracas in shops, restaurants, bakeries. There also arose an element of prejudice, particularly against the Portuguese, who were resented for allegedly displacing Venezuelan workers and being too subservient to employers. Pérez Jiménez knew that foreigners were vulnerable, and he fostered their dependence on his government by funding immigrant associations. Many of the latter took out proregime newspaper advertisements in the weeks before the 1958 plebiscite, which contributed to a mild, xenophobic backlash during the 1960s.[8]

The hyperurbanization of Venezuelan society, especially Caracas, can be attributed in large measure to the concentration of government spending in the cities. Expenditures on public works came to account for 80 percent of all private and public construction, tripling between 1949 and 1958, with the greatest increases coming after 1954. In rural areas, the regime lavished credit and subsidies on "agricultural entrepreneurs," that is, owners of large modern farms, but agricultural production never kept pace with demand, and the campesinos continued

TABLE 4.1 Work Force According to Area of Economic Activity, Selected
Years

Sector	1936	1950	1961	1971	1982
Total work force	1,083,992	1,599,368	2,042,546	2,978,207	4,351,373
Agriculture	662,411	704,704	721,203	611,536	644,468
Nonagriculture	461,581	894,664	1,321,343	2,366,671	3,706,905
Petroleum and mining	15,404	49,276	45,609	38,356	64,705
Manufacturing	146,812	167,726	246,893	403,104	672,464
Electricity, gas, water	808	5,219	21,206	34,004	50,684
Construction	29,413	91,104	81,565	158,622	408,531
Transport and communications	26,447	52,329	96,478	124,217	313,204
Commerce, finance	64,305	149,678	266,229	378,844	1,018,008
Services	178,392	342,114	505,353	776,229	1,174,405
Nonspecified	--	37,213	58,010	453,295	4,904

Source: For 1936, Banco Central, *La economia venezolana en los últimos
treinta años* (Caracas, 1971). For other years, general and housing
census data provided in Hector Valecillos, "La dinámica de la
población y del empleo en la Venezuela del siglo XX," pp. 54-55, in
eds. M. Naim and R. Piñango, *El caso Venezuela, una ilusión de armonía*
(Caracas: Ediciones IESA, 1985).

to toil in extreme penury without access to adequate capital and technology. Ninety-four percent of peasants had no familiarity with the use
of chemicals in agriculture. Other than a few colonization schemes for
immigrants and highly capitalized farmers, no significant land reform
occurred. Hence, peasants continued to migrate to the cities, especially
Caracas, where new arrivals sought jobs in services and construction.[9]
The agricultural work force remained virtually the same size between
1936 and 1982, while nonagricultural employment increased by a factor
of nearly nine (see Table 4.1).

After oil and mining, construction emerged as the leading growth
sector of the economy. Opportunities for making quick fortunes in real
estate speculation and lucrative government contracts abounded. In 1955,
Venezuelans paid a higher percentage of their income on housing than
any other Latin Americans or Europeans. In 1961, the housing shortage
reached an estimated 675,000 units. Caracas now displayed a problem
common to other parts of South America but new to Venezuela—a
large marginal sector consisting of perhaps 35 percent of the urban
population. There were 800,000 people clustered on the hillsides of
Caracas alone. Pérez Jiménez sought with limited success to cultivate
support among the swelling ranks of urban poor by constructing huge

housing blocks, including the enormous one which is known today as "23 de enero" (January 23) in commemoration of the date of the dictator's flight from the country in 1958. Police and soldiers cleared squatters from land, then herded them into the shoddily built high-rises lacking basic services. Thousands of recent immigrants from the countryside continued to raise chickens and maintain other practices of rural life inside the blocks.

The dictator and his clique, many from his native Táchira, plundered the public treasury. The government lavished money on luxurious officer clubs and extravagant hotels and theaters. Bribes and kickbacks became a normal part of doing business with the government, whether the matter involved winning contracts in construction, securing credit, or obtaining licenses. Throughout most of the period the bourgeoisie was content to help itself to the sumptuous financial banquet laid out for them by the dictatorship. The amount of capital underwritten in private companies rose from 1.14 billion bolívars (Bs.) to Bs. 2.03 billion; the jump in the construction sector alone was from Bs. 157 million to Bs. 756 million as 232 new companies registered with the Chamber of Construction. Entrepreneurs like Eugenio Mendoza, Venezuela's cement baron, profited handsomely from the construction craze. Oil exports provided enough money to fend off a crisis, and when it did not, the regime hid deficits by manipulating national accounts.[10] Toward the end of the era, the dictatorship began to resort more often to outright extortion. Public functionaries, playing off competitors for licenses and contracts against one another, turned the common practice of bribery into auctions. Many businessmen, especially immigrants, paid protection money to Estrada's secret police.[11]

The regime showed little interest in stimulating industrialization through import substitution. Despite entreaties from some Venezuelan investors, Pérez Jiménez decided to exclude the private sector from the new basic industries, including steel, which the state intended to foment in Guayana. Nonetheless, there were plenty of new entrepreneurial opportunities in manufacturing as the consumer market continued to expand and oil rents provided a surplus of capital. In 1958, per capita consumer spending in Venezuela was US$516, highest in Latin America, more than double that of Chile, an early adherent to the import substitution model. The strong bolívar made export markets unattractive, so domestic producers had to orient themselves toward the domestic market.[12] Imports satisfied a smaller proportion of private demand for food and finished goods in 1957 than they did in 1950 (see Table 4.2). Production in food processing more than doubled; production of textiles and leather goods tripled; production of metal, mechanical, and transportation goods and of chemicals nearly quadrupled.

TABLE 4.2 Private Consumption, Imports, and Domestic Production, 1950-1957

Year	Total con-sumer spending Bs. million	Total imports		Domestic production					
				Agriculture		Industry		Total	
		1	2	1	2	1	2	1	2
1950	6,808	2,020	100	786	100	1,453	100	4,259	100
1951	7,256	1,924	95.2	935	119.9	1,691	116.3	4,550	106.8
1952	7,599	1,729	85.5	956	121.6	2,081	143.2	4,766	111.9
1953	8,775	2,035	100.7	1,053	133.9	2,462	169.4	5,550	130.3
1954	9,306	2,065	102.2	941	119.7	2,855	196.4	5,861	137.6
1955	10.107	1,924	92.2	1,106	140.7	3,417	235.1	6,447	151.3
1956	10,375	1,669	82.6	1.122	142.7	3,640	250.5	6,431	150.9
1957	11,572	2,143	106.0	1,286	163.6	3,954	272.1	7,383	173.3

1 = Millions of bolívars in 1957 prices
2 = Numerical index, 1950 = 100
Source: Banco Central de Venezuela, La economía venezolana en los últimos treinta años (Caracas, 1971), pp. 183, 191. Manuel Rodríguez Campos, Venezuela 1948-1958 (Caracas: Alianza Gráfica Editorial, 1983), pp. 48-49.

However, Venezuelan industrialization and prosperity was not so firmly and deeply rooted as these figures suggest. Domestic industries relied extensively upon imports of capital goods and intermediate goods, which approximately doubled. Not all domestic growth could be attributed to national investment, particularly in manufacturing, where foreign investment, two-thirds of it from the United States, rose from 12.3 percent of all direct and indirect investments in 1951 to 24.4 percent in 1957. Some products, like cigarettes and soft drinks, were (and are) often labelled "Made in Venezuela" when only packaging or final assembly were completed inside the country.[13]

Imports slumped mildly between 1948 and 1950 but were rising again already when in 1952 the government signed a modification of the 1939 Reciprocal Trade Agreement with the United States. Although the revisions introduced some modest protection for domestic manufacturers, Venezuela remained virtually a wide-open, free market economy, a feature which Vallenilla Lanz promoted tirelessly to an appreciative Republican administration in Washington. The United States was the source of 63.5 percent of imports in 1953. Overall, imports rose from US$749 million in 1948 to nearly US$1.8 billion in 1957.[14]

The capital-intensive nature of growth and competition from imports hurt traditional sectors of society. Artisans found that the priorities of Venezuelan elites had changed little since the nineteenth century. Their share of production fell from 15.2 percent in 1955 to 10.4 percent in 1959, while their share of industrial employment fell from 57.2 percent to 49.7 percent. Employed workers did little better. Labor's share of national income fell from 59.8 percent in 1950 to 47.6 percent in 1957. Even though productivity for each worker in manufacturing rose 68.6 percent, real wages in 1957 were approximately the same as they were at the start of the decade.[15]

The economic growth rate depended upon the continued injection of oil earnings into the economy, not the expansion of a domestic market of productive laborers or increased circulation of capital within the domestic economy. This is reflected in the extraordinary shift of employment toward the service, commercial, and financial sectors (refer to Table 4.1). The percentage of the work force employed in these sectors jumped from 34 to 42 percent of the work force between 1950 and 1961; the percentage employed in agriculture declined and the percentage employed in petroleum, mining, construction, and manufacturing remained virtually unchanged. The limited internal circulation of capital is reflected in the fact that during this period reserves in commercial banks increased at twice the rate of new capital investment and earnings from portfolios.[16]

With a fiscal crisis threatening to halt this demand-driven economy, Pérez Jiménez moved to open the oil spigot wider. In 1956, the regime offered a new round of concessions to the oil companies, which had suddenly rediscovered the importance of Venezuela after the Suez Crisis in the Middle East. The result was an extraordinary influx of revenues (over Bs. 2 billion) into the state treasury for two years, which the government presented in national accounts as rising reserves and a trade surplus. This positive picture was a mirage created by new investments in oil. The "trade surplus" was an accounting trick conjured up by allowing the companies to deduct the amount paid for new concessions from future taxes on actual production. Behind the accounting charade, profit remittances abroad, soaring imports, and capital flight were draining the country of many of its petrodollars. The regime quickly dissipated the economic windfall produced by the new round of concessions.[17]

By 1957, as a result of its decentralized, unmonitored, and corrupt contracting system, the amount owed by the government to lenders and contractors exceeded government spending on all other normal operations. When holders of debt began to sell it to foreign creditors at a discount, Pérez Jiménez tried to halt the practice, which earned him the enmity of many previously complacent members of the bourgeoisie. Administrative incompetence, deliberately deceptive national accounts data, populist spending policies, and massive corruption were brewing an explosive economic crisis.[18]

Such a dysfunctional state was not compatible with the increasingly complex and modernized structure of the Venezuelan economy and society. Families and economic groups like Vollmer, Zuloaga, Mendoza, Phelps, Boulton, Polar, etc., now had diversified holdings, often including modern industries subsidized or financed by the state or closely linked to foreign capital. FEDECAMARAS (the *Federación de Cámaras de Comercio e Industria*), founded in 1940 primarily to represent commercial interests, now represented a more complex and diversified business establishment. Given the crucial role of the state in capital accumulation, the doctrine of economic liberalism, predominant from the times of Páez through those of Gómez, had few partisans. Nor were the expanding middle and working classes likely to permit the new "oligarchy of money," as critic Domingo Alberto Rangel aptly named the elite economic groups, to control the economy without insisting upon a share of economic and political influence for themselves.[19]

Conditions were right for a new relationship between the bourgeoisie and the noncommunist political parties, especially AD. The business sector openly opposed the dictatorship only as it entered its death throes, but it mightily shaped the nature of the regime to follow. Venezuela's leading capitalists, their views articulated most ably by Eugenio Mendoza, now accepted the need to normalize labor relations and modernize the role of the state. One year after the collapse of the dictatorship, the Cuban Revolution reminded them that a far less palatable alternative (from their perspective) awaited those who resisted reform.

FROM DICTATORSHIP TO "PACTED DEMOCRACY"

In 1956, the dictatorship still seemed secure, founded upon an apparently unified military establishment, an expanding economy, and a complacent society. The first breech in the regime's defenses came about as a result of pressures building in the Catholic church.[20] Religious organizations were one of the few outlets for political organizing in an era of great repression. Two Catholic social action groups, the Young Catholic Workers (JOC) and *Fe y Alegría* ("Faith and Happiness") had undertaken pastoral work in poor barrios. They challenged the church to speak out on the social injustices encountered in their work. The church had welcomed the 1948 coup and benefited from the regime's neglect of public education, which swelled Catholic school enrollments, but it was difficult for the bishops to ignore the crass consumerism and the corruption, brutality, and public immorality of the leading figures in government.

When the Archbishop of Caracas, Rafael Arias Blanco, delivered a pastoral letter on May 1, 1956, expressing mild criticism of the social conditions of workers, few anticipated that this would launch a process leading twenty-one months later to Pérez Jiménez fleeing the country in the midst of massive popular agitation and economic crisis. What accelerated the process was the regime's hysterical response. Vallenilla Lanz launched a vicious counterattack, which led to a running battle of editorials between him and the newspaper, *La Religión*. The regime foolishly escalated the conflict by exiling a prominent priest and repressing other religious activists. COPEI, which was never formally banned during the dictatorship, now became more openly critical of the regime and defensive of the church. On June 11, 1957, just six weeks after the pastoral letter was issued, COPEI joined AD and the URD in accepting the Communist suggestion that all the parties form an opposition bloc, the Patriotic Junta. The detention of Rafael Caldera in August elicited *adeco* criticism, advancing the process of reconciliation between the two bitter rivals from the *trienio* era.

After Congress fixed December 15, 1957, as the date for presidential elections, the Patriotic Junta announced on August 1 that it would present a single opposition candidate. As it became evident that he would lose, Pérez Jiménez announced that he was turning the election into a plebiscite on his rule. Voters were asked to cast either a large card marked "Si" or a small one marked "No." No provisions were announced in the event that the vote was "No," and the government poured millions of bolívars into organizations willing to endorse the general's rule. The regime proclaimed victory on December 20, but at the cost of increasingly bold and visible protest in the streets.

The dimensions of the economic crisis had begun to shake the confidence of the bourgeoisie, which began to criticize the regime and make contact with "responsible" leaders, like Betancourt, Villalba, and Caldera. Eugenio Mendoza was particularly active in this regard. Meetings among political and business leaders in New York City laid the groundwork for a series of political pacts, including the Pact of Punto Fijo, before and after the fall of the dictatorship.[21] Much of the post-1958 direction of Venezuela was shaped by political conversations at places like the New York Athletic Club on Central Park South, far away from the mass actions organized by radical youths within the country itself. This gap between the 1928 generation and younger party militants was one factor behind the guerrilla war of the 1960s.

Through January, the one force that seemed solidly united behind the government was the military itself, but on New Year's Eve 1957 a group of officers launched a coup attempt. It failed, but the revelation of fissures within the military dealt a shocking blow to the regime. Although many officers benefited from the regime's lavish spending and were enmeshed in rampant corruption, others were embarrassed and feared for the long-term viability of the institution. Some officers maintained allegiances or contacts with the parties. An *adeco* veteran of the period claims that 700 officers were involved in party activities in one way or another. The Communists enjoyed very good relations with some holdovers from the government of Medina Angarita.[22]

Pérez Jiménez characteristically overreacted to the coup attempt and unleashed a wave of repression that reached into the highest ranks of the armed forces. This only served to intensify the alienation of the officers corp from the government. The officers' sense of urgency about

the future of their institution increased as they confronted mass demonstrations organized by the Patriotic Junta and as the first clashes with
police occurred. The confident underground was now preparing and
training people for an insurrection, a direct threat to the military's
monopoly over armed violence—and a clear warning to the bourgeoisie
that the struggle was assuming more radical proportions.

On January 10, 1958, several prominent businessmen issued their
first timid call for a change in the political situation; they became bolder
as the weakness of the regime became more apparent. On January 21,
a strike among press workers escalated into a full general strike, and
street fighting became more intense. The United States was not disposed
to save the dictator; instead it offered to accept him should he choose
exile, an offer he accepted on January 23. A five-member military junta
assumed power. (In 1963, partly because he continued to threaten the
Betancourt government, which was strongly supported by the Kennedy
administration, Pérez Jiménez was extradited to Venezuela, where he
was convicted of various crimes and ultimately sent into permanent
exile in Spain.)

The departure of the dictator did not end the strife. More demonstrations and violence forced the original junta to discharge two officers
closely associated with the dictatorship. In February, a new junta took
firm control; it was composed of Admiral Wolfgang Larrazábal, two
other military officers, and two civilians (Mendoza and a prominent
engineer) closely linked to the paralyzed construction industry. Still, the
situation was fraught with uncertainty. The petroleum market was
contracting and the construction and financial sectors were in crisis.
Foreign and domestic creditors expected to be paid. The mass resistance
to the dictatorship had awakened popular expectations of a substantial
improvement in the standard of living. Right-wing military officers
awaited an opportunity to stage a coup.

But the unity forged among the political parties during the antidictatorial struggle and the new outlook of the bourgeoisie enabled the
transition process to proceed. AD, although not directly represented in
the junta, took the lead in negotiating the terms by which it would pay
US$1.4 billion of debt accumulated with domestic creditors. On April
24, 1958, the political and economic elites signed the *Avimiento Obrero-
Patronal,* a social pact which called for business elites and unions to
ensure labor peace and the survival of democracy.[23] Although far from
as generous as the economic relief afforded to the bourgeoisie, the
Larrazábal government announced an Emergency Plan, consisting mostly
of construction projects to generate short-term employment in the cities.
Even so, the Bs. 400 million (Bs. 3.33 = US$1) allocated to the plan
was paltry compared to the Bs. 2.4 billion allocated to pay debts held

by the foreign and domestic bourgeoisie, who were often complicit in the ousted regime's corruption.

On October 31, 1958, Betancourt, Caldera, Villalba, and other leaders of the three noncommunist parties signed the Pact of Punto Fijo, named after Caldera's residence where the negotiations took place. Under the pact, the three parties agreed to share power regardless of which won the December elections. As part of the minimum program that accompanied the pact, the business community was promised protection from imports, the church was guaranteed a financial subsidy and legal autonomy, and the military was assured that officers would not be subject to prosecution for their past actions. The agreement ensured that COPEI and the URD would be incorporated in the new political system. Indeed, COPEI proved to be the most reliable ally of AD in the subsequent decade, maintaining the coalition with AD after the URD went into opposition over Betancourt's handling of the leftist opposition and relations with Cuba.

There is good reason for calling the present constitutional regime a "pacted democracy."[24] However, it is important to keep in mind that underlying social forces made the pacts possible, inducing political leaders to set aside the sectarianism that characterized the *trienio* and inducing economic elites to accept a new relationship with labor and the state, respectively. Foreign capital was already prepared for this new relationship, as we noted in reviewing the events of the *trienio*. Although not all Venezuelan capitalists shared the outlook of Mendoza and the leading sectors of FEDECAMARAS, the mass unrest unleashed by the resistance alarmed the bourgeoisie, and AD was the only party capable of taming it. The business sector could also be reassured by the *exclusion* from the new political pact of the Communist party, despite the major role it had played in the antidictatorial struggle, including having initiated the Patriotic Junta.

Betancourt had been in exile for ten years, but as titular head of the AD and an enormously popular figure, he had little difficulty securing the nomination for the presidency for the December 1958 elections. COPEI nominated Caldera, and the URD and the PCV supported Admiral Larrazábal. In the legislative and presidential contests, AD collected 49 percent of the presidential vote, enough to elect Betancourt president and assure *adeco* control of Congress and most state legislatures. Though not as resounding as its triumphs during the *trienio*, AD had won a clear victory. The key electoral base of AD, judging from the geographic distribution of votes was rural (see Table 4.3). AD and Betancourt performed poorly in metropolitan Caracas, where the populist Larrazábal won more than two-thirds of the vote. This was a harbinger of the discontent that followed Betancourt's cancellation of the Plan of Emergency.

TABLE 4.3   Presidential Vote by Type of Community, 1958

Community type	Total vote (%)	Percent for each presidential candidate		
		Betancourt (AD)	Caldera (COPEI)	Larrazábal (URD, PCI)
Metropolitan Caracas	434,715 (17%)	13%	19%	68%
Districts with other large cities	506,303 (19%)	48	13	39
Districts with small towns and cities	1,277,663 (49%)	57	16	28
Rural districts	392,150 (15%)	66	20	15
National total	2,610,831 (100%)	49%	16%	35%

Source: Adapted from Tables V.1 and V.2 of David Blank, *Politics in Venezuela* (Boston: Little, Brown, and Co., 1973), pp. 142, 143. Original data, Republica de Venezuela, Consejo Supremo Electoral, *Resultado de las votaciones efectuadas el 7 de diciembre de 1963* (Caracas, 1969). Percentages may not total 100 due to rounding.

The weakness of AD in Caracas contributed to the left's miscalculation of the degree of legitimacy conferred on the new regime by the elections. Although Larrazábal ran well, the PCV won only 6.5 percent of the congressional vote. Douglas Bravo, a guerrilla leader who refused amnesty under the reconciliation of 1970, admitted as early as 1963 that the lack of a radicalized rural sector, the economic and demographic importance of urban areas, and the legitimacy conferred by elections all were obstacles to success for Venezuela's *Fidelistas*.[25]

To Betancourt and his supporters, including sympathetic North American scholars and politicians, the resort to armed struggle by the left after its clear defeat in the elections was proof enough of its antidemocratic tendencies.[26] This was at best an oversimplification, at worst a self-fulfilling prophecy. In 1959, the Communist party was still officially committed to supporting the new electoral order and consolidating democratic gains in the face of a continued threat from the right, but Betancourt had already made up his mind. In his inaugural address of February 13, 1959, he insisted that "the communist political philosophy is incompatible with the democratic structure of the Venezuelan State."[27]

THE COLD WAR AND BETANCOURT IN EXILE

Betancourt was part of a generation of social democratic, reformist leaders, like Costa Rica's José (Pepe) Figueres and Peru's Victor Raúl Haya de la Torre, who had embraced Roosevelt's New Deal and Good

Neighbor policies. They took seriously the promises of a new deal for Latin America in return for its loyalty to the Allied cause in World War II. During the *trienio* this informal alliance manifested itself in a foreign policy hostile to military dictatorship, but firmly anticommunist. The *trienio* government embraced Pan-Americanism and stressed nonintervention, but it also supported the establishment of the Organization of American States, headquartered in Washington, D.C., and funded mostly by the United States, and it acquiesced to the U.S. plan to establish a military alliance with the United States under provision of the 1947 Rio Treaty.

Pérez Jiménez was even more in accordance with Washington's priorities during the Cold War. The Truman administration purged the State Department of many capable foreign policy experts and increased the influence of right-wing sectors unwilling to discriminate between reformers and Communists. McCarthyism put U.S. foreign policy under the control of ideological warriors like John Foster Dulles and Allen Dulles, lawyers with close ties to corporations (like United Fruit) with major Latin American investments. As an anticommunist and advocate of a wide-open investment climate, Pérez Jiménez was fervently embraced by such men. U.S. support for the dictator was deeply resented by Venezuelans, which became obvious in the famous incident of 1958 when an angry Caracas mob spat upon Vice-President Richard Nixon as his limousine was attacked. But Betancourt had a keen grasp of U.S. politics. Rather than break with the United States over its support of the dictatorship, he sought alliances with Democrats and labor union officials, like George Meany, who were hardline anticommunists but opponents of the unabashedly probusiness Eisenhower administration.

Betancourt sharply criticized the United States for its unseemly, hasty recognition of the government formed by Pérez Jiménez after the 1952 electoral fraud and for presenting the dictator its highest civilian award, the Legion of Merit, in 1954. When the International Labor Organization sent a delegation to Venezuela in 1950 and produced a highly critical report of labor conditions, Betancourt secured a vote of condemnation from the AFL-CIO. He encouraged old friends in government in Costa Rica to test the limits of the dictator's tolerance for criticism at the InterAmerican Conference in Caracas in 1954.

In his book on oil, published just before his return to Venezuela in 1958, Betancourt rebuked U.S. Secretary of the Treasury George Humphreys for praising Pérez Jiménez as a "profoundly nationalistic" ruler who had made Venezuela "an example of what can be done when private enterprise is promoted by a climate of economic freedom," but Betancourt avoided suggesting that U.S. support might have systemic roots. In contrast, he hurled vitriolic criticism at the Soviets, who had little to do with supporting the regime. For example, he alleged that Soviet representatives of a United Nations human rights delegation had failed to speak out on the Guasina prison because it might raise issues about labor camps in Siberia.[28]

Betancourt thus contained his critique of U.S. policy within bounds acceptable to the liberal establishment in the United States. Calling for a "free Venezuela within a just America," Betancourt proposed "an organic Latin American integration which would help stabilize the representative, democratic system of government without interfering in the sovereignty of each nation. A front of this nature would be supported by public opinion in Latin America and would have the sympathy of those in the United States who profess to liberal democratic beliefs."[29] By 1958, the international winds were shifting again. McCarthyism had run its course in the United States and military dictatorships had been toppled in a number of countries, including Peru. Two years later, Betancourt's work in exile paid off when a liberal Democrat, John Kennedy, became president of the United States.

Events in Venezuela, Cuba, and the United States between 1958 and 1962 intertwined with one another in a way that favored a tight political alliance between Betancourt and the U.S. government. The Provisional Government had welcomed the January 1, 1959, seizure of power by Fidel Castro and his followers. Castro received a wildly enthusiastic welcome when he visited Caracas in January 1959, within a month of taking power, to thank the Venezuelan people for their support in the struggle against the Cuban dictator, Fulgencio Batista. The Cuban leader reviewed in detail the many parallels between the two countries' experiences, which could only have served to heighten the disappointment of leftist youths when Betancourt's government revealed opposite priorities. After Betancourt assumed power one month later, relations with Cuba began to deteriorate, particularly after the revolutionary regime tried and executed followers of Batista, enacted measures that strengthened the public and weakened the private sector, and announced its intention to seek normal and friendly relations with the Soviet Union. Subsequent events drew the United States and Betancourt's government even closer.

On June 20, 1960, Betancourt was seriously injured by a bomb planted in an assassination plot authored by Gen. Rafael Trujillo, dictator of the Dominican Republic. Betancourt sought and received an assurance from the United States that it would act (as it subsequently did) to remove Trujillo from power. At the same time, Venezuela agreed to vote to expel Cuba from the Organization of American States in August 1960 and to break diplomatic relations with Cuba in November of 1961. During the Cuban Missile Crisis of 1962, Venezuela sent two destroyers to participate in the U.S.-organized blockade.[30] In 1965, although it reacted with coolness, Venezuela failed to criticize the U.S. invasion of the Dominican Republic.

THE ROAD TO OPEC

Venezuela's relations with oil-producing states took on a new character after World War II, a development encouraged by shortsighted policies on the part of the United States. In 1956 and 1957, with the crisis in Suez fresh in mind, Creole alone acquired nearly one-fourth of the new concessions authorized. However, it is not clear that the new round of concessions was welcomed by the three traditional giants (Creole, Lago, and Mene Grande, of Standard Oil, Gulf, and Shell, respectively), who acquired altogether only 43.4 percent reserves allotted and faced new competition from independents.[31]

By the time the dictatorship fell, the conjuncture was less favorable to Venezuela. The U.S. economy was in recession, and the government was under pressure from domestic producers for protection from imported oil. The Provisional Junta of Government, headed by Larrazábal, had to deal with an aroused populace in what was a highly unfavorable economic conjuncture. The government's fiscal situation was critical. Foreign creditors held US$1 billion of immediately recallable debt. The termination of the dictatorship's wasteful construction projects had created a jump in unemployment to 250,000, and the (inadequate) Plan of Emergency was going to cost money. Despite the dire fiscal straits, in August, Minister of the Treasury J. A. Mayobre, the only *adeco* in the cabinet, announced that the provisional junta would reject any new taxes on petroleum because this would violate the principle of "fifty/fifty"— an inadvertent admission that the policy was not a unilateral victory achieved by AD in 1948. Betancourt articulated an ambiguous position in his campaign, promising only to seek a higher share of company profits through negotiations.[32]

Despite AD's reluctance to press the issue, nationalist feelings against the companies were running high, fed in part by the oil companies' announcement that they would respect the voluntary import quotas established by the Eisenhower administration. Edgar Sanabria, a law professor who had assumed leadership of the provisional government after Larrazábal launched his candidacy for the presidency, decreed on December 9, two days after the elections (there was still no elected Congress), that the tax rate on income over Bs. 28 million would rise from 26 to 45 percent. Immediately, the Venezuelan share of oil profits rose to 64 percent.[33] For the first time in Venezuelan history the government had unilaterally asserted its right to raise taxes on the companies without negotiation. Betancourt was deprived of the opportunity to embellish the *adeco* record on oil, but he had at least been handed a major victory without political cost, one that once again put Venezuela in the vanguard of the oil-exporting nations of the Third World.[34]

The Betancourt government (1959–1964) was rebuffed in its attempts to convince the United States of the wisdom of increasing the share of oil imports allocated to Venezuela, even after it offered to discount Venezuelan oil in exchange for larger quotas. The powerful domestic oil lobby in the Southwest United States was determined to protect its share of the North American market despite the entry of imports from new, large, highly productive fields in the Middle East. In this context, Venezuela began to approach other petroleum-exporting states with the idea of organizing a cartel of oil-producing states.

In April of 1959, the Betancourt government sent a delegation to the First Arab Oil Congress (in which Iran also participated) with instructions to put forth proposals to maintain the host country's rate of participation in profits. This was not Venezuela's first initiative to unite the oil-producing states. In 1949, spurred by knowledge that the companies were looking to strengthen their bargaining position by striking favorable deals with the new Middle Eastern producers, many of whom were just emerging from colonial and semicolonial statuses, a Venezuelan delegation had travelled the Middle East to provide advice to the new producing states. This established a pattern of growing cooperation and (perhaps most critical) information sharing among the landlord states.

The companies, present at the 1959 conference as observers, publicly resisted negotiating with a cartel, but secretly they agreed to maintain the share of host country profits at no less than 60 percent, that is, to ratify the Venezuelan victory as the new accepted level for all states. The potential of a cartel of landlord states had been demonstrated, and within a year the Organization of Petroleum Exporting Countries (OPEC) was founded. OPEC would emerge, of course, as an international organization of transcendental importance for Venezuela and for international politics in the 1970s.[35]

Through 1960, Venezuela enjoyed the advantage of proximity to the U.S. market, and its proven reserves were among the most naturally productive in the world. However, the discoveries of massive, high-quality, easily extractable reserves in the Middle East, as well as improved transportation technologies have steadily undermined Venezuela's position (see Table 4.4). Whereas in 1940, Venezuela's share of exports from the nations that would later form OPEC was 54.1 percent, by 1960 that percentage had already slipped to 32.8 percent, a trend that would continue. The average price of Venezuelan oil dropped from $2.65 per

TABLE 4.4   Venezuelan Petroleum Exports as a Percentage of All OPEC Nations' Exports, Selected Years

Year	Percent	Year	Percent
1920	1.5	1965	24.3
1940	54.1	1970	15.9
1950	44.5	1973	10.9
1955	38.4	1979	3.7
1960	82.8		

Source: Adapted from Ramón Rivero, *El Imperialismo Petrolero, III, la OPEP y las nacionalizaciones: La renta absoluta* (Caracas: Fondo Editorial Salvador de la Plaza, 1979), pp. 60-61.

TABLE 4.5   Production of Crude Petroleum by Selected Countries, 1938-1974, in Thousands of Barrels per Day

	1938	1948	1958	1968	1970	1973	1974
MIDDLE EAST							
Saudi Arabia	1	390	1,055	3,044	3,799	7,596	8,480
Iran	215	520	826	2,840	3,829	5,861	6,022
Kuwait	--	127	1,436	2,614	2,990	3,021	2,546
AFRICA							
Algeria	--	--	9	904	1,029	1,097	1,009
Libya	--	--	--	2,602	3,318	2,175	1,521
Nigeria	--	--	5	141	1,083	2,054	2,255
United States	3,327	5,520	6,710	9,095	9,637	9,187	8,373
Soviet Union	572	615	2,208	6,134	7,030	8,477	9,159
Venezuela	515	1,339	2,605	3,605	3,708	3,366	2,976
World Total	5,447	9,380	18,091	38,343	45,370	53,388	55,370

Source: Venezuelan Ministry of Mines and Hydrocarbons, *Petroleo y otros datos estadísticos* (Caracas, 1963 and 1974).

TABLE 4.6   Economic Dependence of Venezuela on Oil Income

	1967	1969	1971
Exports of petroleum and derivatives (US$ millions)	2,333	2,305	2,884
Other exports (US$ millions)	336	416	444
State income from petroleum (Bs. millions)	5,666	5,443	7,643
Total state income (Bs. millions)	8,539	8,661	11,634
Percentage of state income from petroleum	66.4%	62.8%	65.7%

Source: Banco Central de Venezuela, *Informe Económico* (Caracas, 1967 and 1971).

barrel in 1957, to $1.89 in 1965, and to $1.81 in 1969. Earnings from oil exports dropped in 1959 and 1960, critical years in the transition from dictatorship. However, through higher taxes and increased production, they rose again thereafter (see Table 4.5). The percentage of government revenues derived from the petroleum sector, including refining and other operations, rose from 58 percent in 1959 to a peak of 67 percent in 1967.[36] By any measure employed, the Venezuelan economy was still a highly dependent one (see Table 4.6).

The leadership of OPEC began to shift in the 1960s away from Venezuela toward the Middle East. But no other Third World nation could have taken more credit for what had been accomplished through that time.

THE QUEST TO REDUCE DEPENDENCE ON OIL

Beginning with the *trienio* regime, Venezuelan governments have been searching for ways of reducing the country's extreme dependence on oil exports. Some governments have placed more stress on developing alternative export industries, and others have stressed import substitution as a higher priority. In either case, tendencies in the world economy and distinctive features of Venezuela's own economic development have encouraged a high degree of integration with foreign capital in these endeavors.

The development of the mining industry in the Orinoco set a pattern for the relationship of the Venezuelan economy to the metropolitan center as postwar governments attempted to reduce the dependence on oil. Initial contracts between the government and affiliates of U.S. Steel were signed during the *trienio*, and production began in earnest in 1950. By 1957, Venezuela was the seventh-largest producer of iron ore in the world. Between 1950 and 1957 over 46,000 metric tons were produced, including over 15,000 tons in 1957 alone. Almost all production was exported, 80 percent to the United States. The enterprise was a bonanza to U.S. Steel Corporation, which was seeking new sources of iron to replace declining, lower-quality reserves in the Mesabi range near Lake Superior. Whereas the cost of extracting ore was approximately 15 cents per ton in the Mesabi, Venezuelan ore could be extracted for 7.2 cents.[37]

The *adeco* governments of Betancourt and Raúl Leoni (1964–1968) continued to "sow the oil" in new mining and metallurgical industries in Guayana, but they also had committed themselves to the bourgeoisie in the pacts of 1958 to promote import substitution. The imposition of oil import quotas by the United States, breaking the spirit if not the letter of the 1952 reciprocal trade agreement, further encouraged a shift in policy toward protectionism. With oil earnings relatively stagnant, import substitution also offered an alternative approach to widening the market for domestic industrialization.

Thus, in the 1960s, just as the strategy of import substitution was reaching its point of exhaustion elsewhere in Latin America, Venezuela was embarking on its first true experiment with this strategy. Betancourt's government established policies exonerating customs taxes on imports (machinery, raw materials, intermediate goods) destined for the manu-facturing sector, authorized the sale of land cheaply to industrial en-

TABLE 4.7   Gross National Product in Venezuela, 1957-1969, by Sector,
Selected Years, Millions of 1968 Bolívars

Sector	1957	1959	1961	1963	1965	1967	1969
Agriculture	1,507	1,642	1,999	2,220	2,546	2,798	3,030
Petroleum	7,135	7,154	7,493	8,336	8,915	9,093	9,222
Mining	383	420	358	282	425	411	454
Manufacturing	2,766	3,418	3,548	4,148	5,049	5,375	5,917
Construction	1,581	1,707	1,471	1,340	1,545	1,682	1,975
Water, electric	283	336	422	590	738	894	1,147
Commerce	3,933	4,003	3,811	4,315	5,455	5,907	6,501
Services	5,364	6,295	8,381	10,946	12,665	13,555	15,075
Transport and communication	940	1,090	996	1,045	1,267	1,370	1,466
Total	23,892	26,065	28,479	33,222	38,605	41,085	44,787

Source: Banco Central de Venezuela, La economía venezolana en los
últimos treinta años (Caracas, 1971).

terprises and reduced their taxes, allocated state subsidies and credits
for investments, and imposed tariffs on products where domestic industries might become competitive using Venezuelan inputs.

The policy began in difficult circumstances. In the uncertain economic and political climate of the early 1960s, there was a marked
decline in investment, particularly between 1957 and 1961 when gross
fixed investment fell from Bs. 5.6 billion to Bs. 4 billion.[38] As it became
clear that the government would prevail over the guerrilla movement
in the early 1960s, investor confidence rose. The economy began to
recover and grow (see Table 4.7). Although the decade had begun with
a recession, the 1960s proved to be an era of stunning economic growth
in manufacturing; the annual rate of expansion averaged 10.5 percent
between 1960 and 1965 and 6 percent from 1966 to 1970. Most of the
industrial expansion took place in the central zone, from Puerto Cabello
through Valencia (in the state of Aragua) and the port of La Guira,
which became centers for textiles, food processing, and other manufacturing enterprises.[39]

It is difficult to know how much of this growth can be credited
to the policy of import substitution. As in the 1950s, the percentage of
consumer demand satisfied by imports declined, but imports of capital
goods and intermediate goods once again increased. Many manufacturing
industries produced durable goods intended for consumption by the
middle and upper class with few inputs of raw materials and products
(except energy) produced domestically. Toward the end of the decade,
some progress toward the development of sectors producing capital and
intermediate goods sectors was achieved, but there was little to indicate
that industrialization in Venezuela was proceeding in an integrated way
under control of the domestic bourgeoisie. In not one major area of
industrial growth was private, national capital more significant than

foreign and state investment. The process of import substitution in Venezuela was even less "national" than it was elsewhere in South America.[40]

Heavy industries created to produce intermediate goods, like steel and aluminum, were often founded as joint ventures between the state and foreign capital, with little participation of private, domestic capital. For example, a new aluminum industry was developed in association with Japanese corporations eager to assure a steady supply for that country's expanding economy.[41] This, of course, was consistent with the experimental partnership forged between the government and foreign capital during the *trienio*, but hardly consistent with the conception envisioned when Betancourt, Uslar Pietri, and others advocated "sowing the petroleum" in the 1930s.

Manufacturing was highly concentrated in capital-intensive industries in a way that deepened dependence on foreign technology and limited employment. Between 1960 and 1969, industrial expansion generated around 10,000 new jobs per year, but 100,000 new job seekers were entering the work force annually.[42] Each automobile sold in Venezuela generated more employment abroad than domestically. Although wages in Venezuela were higher than in other semiindustrialized countries of Latin America, inequalities were still pronounced. Income accruing to labor relative to capital fell drastically (from 60:40 to 43:57) between 1960 and 1973, frustrating hopes that import substitution would create a broad domestic market capable of generating demand for manufactured goods. Consumer demand continued to depend upon the injection of oil rents into the economy.[43]

Most of the technology needed for industrialization remained firmly in the control of foreign enterprises. Between 1965 and 1969, 96.2 percent of patents registered in Venezuela were of foreign origin, more than one-half from the United States. Parent companies of foreign firms often completely recovered the value of their investment in Venezuelan partnerships within two or three years in the form of payments for patents alone. In the chemical industry, one of the most dynamic growth sectors, enterprises remitted an average of 35 percent of the value of their fixed investment abroad as payment for patents; one foreign firm recovered all of its initial investment in four-and-one-half months via this device.[44] A study of industrial development for the government estimated that the net loss of capital in Venezuela between 1960 and 1969 via licenses and profit remittances could have generated 1.2 million new jobs had it been invested instead in the domestic economy.[45]

The urban sector continued to expand, but the bulk of employment was absorbed by services, transportation, and the financial-commercial sectors. Women continued to enter the work force in greater numbers,

TABLE 4.8 Number of Men and Women Employed in Professional or
Clerical Occupations, 1950-1977, Selected Years

	1950	1961	1971	1977
Men	41,699	89,174	135,032	146,387
Women	17,711	47,270	110,621	186,753

Source: Ministerio de Fomento, IX and X Censo de población y vivienda,
encuestra de hogares por muestra (Caracas, 1977).

especially in professional and clerical occupations. As Table 4.8 illustrates, the gap between male and female employment in the service sector dropped considerably between 1961 and 1971 after having remained relatively constant in the prior decade. In the next six years, a period of phenomenal economic expansion due to the oil boom that commenced in 1974, this trend accelerated to the point where the number of women employed in office work came to exceed the number of men.

Overall, then, economic growth in Venezuela was having a dramatic effect on the social structure, but the expansion of the service sectors was far outstripping the development of manufacturing and other industries. Venezuelan intellectuals, like Uslar Pietri, continued to warn that this type of development would bring the nation to ruin once the oil ran out. In fact, even today there is little chance that the oil will "run out." However, the collapse of oil prices in the 1980s has had virtually the same effect.

LAND REFORM: POLITICAL SUCCESS, ECONOMIC AND SOCIAL FAILURE

Upon returning to power in 1959, the *adecos* undertook once again to redistribute former Gómez properties now owned by the state. In many instances, peasants forced the government's hand through land seizures. In early 1960, the Betancourt government secured passage of a reform bill that led to further expropriation (with compensation) from private owners in the central states of Miranda, Aragua, and Carabobo, where peasant pressure was most intense. In exchange for the law, the *adeco*-controlled Peasant Federation, reorganized after ten years of illegality, agreed to cease land seizures. During Betancourt's administration, 62,000 peasant families were settled and more than 1.5 million hectares distributed. By 1971, 140,289 families had received 3,505,300 hectares. In addition, the AD government could boast of having made significant investments in health, education, and water for hundreds of thousands of peasants.[46]

The *adeco* objective, according to John Powell's study of the reform, was to "mold about 300,000 subsistence farm families into a productive sector of the national economy."[47] By its own terms, then, the reform

TABLE 4.9 Distribution of Landholdings by Size and Area, 1971, 1961, 1950

Size of parcel in hectares	1971 Number of parcels	Area[a]	1961 Number of parcels	Area[a]	1950 Number of parcels	Area[a]
Less than 10	171,173	577	213,419	753	168,004	544
10 to 50	73,772	1,429	69,987	1,324	46,451	911
50 to 200	22,648	1,971	18,899	1,662	11,407	1,004
200 to 1000	11,786	4,825	8,949	3,611	5,446	2,265
1000 to 5000	4,034	7,719	3,383	6,919	2,512	5,049
More than 5000	870	9,949	840	11,736	910	12,354
Total	284,283	26,470	315,477	26,005	234,730	22,127

[a]In 1,000 hectares.
Source: Ministerio de Fomento, IV Censo Agropecuario 1971 (Caracas, 1971).

failed to reach one-half of its goal in terms of numbers. Furthermore, only a few of the 800 new peasant communities created by the reform benefited from the entire range of inputs—credit, infrastructure, medical and educational facilities, etc. In contrast to the reform contemplated during the *trienio*, noted Powell, "the 1960 law was the product of a deliberate, extended process of consultation and consensus among other electoral elites, and even among representatives of traditional elites. The result embodied legitimacy at the price of restraint in the partisan pursuit of peasant interests."[48]

Most of the distributed land came not from the private sector, but from vacant land or former *gomecista* properties. When expropriation touched private landowners they were placated by generous compensation, providing many with funds to invest in the booming urban real estate market. Peasant militancy did result in labor's share of income relative to other factors of production in agriculture rising from 67.4 to 77.2 percent between 1957 and 1960. However, the gains proved short lived. The reform served to mute rather than to advance peasant militancy, and AD came to dominate the Peasant Federation much the way that it exercises hegemony within the urban labor movement.[49]

Ten years of reform failed to reduce significantly the maldistribution of land (see Table 4.9). Nonetheless, the countryside was in transition. Cultivation of the bulk of agro-industrial and dairy products, grains, poultry, and many other crops and products was being concentrated on large, capital-intensive, though not necessarily efficient, farms. Large domestic and foreign firms (e.g., Nestle, Boulton, International Multifoods, Ralston Purina, state-controlled cooperatives) came to dominate processing and distribution of animal feed, poultry, sugar, butter and cheese, milk, vegetable oils, processed corn, chocolate, flour, and processed wheat.[50] As in manufacturing, domestic production expanded and imports of food as a percentage of consumption fell from 32 to 21 percent

Despite promises by many governments to "sow the petroleum," most peasants continue to cultivate the land by traditional methods (photo by Alejandro González)

between 1960 and 1969. However, total imports of food still rose 26 percent in absolute terms.[51]

Private banks devoted only 4.4 percent of their investments to agriculture in the 1960s, in contrast to 53.3 percent to commerce, industry, and services, and 35.7 percent to real estate. The state granted only an average of 54 percent of requests for agricultural credits between 1963 and 1969.[52] Much agricultural credit is siphoned into real estate or financial speculation or into the pockets of middlemen. For example, it was estimated around 1970 that the profit realized on one common class of tractors by Venezuelan merchants was 35 percent.[53]

It could hardly be said that the agrarian reform had met the goal of "molding" the peasantry into the modern economy. The peasantry continues to be squeezed, on the one hand, by creditors and suppliers and, on the other, by those who controlled marketing, transportation, and processing. By 1969, the peasantry's share of national income had fallen from 77.2 percent in 1960 to 38 percent in 1972. In 1976, two-thirds of rural households earned less than $25 per month. A government study in 1974 showed, ironically enough, that peasants in the reform sector received the lowest income of all those economically active in

TABLE 4.10   Yields of Coffee and Cacao, Kilograms per Hectare,
Venezuela and Other Major Producers, 1978

	Venezuela	Costa Rica	Colombia	Brazil	World
Coffee	149	971	558	480	478
Cacao	229	400	470	553	300

Source: United Nations, Food and Agriculture Organization, 1978,
cited in Alberto Micheo, La agricultura en Venezuela (Caracas: Centro
Gumilla, Curso de Formación Sociopolítica 12, 1987), pp. 34-35.

agriculture. Fifty-seven percent of all rural children between the ages of seven and thirteen, a group covered by the compulsory education law, were not being provided schooling. Not surprisingly, of 150,000 families that received land (of 300,000 originally targeted), it has been estimated that one-third have left the land and migrated to the cities.[54] The traditional export sectors, coffee and cacao, where Venezuela enjoys considerable natural advantages, remain stagnant and inefficient compared to other exporting nations (see Table 4.10).

Perhaps nowhere has the state and political elite failed so miserably to "sow the petroleum" for development as in the countryside. Yet in political terms, the agrarian reform was successful. Enough peasants received land and other benefits to forestall widespread support for guerrillas. The reform did manage to cement an alliance between a modernizing urban elite (AD) and the peasantry, one which was vital to the success of Betancourt's political project in the 1960s.[55] Peasants provided the crucial votes that AD needed to defeat the populist challenge of Larrazábel, who carried the vote in Caracas in 1958. When Venezuela's young Fidelistas turned from urban to rural guerrilla warfare in 1964, they were turning down a blind alley.

THE LEFTIST INSURGENCY AND DEFEAT

By excluding the Communist party, whose ranks had swelled from 500 to 25,000 members within two years, Betancourt had signalled that a social and economic revolution was not part of his agenda. Simultaneously, he undermined the position that the Moscow-oriented Communists had maintained since Medina, that is, that of uniting with democratic, bourgeois sectors against the threat of the right. As Betancourt's government imposed austerity to deal with the country's economic problems and as the Cuban Revolution turned left, some Communists, especially younger ones, became dissatisfied with the pragmatic, cautious approach of the PCV. In August 1959, Betancourt announced that his government would end the Emergency Plan as well as the freeze on rents that had been decreed by the Provisional Government—the only two measures from that period that were subsequently repealed. This led to widespread, violent demonstrations, a factor in persuading the left that armed struggle would be as successful in Venezuela as it had been in Cuba.[56]

Betancourt's policies also evoked consternation among more radical and youthful members of AD. While the Old Guard was in exile, many young *adecos* had assumed positions of leadership, as they worked to build mass resistance to the dictatorship. Many had worked closely with the Communists, whom Betancourt continued to abhor. Betancourt and the Old Guard also faced a challenge from a group known as the ARS faction, composed mostly of members who were young militants during the *trienio*. (The name, "ARS," was taken from an advertising firm that had played a role in the 1958 campaign.) Much of the ARS group later did split from AD (in 1961), and a few joined the guerrilla movement. However, in 1960 the ARS faction supported Betancourt against the even younger generation of *adecos* who had led the struggle against Pérez Jiménez. Together, they were able to regain control of the party's leadership posts. When only the Youth Bureau remained outside of his control, Betancourt expelled the elected leadership, inducing the young radicals, joined by a few veteran leftists, to form the Left Revolutionary Movement (MIR) in August 1960.

The political situation in 1960 was highly charged. Several abortive coup attempts were launched by rightist military officers. The most serious was launched on April 20 in Táchira, but was brought under control within one day. On June 24, Armed Forces Day, Betancourt was nearly killed in the bomb attack in which the Dominican dictator, Trujillo, was implicated. Despite serious injuries, Betancourt insisted on appearing on television to verify that he had survived. His reputation for honesty and personal courage were tremendous assets in the struggle with the left. Betancourt ably projected his government as a centrist, reformist, democratic alternative under siege from both the right and left.

Unlike the *trienio* government, the new regime could count on important allies. COPEI played the role of loyal opposition, a choice that would shortly pay political dividends. The country's powerful economic groups extended support to the *adeco* regime as it coped with these problems, in marked contrast to their attitude during the *trienio*. The U.S. government was eager for the reform project to succeed and in preventing "more Cubas" in the hemisphere. Even the departure of the URD from the government coalition in September 1962, failed to produce the climactic crisis that the government's opponents hoped would materialize.

On the other hand, the economic crisis engendered considerable discontent in the poor barrios, encouraging bolder actions on the part of students and radicalized sectors of the intellectuals, professionals, and elements in the military. A decisive moment came on October 19, 1960, when the editors of MIR's newspaper, *Izquierda*, were detained for having suggested that conditions for popular insurrection were developing. Demonstrations broke out on the Central University campus and in the barrios where the leftist youth retained influence from the days of the antidictatorial struggle. The demonstrations were severely repressed by the police, leading to more violent confrontations. Betancourt blamed Communist agitation and temporarily suspended constitutional rights. Many barrios were cordoned off by the police or subjected to military occupation.

In November 1960, violence flared again after the government declared illegal a strike by telephone workers. Betancourt again blamed the unrest on leftist agitation and suspended constitutional guarantees, this time indefinitely. On November 30, the offices of the Communist party newspaper were occupied by the military. Barricades went up again in many barrios, and fighting brought widespread death and destruction. The PCV, over the objections of many of its own "Old Guard," who continued to fear the threat of a rightist military coup, formally endorsed the thesis that revolution was possible. No clear strategy was presented, but the party began to cultivate support among leftist military officers and to train, both at home and abroad, guerrilla cadre. After two coup attempts by leftist military officers, in Carupano and Puerto Cabello, were defeated in May and June 1962, respectively, the government formally moved to ban the MIR and the PCV and to break relations with Cuba, inducing some leftist members of the URD to join the revolt.

The MIR and the Communist party had called for revolution, but neither had a clear idea of what strategy—urban or rural, insurrectionary or patient accumulation of forces—should be pursued. Not until mid-1962 was a centralized, coordinated guerrilla command structure created. At that time, various guerrilla and political leaders agreed that military operations would be coordinated by the Armed Forces of National Liberation (FALN); political affairs and organizing were placed under control of the National Liberation Front (FLN). Both fronts were subordinate to a Political Military Directorate headed by the leaders of the FALN, the MIR, the PCV, the revolutionary sector of the URD, and some independents.

In 1962, the left still believed that revolution was virtually inevitable. This false optimism was based upon a conviction that the popular unrest generated by the antidictatorial struggle and the economic crisis had created conditions comparable to those prevailing in prerevolutionary Cuba. However, the government of Venezuela under Betancourt was not a corrupt, personal dictatorship, but a constitutionally elected regime with a politically astute leader who possessed personal integrity, prestige, and physical courage.

Many urban dwellers were recent migrants from the traditional countryside. Although they supported the overthrow of Pérez Jiménez and felt discontent with the economic situation, they were not thereby automatically inclined toward revolution. Over decades, the PCV had placed little stress on rural areas, and the new migrants were highly susceptible to anticommunist propaganda. Despite a widespread (and improvised) call disseminated by Cuban radio broadcasts for an insurrection to accompany the military revolts in Carupano and Puerto Cabello, the population for the most part remained loyal to the government. Although the PCV had emerged with great prestige from the antidictatorial struggle, the government made deft use of fear of communism, blaming Communist subversion for the climate of violence.

The social historian Elena Plaza, based on interviews with barrio residents, concluded that the left was effectively defeated when the urban sectors failed to rise in support of the leftist barracks revolts.

> The left had already embarked on the process of marginalizing itself from the masses. . . . Insofar as the left was radicalizing itself progressively toward violence; insofar as the government was increasing its political repression, insofar as the phantasm of communism was raised (with the efficient use of media, among other things) as responsible for everything that was happening, the people—with scarce political consciousness— were terrified and retreated. On the one hand, the left became more radical in the name of popular conquests, and on the other hand, the people were not disposed to continue struggling by means of violence.[57]

In effect, the left was defeated even before the FALN and FLN were officially constituted; the guerrilla *focos* were from the start isolated from the people. However, the left continued to act as though armed struggle were viable.

For much of the 1960s, Venezuela was a violence-ridden society. Since human rights reports were much less commonly and scientifically reported, it is difficult to quantify abuses on the part of the regime. Ex-guerrillas and political activists of the period, many of whom are today extremely critical of the decision to undertake arm struggle, are able to recount numerous instances of unnecessary, if not deliberate, killings by military forces and of torture. However, the record of the left in this period leaves much to question on moral as well as pragmatic grounds. Between 1962 and 1964, the FALN carried out spectacular actions, including the sabotage of the U.S. embassy, the sacking and burning of the U.S. military mission, the kidnapping of a prominent soccer player and a U.S. army colonel, the burning of the Sears department store in Caracas, the capture of a few towns on the outskirts of Caracas, and the seizure of several barrios, followed by distribution of food stolen from supermarkets. Often these action were followed by pitched battles with the military in which residents suffered the worst consequences. This violence impeded efforts by some leftists to negotiate an end to the armed struggle before total defeat.

For example, in September 1963, it appeared as though a negotiated solution with part of the left might be achieved before the December elections. However, the negotiations collapsed after five National Guardsmen were killed thwarting the attempted takeover of a commuter train by guerrillas. Under pressure from the military, the government arrested several PCV and MIR politicians, including several members of Congress, violating their constitutional immunity from prosecution. The left responded by urging a boycott of the elections, backed by violent attempts to disrupt them. However, voters turned out in massive numbers. Still, the left pressed on with the armed struggle.

In 1964, the guerrilla movement turned more frequently to terrorism, which attracted massive police and military violence against guerrilla strongholds, including the razing of entire neighborhoods where they were ensconced. A major leftist stronghold was eliminated in 1966 when the Central University campus in Caracas was militarily occupied. In some contexts (e.g., contemporary Central America), such a response might have swung hearts and minds over to the revolutionaries. However, in the Venezuela of 1966, state violence only made the guerrillas less welcome in the barrios. Combining a carrot with the stick, the presidential administrations of AD's Raul Leoni (1964–1968) and COPEI's Rafael Caldera (1969–1973), sponsored a community development program to provide political training and salaries for barrio leaders, which further undercut the influence of the left.[58]

As the urban front collapsed, the guerrillas turned to a rural strategy, a process described by former guerrilla leader Alfredo Maneiro as "leftist irrealism."[59] The turn to the countryside was inspired by popular conceptions of the revolutionary process in Cuba and by the success of rural guerrillas in Vietnam. This ignored the strong base that AD had built in rural areas and the political importance of the modest land reform effort undertaken by the government. Venezuela's young *Fidelistas* believed that sacrifice and courage would suffice to win a revolution, but they were relatively easy marks for the Venezuelan military, now indoctrinated by U.S. advisers in the counterinsurgency techniques being used in Vietnam, for example, rapid deployment of special hunter battalions. These proved effective in rural Venezuela, where the young guerrillas found an unenthusiastic peasantry and a harsh physical environment.

After 1966, the PCV haltingly began to explore ways of returning to legality. This produced tensions between veteran PCV leaders and, respectively, the MIR and younger cadre within the party. This was also the period of conflict between traditional Communists and *Fidelistas* throughout the hemisphere, culminating at the Tri-Continental Congress of Havana in August 1967 in the triumph of the thesis that "the revolutionary route is valid for all countries and all revolutionaries in Latin America." Of course, this was absolutely false for Venezuela, but it encouraged some guerrillas to continue the struggle even as others were abandoning it.

The Venezuelan political elite, especially Presidents Leoni and Caldera, wisely adopted a flexible approach to ending the civil unrest. Betancourt had voluntarily left the country after completing his term of office in 1963, a gesture intended to leave no question about the authority of Leoni. Leoni decided to negotiate with those guerrillas seeking a way to reintegrate themselves into political society. Leoni had some political incentives to be generous toward the PCV. At the time, AD was locked in a battle for votes and control of the labor movement with Prieto Figueroa's *Movimiento Electoral del Pueblo* (MEP), which had split from AD in a dispute over the 1968 presidential nomination. Communist participation in the elections could only divide the leftist vote and hurt MEP, which had taken many key labor leaders from *adeco* ranks. With the tacit consent of Leoni, the PCV presented candidates in the December elections through a front organization, "United to Advance."

Caldera, who took advantage of the MEP defection from AD to win the 1968 election with only 27 percent of the vote, had campaigned on a platform of reconciliation. In the context of extreme labor unrest, and with AD and MEP continuing to battle for control of the union movement, the *copeyano* president decided that by ending the guerrilla war he could leave his mark for social peace. Ironically, then, it would be Caldera, known for his anticommunist attitudes in the past, who would put an end to the insurrection by decreeing a policy of pacification through amnesty and relegalization of leftist parties. Most of the left accepted the opportunity to return to legal status.

Since 1969, the only guerrilla activities have been carried out sporadically and ineffectually by small groups, the most notorious of which is called *"Bandera Roja."* The existence of *Bandera Roja*, has done little more than provide the government with a scapegoat by which it can attribute protest activities to subversion rather than genuine popular discontent.

Who Was Responsible for the Violent 1960s?

Not surprisingly, the question of responsibility for the guerrilla war remains today a politically charged issue for Venezuelans. A popular explanation among admirers of Betancourt is that the insurrection was exported to Venezuela by Cuba. However, Cuban involvement through the early years was mostly limited to moral support and training. By the time (1968) that Cuba apparently turned to open material support, the outcome was already decided. Cuba may have intervened, but Venezuelan foreign policy was hardly a model of probity either. Betancourt's government had cooperated fully with U.S. attempts to isolate and reverse the Cuban Revolution. His decision to exclude the PCV from the Pact of Punto Fijo made it difficult for veteran Communist leaders to resist the pressure from their youth for a strategy of armed struggle inspired by Cuba.

It is difficult to accept the government's claim that the strikes, protests, and violence were merely the product of subversion. While the economic crisis was not of its own making, the Betancourt government did make choices regarding who would bear the burden of recovery. Its predilection was to reassure the foreign and domestic bourgeoisie that they would not pay the price of the dictatorship's mismanagement and corruption, even though business elites had been among the last to join in opposition to the dictatorship and had profited handsomely from its profligacy. Meanwhile, the poor and working class, who had risked the most in confronting the violent and brutal dictatorship, saw the sole concession to their economic plight, the Plan of Emergency, cancelled.

To recognize the government's share of responsibility is not to endorse the opposite myth that the armed struggle was inevitable or forced upon the left. The PCV had denounced Betancourt for accepting overtures from the military to overthrow Medina in 1945, yet the PCV sought opportunistically to exploit divisions in the military in the post-1958 era, endorsing the barracks revolts of 1962. Inspired by the Cuban example, confident that the mass mobilization against the dictatorship could be converted into a genuine social and economic revolution, the radical and youthful cadre of PCV and the MIR took up the call to arms with enthusiasm, patriotism, a spirit of sacrifice, and overconfidence. However, to have continued with violent tactics after the clear rejection by the people of the call for electoral abstention in 1964 raises even more serious questions of judgment and morality. The left presented no clear program or coherent strategy to their civilian supporters, who suffered the consequences when the government unleashed violent repression in neighborhoods where *focos* had been established. In the end, Venezuela's *Fidelistas* lacked, despite their Marxist inclinations, the realistic type of class analysis of Venezuela that their nemesis, Betancourt, had developed thirty years earlier.

The left paid dearly for its errors. The war marked the definitive end of the PCV as a serious contender for control of either the government or the union movement after more than forty years of active struggle. One national survey study done in 1973 categorized 82 percent of the population as "anticommunist." This is even more remarkable considering that 67.5 percent of the respondents expressed little or no fondness for Rómulo Betancourt and that 79 percent believed that the government "doesn't concern itself with what people like me think."[60] That no force on the left was able to exploit such alienation is one manifestation of the magnitude of the defeat sustained by the left in the guerrilla war.

Many former guerrillas returned to party politics after 1969. Teodoro Petkoff and other Communists, disillusioned by the failure of the guerrilla war and by the 1968 Soviet invasion of Czechoslovakia, formed a new party, the Movement for Socialism (MAS), which has since emerged as the largest leftist party. Alfredo Maneiro, after breaking with MAS, helped to found CAUSA R, which has developed into the largest working-class party in the important industrial zone of Guayana. One of the MIR's most important guerrilla leaders, Américo Martín, led the party after it return to legality, but later reentered the ranks of *Acción Democrática*. (The MIR itself underwent several more splits, and in 1988 merged with MAS.) Even more spectacular was the reintegration of former guerrilla Gumersindo Rodríguez, who rose to prominence in 1973 as part of the campaign of Carlos Andrés Pérez and subsequently became minister of planning. The best-known guerrilla leader never to accept an amnesty is Douglas Bravo. Since his release from prison, he has limited his political work to public commentary and writing.

THE *GUANÁBANA* MATURES

AD and COPEI emerged the clear victors of the political and civil wars of the 1960s. The URD, the third major signatory to the Pact of Punto Fijo, mistook the support for Villalba in 1952 and for Admiral Larrazábal in 1958 as evidence that it could contend for political hegemony with AD. But Villalba's success in 1952 was as a unity candidate against an unpopular dictator, and Larrazábal was a popular independent, not an *urdista*. The bourgeoisie had rallied around AD, and the URD's connections to the guerrilla movement did not enhance its prestige.

COPEI had contributed to the stability of the Betancourt government by guaranteeing church support. COPEI chose to offer Caldera as its candidate in the 1963 elections rather than to accept Leoni, whom it viewed as too close to AD's labor wing. However, COPEI agreed to continue the principles of the Pact of Punto Fijo regardless of who won. The formal alliance embodied in the pact ended with Caldera's victory in 1968. Nonetheless, both major parties agreed not to make unilateral changes that would disenfranchise the other. The spirit of the Pact of Punto Fijo has remained the basis for the constitutional regime since 1958. Caldera grew in stature and since the death of Betancourt stands with Gonzalo Barrios, the nonagenarian president of AD, as a patriarch of the present system.

Participating in government enabled COPEI, which had renounced its pretensions as a confessional party while maintaining its ties to the international Christian Democratic movement, to expand its base of support beyond its traditional base in the Andes and Zulia. This position enabled Caldera to take advantage of a serious split in *adeco* ranks in 1968. The powerful Labor Bureau within AD had supported the leftist teacher, Luis Beltrán Prieto Figueroa, in the struggle for the party's presidential nomination. Betancourt rejected the candidacy of Prieto and intervened with a letter from Berne, Switzerland, accusing key supporters of Prieto in the labor movement of corruption and abuse of power.[61] He sought to impose his lifelong associate, Barrios, as the party's nominee. When AD's National Executive Committee voided the primary won by Prieto and ceded the nomination to Barrios, Prieto's supporters left to form the People's Electoral Movement (MEP). The split opened the way for Caldera to win the election, and for the first time in Venezuela's history, one political party passed the presidential sash peacefully to an opposition party.

The shift of AD to opposition in 1968 and the competition between AD and MEP for control of the Confederation of Venezuelan Workers (CTV) unleashed a period of serious labor unrest just as the civil war was reaching its denouement. For ten years, *adeco* administrations had maintained labor peace through party discipline and control of the Labor Ministry. With a *copeyano* in the presidency, *adeco* union leaders, spurred on by competition from MEP, did not hesitate to demonstrate their militancy. However, AD and COPEI also had reasons to cooperate with one another. Caldera lacked a congressional majority and wanted social peace; AD wanted to repel the MEP challenge. As a result, the two parties struck a deal. AD agreed to moderate its congressional opposition, to mute strike activity, and to concede a measure of influence in the CTV to COPEI; in return, *copeyano* union leaders and Caldera's Labor Ministry agreed to help AD reestablish its hegemony in the CTV.[62] In subsequent years, MEP would decline as an electoral force and accept its own power sharing arrangement with AD in the CTV.

In his famous letter opposing the nomination of Prieto Figueroa, Betancourt complained about the ascendancy within AD of party members motivated less by ideology than by "appetites, directed toward control of power at whatever price."[63] In reality, there was little basis for the charge that supporters of Prieto had "appetites" greater than the Old Guard itself. The politics of greed were becoming prominent within the ranks of virtually all political parties as they competed for votes and for control of the unions, professional associations, universities, etc. Electoral victories, no matter what the arena, brought jobs, money, and prestige to party workers, and these in turn strengthened the party in future contests. The four traditional leftist parties (PCV, MAS, MIR, and MEP) rationalized their participation in this game as "accumulation of forces," that is, the mustering of power to make possible an eventual socialist breakthrough. The discipline of democratic centralism, the organizational framework of all the significant parties, was now being applied not to the politics of class struggle, but to the politics of patronage and clientelism. The goal was no longer to mobilize or to represent citizens, but to incorporate them under the umbrella of the party as pawns in the larger populist game.

Before oil rents could pass into the pockets of Venezuela's capitalists, they had to pass through the coffers of the state, providing plenty of opportunity for corruption and patronage. In 1971, Venezuelan capitalists could expect an annual rate of profit *after taxes* of 20 percent in manufacturing, compared to 5.4 percent in the United States and 9.6 percent in Argentina. This rate would rise to 36.1 percent (1975) as a result of the oil boom. As dollars cascaded into the economy after 1973, the problem of corruption took on an entirely new dimension.[64] To Betancourt, the problem was basically one of moral rectitude. The *adeco* patriarch failed to accept that the problem had become systemic, related to the political edifice for which he had served as principal architect.

Of course, as the 1973 elections approached, no one realized that an economic windfall lay around the corner. In fact, it seemed as though the day of reckoning might be approaching for Venezuela's "democratic experiment." The economy was sluggish, slowing down from the expansion of the 1960s. Middle East producers were grabbing an ever-larger share of the world market and driving down the price of oil, threatening the economic basis of populist, patronage-driven politics. The possibility of prolonged economic decline loomed.

Both parties experienced bitter internal competition for the 1973 nomination. The great Dons of the Generation of 1928 were being challenged by upstart, ambitious politicians from within. The left seemed fortified by the split within AD and ready to test its strength in elections for the first time; the profundity of its defeat in the guerrilla war was not yet clear. Pérez Jiménez seemed poised to make a comeback. He was formally prohibited from running for president, but his followers hoped to launch a symbolic candidacy in the style of the Argentine Peronists. Polls indicated some popular sympathy in Caracas for the ex-dictator, who had presided over a period of economic expansion and extensive public works projects.

However, the results of the 1973 election suggested that the system was actually growing stronger and more stable. Carlos Andrés Pérez won the presidency handily, and AD and COPEI together won 85.5 percent of the presidential vote and 73.3 percent of the congressional vote. The left failed to find a formula for unity, and no one leftist candidate received more than 5 percent of the vote. The MAS received the highest congressional vote, only 5.24 percent. The URD fared even worse, and no party on the right, including those that courted Pérez Jiménez, posed a significant challenge. Thus, the Venezuelan party system arrived at the configuration that it has maintained to this day—the "guanábana" (a pear-shaped fruit), that is, a system dominated by the two large parties, generally inclined toward an *adeco* majority, with COPEI as the only opposition party capable of winning the presidency.[65]

The Governmental System

Under the 1961 Constitution, Venezuela is a federal state with a president and a bicameral legislature. Until reforms enacted in 1988, only state legislatures, not governors, were elected. All revenues are provided by the central government, so even with the direct election of governors, the central government continues to exercise great control over state and local priorities. The system is intentionally weighted toward a strong executive. The president is commander of the military, can decree a wide range of monetary and fiscal policies, is in charge of exploitation of oil and mining concessions, and enjoys virtual autonomy in foreign affairs. The president can assume additional powers under a state of emergency and has broad powers of appointment in public institutes, enterprises, and foundations. Even more so than in developed parliamentary democracies, legislation tends to set objectives and leave implementation to the executive through *reglamientos* (executive orders).

A clause in the 1961 Constitution mandates that no president can run again for the office until two subsequent terms have passed. Betancourt's magnanimous gesture of leaving the country after passing the presidency to Leoni breathed life into this provision, which has served as a somewhat effective check on personal power. However, the system of checks and balances between the legislative and executive branches has worked only exceptionally. When confronted with an opposition majority, the president can occasionally be overruled, as when AD and the left combined to pass a national wage hike over the objections of the *copeyano* president, Luis Herrera Campins (1979–1983). Most of the time, however, the president has a working majority or near majority and can cajole additional support by using the resources of the state to induce cooperation from smaller parties. In the first four years of a term, the power of the president is usually overwhelming. In 1990, for example, almost the entire Congress, including AD, were united in opposing Pérez's plan to raise gasoline taxes, but the legislators preferred to defer to executive authority rather than to confront Pérez with legislation contrary to his economic austerity plan.

The system of representation used in legislative elections at all levels is proportional. The formula used to allocate seats is weighted toward the larger parties, but parties are awarded additional representatives according to their share of the total national vote. Each party prepares a list of candidates, a *plancha*. Since 1988, voters have had the right in state and local elections to indicate a preference among names listed on the *plancha* they choose, but the manner of voting discourages voters from choosing this option.

A similar system of party competition through lists is employed throughout Venezuelan civic society—in neighborhood associations, unions, professional associations, peasant leagues, cultural institutions, student organizations, etc., partly as a device to dissuade parties from forming their own separate organizations. Since virtually all such organizations are subsidized through the central government budget, they are targets of control by parties of all ideological stripes. Whatever the rhetoric, the contests are more often about patronage than about ideology. For the parties in opposition, control of civic organizations, especially unions in critical economic sectors, can be a useful tool for negotiating with the government, a temptation that induces all of the parties, large and small, to put the welfare of constituents second to the welfare of the party.

CONCLUSION

Venezuela hardly seemed likely to consolidate stable electoral democracy after the fall of Pérez Jiménez in 1958, but it was one of the few South American countries to escape the wave of military dictatorships that swept across the continent in the 1960s and 1970s. Venezuela provided a successful experiment for the combination of counterinsurgency tactics and reform that U.S. policy makers hoped would stem the tide of revolution in the Third World. It should be obvious, however, that the conditions that produced both defeat of the insurgency and avoidance of military rule were quite specific to Venezuela's own historical experience. Already, by 1973 doubts about the viability of the Venezuelan model had begun to surface. However, the extraordinary events in the Middle East would produce one more opportunity for Venezuelan elites to prove that the Venezuelan model could effectively "sow the petroleum."

5

From the Oil Boom to the Postpetroleum Era

Venezuelan society, with its secular and materialistic culture, egalitarian norms, partisan politics, and commercial mass media seems a world apart from the oil-based economies of the Persian Gulf; however, like other oil-rich nations, Venezuela reaped a bonanza from the "oil crisis" of 1974 to 1981. This reality was captured for the public imagination in the cover of a book, *Venezuela Saudita*, depicting Carlos Andrés Pérez, president from 1974 to 1978, in the robe and headdress of an Arab prince.[1]

Between 1974 and 1978, Andrés Pérez, popularly known as "CAP," attempted to implement his grandiose vision of *"Gran Venezuela"* as laid out in the Fifth National Plan (*Plan V*). *Plan V* called for a dramatic acceleration of heavy industrialization projects in order to reduce the nation's dependence upon oil. By 1978, however, Venezuelans were disillusioned with the inefficiency and corruption of Pérez's administration; they elected a *copeyano*, Luis Herrera Campins, to the presidency. Despite a second round of oil price increases, Herrera Campins fared little better. As oil prices dropped toward the end of his term, the country faced an economic crisis, crystallized in the decision on February 28, 1983 ("Black Friday"), to devalue the bolívar, which exacted a devastating toll on the middle and working classes and on the poor.

A brief economic surge in 1986 and 1987 helped *adeco* President Jaime Lusinchi leave office as a relatively popular president, but he bought this "prosperity" at a high price to be paid by his successor, Pérez, who became in 1988 the first president to achieve a second term. Pérez announced almost immediately that he would implement an austerity package designed to satisfy the International Monetary Fund (IMF); Venezuelans responded on February 27, 1989, with a violent, spontaneous mass revolt.

THE OIL BONANZA AND NATIONALIZATION

Under Betancourt and Leoni, it was Venezuelan policy to pursue both a special trading relationship with the United States as well as a strengthening of OPEC, two somewhat contradictory goals. Over time, OPEC became the higher priority. The need for a more effective cartel was made urgent by the fall in proven reserves to a point where they were only expected to last seventeen years, by falling prices, and by the U.S. decision to make Canada more than Venezuela its preferred supplier of oil. Caldera ended this futile quest to resolve a conflicting policy when, in the face of considerable opposition from the Federation of Chambers of Commerce and Industry (FEDECAMARAS), he abrogated the 1951 Reciprocal Trade Treaty. Hence Venezuela worked within OPEC to establish more effective limits over production. Although this was largely unsuccessful, growing consumption of oil and dependence on OPEC suppliers on the part of the industrialized countries and the political crises of 1973 in the Middle East would eventually bring about results beyond Venezuela's wildest expectations.

An important prelude to the post-1974 bonanza was OPEC's successful struggle in the 1960s to gain the right to set reference prices— that is, the right to unilaterally set the price on which royalties and profits (the basis for applying general taxes) would be calculated, regardless of the actual (posted or discounted) price of oil on the world market. This reference price system was formalized for all the oil-producing nations in 1971 in the Teheran Agreements. From this point on, host countries had the power, within limits set by the market and their cohesiveness as a cartel, to determine prices. That is, no longer did the host countries have to be content with capturing profits determined by price, they could now drive up their incomes by driving up prices. From this point forward, their principal opponents were not the companies themselves, but the governments of the industrial consuming economies.

The fourth Arab-Israeli War of 1973 and consequent Arab oil embargo, which removed oil from the world's most productive fields from Western markets—permitted the landlord states to exercise their newly won power to the maximum. The price of Venezuelan crude, which had fallen to its nadir of US$1.76 per barrel in 1970, had already recovered to $3.56 by 1973.[2] The price per barrel shot up to $10.31 in 1974. Even though Venezuela reduced oil exports (in the interest of conservation and fiscal prudence) by nearly one-third over two years, revenues flooded into the state treasury. In 1974 alone national income increased 40 percent and government revenues by 170 percent. Between 1973 and 1983, the petroleum boom earned Venezuela's 16 million people

TABLE 5.1 Petroleum Exports, Government Income, Government Spending, Government Investment, 1972-1986

Year	Petroleum exports, US$ million	Government Income: Total Bs. million	From oil	Total government spending, Bs. million	Government investment, Bs. million
1972	3,202	12,546	7,881	12,413	3,489
1973	4,803	16,432	11,180	14,572	4,485
1974	11,290	42,800	36,445	39,471	24,103
1975	8,982	41,001	31,648	40,015	20,749
1976	9,342	43,143	28,012	37,351	17,651
1977	9,661	51,179	29,421	48,803	24,378
1978	9,174	50,663	25,174	47,341	19,795
1979	14,360	48,432	33,308	43,092	10,935
1980	19,360	71,507	45,330	62,196	21,987
1981	20,181	95,585	92,672	87,369	32,753
1982	16,516	82,101	49,223	82,404	27,964
1983	14,759	80,492	40,546	78,464	24,434
1984	15,967	102,769	60,561	86,865	19,665
1985	14,178	118,040	62,071	98,130	24,380
1986	8,686	115,925	42,873	103,336	31,112

Source: Banco Central de Venezuela, *Anuarios de Cuentas Nacionales* (Caracas, 1972-1986).

over US$150 billion. The era of "Saudi Venezuela" had arrived (see Table 5.1.).

It is within this context that one must also judge the most important measure undertaken by Carlos Andrés Pérez, the nationalization of the petroleum industry in 1976, one year after nationalization of the iron industry. By 1974, the host countries had established their own companies, which provided vital experience and preparation for nationalization. The companies had never owned the petroleum reserves themselves; they only paid a royalty to the landlord state for permission (a "concession") to extract oil from the ground. Once the OPEC nations had gained the right to establish reference prices and determine production levels, the oil companies became side players in the struggle between the landlord states and the industrial consuming nations. This development itself was made realistic by the unity provided by OPEC.

While they hardly welcomed nationalization, nothing like the bitterness in struggles over expropriation and compensation elsewhere in Latin America characterized the process of nationalization of oil in Venezuela. In 1974, Pérez appointed a commission composed of virtually all sectors, including FEDECAMARAS, to make arrangements with the companies. The companies, whose forty-year concessions were due to expire in 1983 in any case, signalled their acceptance of the process. The main issues for negotiation were compensation and the terms of transition.

The PDVSA (Petroleos de Venezuela, Sociedad Anómina) was created as a state holding company for smaller enterprises corresponding to each of the subsidiaries of the major companies. These new subsidiaries were prohibited from transferring information and technology to one another. Under service and technology agreements (unintentionally revealed by the government in 1977), the companies were paid twenty cents per barrel, half of the profit per barrel they were obtaining before nationalization. Since the companies no longer provided any investment (or assumed any risk), their overall profits on service agreements on Venezuelan operations were roughly equivalent to what they earned before nationalization.[3]

Commercialization agreements assured that 88 percent of PDVSA production would be allocated to the former companies in proportions equivalent to their previous status, leaving the new state company little margin for developing competing markets without boosting production. In fact, production had been falling steadily because the companies had been making few new investments—partly because they were increasingly oriented toward the higher grade, more easily extractable deposits in the Middle East, and partly because the concessions obtained in 1943 were approaching their forty-year expiration. Hence, the PDVSA faced the immediate need to make new investments in exploration and extraction.

However, the deal was not entirely one-sided. The US$1 billion paid the companies as compensation represented only 13 percent of revenues realized by the PDVSA in 1976 alone. By taking control of the companies seven years in advance of the 1983 reversions, the PDVSA was able to make investments needed to keep the Venezuelan industry competitive. As the state company has acquired experience, and as contracts have come up for revision, it has been able to strike better arrangements. It has also extended its operations into new phases by entering into marketing and joint ownership arrangements overseas. The PDVSA has generally avoided the taint of corruption and favoritism associated with many other state industries, demonstrating that Venezuelans are indeed capable of running a complex, technologically sophisticated industry. With nationalization Venezuela laid the basis for transforming itself from a mere *landlord* (host) nation interested in little more than maximizing rents to a *producing* nation with an industry with potential to generate many forward and backward links with the rest of the economy.

FROM BOOM TO BUST IN THE ECONOMY: AN OVERVIEW

The boom and bust path of the Venezuelan economy between 1970 and 1986 is evident in Figure 5.1, which shows the tendencies of several major economic indicators between 1971 and 1986. Despite the massive

Figure 5.1 Tendencies in the Venezuelan Economy, 1972-1986

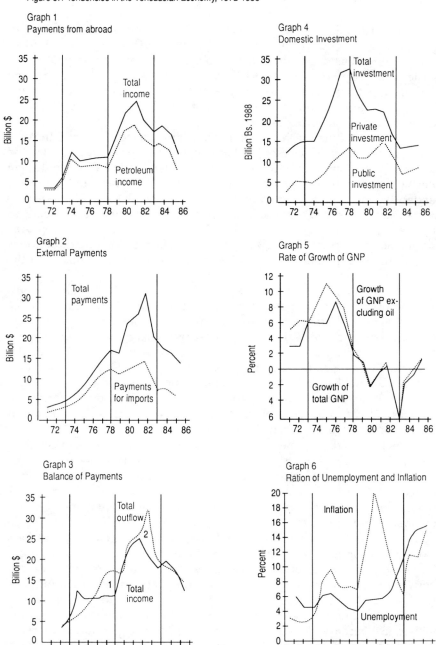

Graph 1
Payments from abroad

Graph 4
Domestic Investment

Graph 2
External Payments

Graph 5
Rate of Growth of GNP

Graph 3
Balance of Payments

Graph 6
Ration of Unemployment and Inflation

Source: Adapted from Ramón Espinasa, "El déstino de renta petrolera 1974–1976"
Revista SIC, 50 (February 1987): 54-56

flow of petrodollars into the economy, by 1978 the positive balance of payments generated by the boom had been overtaken by the export of capital abroad and by imports for consumption and for expansion of basic industries. Hence, in 1978, the government undertook the first fateful step toward the crisis of the 1980s when it contracted several large, short-term loans to cover the balance of payments deficit and to continue industrial expansion projects.

President Luis Herrera Campins, whose electoral slogan in 1978 was "*¿Dónde están los reales?*" ("What happened to the money?"), planned to scale back spending; however, the years 1978 to 1981 saw the Iranian Revolution and outbreak of war between Iraq and Iran, and oil prices underwent a second jump, from $13 to $34 per barrel. The *copeyano* administration ended up spending as much in its first three years as the Pérez administration had in five. The last two years of the *copeyano* presidency of Herrera Campins saw the end of favorable market conditions for OPEC, but the government failed to adjust spending policies to the new reality.

The reasons for the collapse of oil prices in the 1980s are various. The industrialized consumer countries responded to OPEC's challenge with their own cartel of consumers, the International Energy Agency; fuel efficiency, conservation, and alternative energy technologies were developed to reduce consumption. Non-OPEC sources of oil were developed in Mexico, Alaska, and northern Europe. OPEC found itself unable to establish effective production quotas in order to prevent a glut, while its share of world production of oil fell from 70 percent in the early 1970s to 50 percent ten years later. (Venezuela's own share of the exports fell to 5 percent in 1984.)

As prices fell, income from petroleum exports dropped from slightly below $20 billion in 1981 to $11 billion in 1983, just as large, short-term debt payments were coming due. The value of the bolívar remained pegged at 4.3 to 1 U.S. dollar despite the deterioration in the country's trade and reserves, but Herrera Campins resisted devaluation—for very understandable reasons. Debts held in dollars would suddenly double or triple their size in bolívars. Merchants and industrialists would pass along to consumers the higher price (in bolívars) of imported goods. Since the prices were regulated, the government would find itself caught between the interests of consumers and suppliers. Inflation had already reached 22 percent in 1980; devaluation was certain to intensify it.

But the more the government postponed the day of reckoning, the more grave became the crisis. The overvalued bolívar discouraged foreign investment, while the domestic bourgeoisie continued to act with short-sighted avarice. By 1983 domestic investment had fallen to one-fifth of its level of 1977. Net short-term outflows of capital rose from $1.3 billion in 1980 to $5.3 billion in 1982. Foreign reserves fell $6 billion in the first eleven months of 1982, reaching $11 billion.[4] Dollars obtained licitly or illicitly from the central government at a ridiculously low rate of exchange were being invested in U.S. banks at the era's extraordinarily high rates of interest and in the booming Miami real estate market. In the first two months of 1983 alone, Venezuela's capitalists exported $2 billion, compared to $1.3 billion in all of 1978.[5]

On February 28, 1983, "Black Friday," Herrera Campins relented and announced the implementation of a new, three-tiered, exchange system. The rates were 4.3 to 1 for repayment of public debt and imports of essential goods; 6 to 1 for other trade transactions (subject to additional controls); and a free-floating rate for travel, financial, and other transactions, including private debt. The private sector protested the exclusion of private debt from the preferential rate. Despite the fact that a large portion of this borrowing was for little more than speculation, the government bowed to pressure and allowed transactions for payments on the private debt to be conducted at the preferential rate, provided debts were renegotiated to mature within three years.

With devaluation, the economic bubble was pricked. By the end of the year the free market rate for the bolívar had tripled. Imports and gross investments plunged 50 percent. The real gross domestic product (GDP) fell 5.6 percent. Construction declined by 13.3 percent in 1983 and 34.4 percent in 1984. Official rates of unemployment in the urban sector (80 percent of the work force) rose from 7.8 percent to 14.3 percent over these two years, while real wages fell 7.2 percent and 7.6 percent, respectively. Underemployment, already at 44 percent of the urban work force in 1981, also rose.[6] And things were to get worse. Between 1987 and 1989, oil exports earned only $8.5 billion on average, and two additional devaluations took place in 1985 and 1987. Overall, between 1981 and 1989 GDP fell by 3.8 percent—almost 25 percent in per capita terms. In 1989 the GDP contracted by more than 8 percent; inflation reached 81 percent; and unemployment and underemployment (unofficially) reached 50 percent.[7]

At the same time, wealthy Venezuelans who had already moved their funds into New York and Miami reaped a bonanza, tripling the worth (in bolívars) of the money they had exported between 1974 and 1983. The three-tiered (four-tiered from 1984 to 1986) exchange rate system created speculative opportunities for those able to get their hands on dollars at preferential rates; they merely had to convert them back to bolívars at the free market rate to make enormous profits. With short-term profits of 100 percent available for merely circulating money in and out of the economy, corruption was almost inevitable. In 1988, *adeco* president Jaime Lusinchi found himself in the midst of a major money laundering scandal involving the agency (RECADI) created to manage the three-tiered exchange system.

The government turned to the international banks to fill void. Between 1974 and 1983, government ministries, autonomous institutes (e.g., for housing, culture, technical training, etc.), local governments, and public enterprises contracted huge debts, often in violation of the constitution, which requires approval of Congress for certain types of financing.[8] Until 1983, the true size of the external debt was unknown. In 1982, the government announced that only one-half of the total public debt had been recorded and approved by Congress. In 1984, after some of the decentralized debt had been refinanced, the total disbursed public external debt stood at $34.2 billion, nearly double the figure for 1978, making Venezuela the fourth-largest debtor (after Brazil, Mexico, and Argentina) in Latin America.[9]

A high proportion of the debt was short term. Forty-five percent of Venezuela's obligations were due in 1983–1984, compared to 19 percent for Brazil and Argentina, and 30 percent for Mexico. In 1982, the minister of finance estimated that $13.1 billion would fall due in 1983, constituting 94 percent of oil export earnings that year. Another $6.8 billion was due over the next three years, and $5.1 billion beyond 1987. Lusinchi, believing that he could entice new foreign investment by proving Venezuela a good credit risk, refused to consider a moratorium or a cap on payments of interest. Venezuela not only paid interest but principal during his administration, an "achievement" matched only by Pinochet's Chile. The government did manage to reschedule $21.2 billion of its debt in 1984 on relatively favorable terms; between 1983 and 1989 Venezuela reduced the size of its external debt from $36 billion to $26.7 billion.[10] However, the policy failed to attract new foreign investment and earned Venezuela sharp criticism from the Cartegena Group, a coalition of major Latin American debtors attempting to develop a common front against the banks. By late 1989, Venezuela was once again negotiating for rescheduling and debt relief.

Remarkably, Lusinchi seemed to resuscitate the economy and to service the debt at the same time. In 1986, a year in which oil prices fell from $26 per barrel to less than $13, the gross domestic product grew by 6.8 percent, and there were modest increases in 1987 and early 1988. Some of this growth can be attributed to the devaluation, which served to make domestic producers more competitive with foreign imports. More important, however, were large state investments in basic industries, subsidies to agriculture, and new protectionist measures to promote import substitution. But from what fiscal resources had Lusinchi drawn to stimulate the economy and amortize the debt simultaneously?

As Andrés Pérez would learn to his great discomfort, Lusinchi had purchased economic growth and political popularity by exhausting the country's savings. Venezuela's noncommitted monetary reserves dropped from $8.98 billion in 1985 to $1.77 billion in 1986. A positive balance of payments of $1.7 billion in 1985 turned into a deficit of $3.8 billion in 1986 and $4.4 billion in 1987. Not only was Lusinchi unwilling to make spending cuts in an election year, government spending actually increased 9.9 percent in 1988, while government income fell 4 percent. As a result, the budget deficit rose from Bs. 234 *million* to Bs. 15.7 *billion*. The overall balance of payments deficit was nearly $4.4 billion in 1988, leaving only $2 billion in operating reserves as the new year loomed. Debt service alone required $1.3 billion for amortization and $2.2 billion for interest, amounting to 45.4 percent of export earnings.[11]

The country experienced a net capital loss of $17.3 billion between 1983 and 1987. The trade deficit turned negative for the first time in ten years. The government maintained interest rates well below the rate of inflation; when regular lines of credit went dry, wealthier consumers resorted to credit cards. By the end of 1988, the Central Bank owed international banks $1.2 billion for such charges. Had the Central Bank insisted on charging the commercial banks 14.5 bolívars (well below the free market rate of 37) for each dollar remitted abroad, it would have virtually bankrupted the banking system. The financial system was on the verge of collapse when Pérez took office.[12]

Lusinchi's policies probably helped his fellow *adeco* win the December 1988 elections, but he left Pérez an economic time bomb to dismantle. Every dollar that the central bank paid to the international banks subtracted another 14.5 bolívars from the economy; yet despite the subtraction of currency from the economy, inflation had climbed close to 40 percent, with almost the entire increase coming in the final eight months of 1988. By the end of the year, a psychological dynamic began to exert itself as consumers sought to spend their bolívars quickly or to turn them into dollars, provoking a "dollarization" of parts of the economy. Merchants, expecting the new government to liberalize prices, began to hoard goods, creating the first food shortages of the modern era. By the time Andrés Pérez was inaugurated for the second time in 1989, the state investment corporation had been dissolved, the reserves from the investment fund had been emptied into the general treasury, and the nation's credit rating had slipped so low that Venezuelan notes held by the banks were worth only 30 percent of their face value on the open market.

After the elections, Lusinchi, with Pérez's approval, announced that no more of the debt would be amortized until January 17. The government began talks with its international creditors on restructuring its loans, while the president-elect began to formulate a package of measures to deal with the crisis. José Ignacio Cabrujas, Venezuela's leading playwright, imagined the following conversation between Pérez and banker Pedro Tinoco, who has just informed the president-elect that, "There are $200 million dollars."

> *Pérez:* To buy paper clips, Tinoco?
> *Tinoco:* No, no. In general, Mr. President.
> *Pérez:* I assume you're referring to the petty cash box, Dr. Tinoco.
> *Tinoco:* No. No. I'm talking about the general treasury. That's all we have. There's nothing else.
> *Pérez:* But Jaime . . . he didn't . . . he didn't tell me anything about this. . . . Call Jaime!
> *Tinoco:* Jaime is in Miami, Mr. President.[13]

CARLOS ANDRÉS PÉREZ AND THE DREAM OF PROGRESS

Historian John Lombardi once characterized Venezuelan history as "the search for order, the dream of progress."[14] In 1974, with civil peace restored, electoral democracy consolidated, and export earnings booming, the dream seemed within reach, or so it seemed to President Carlos Andrés Pérez at the beginning of his first presidency. His *Plan V* sought to move beyond import substitution and to "deepen" industrialization, that is, to encourage vertical integration of the economy through development of basic industries producing intermediate and capital goods and to increase nontraditional exports. This would require foreign investment and technology as well as domestic resources. Robust oil earnings induced the government to contract loans at what seemed favorable terms at the time. The government also dictated new nationalistic conditions on foreign investment—for example, limits on repatriation of profits, requirements for technology transfers, local content requirements, etc. A huge new educational effort, the *Gran Mariscal de Ayacucho* program, allocated scholarships for study abroad and technical education.

In Brazil and some countries of the Southern Cone, military governments were also rethinking economic strategy. They had come to power to resolve a crisis of populism generated at least in part by the exhaustion of the import substitution strategy of industrialization.[15] However, in two vital respects, one political and the other economic, Venezuela differed from its semi-industrialized sister countries. First, the radical left had already been defeated, as the 1973 elections amply confirmed; the reassertion of *adeco* control over the Confederation of Venezuelan Workers (CTV) further ensured that no crisis of populism was in the offing in Venezuela. Second, Venezuela's industrialization process came later and owed as much to expanding internal demand as to protection of the internal market. Venezuela's populist and modernizing elites had sought not so much to protect the industrialization process from foreign capital as to associate with it.[16]

In political pacts negotiated during the 1958 transition, the Venezuelan bourgeoisie built import substitution into the economic policies pursued by AD under Betancourt and Leoni. The policies seemed to work as domestic production in manufacturing expanded at an average annual rate of 9.9 percent between 1962 and 1965 and over 6 percent for 1966 to 1971.[17] However, for import substitution to succeed as a long-term strategy, the benefits of this growth needed to be distributed in a way that would expand the domestic market (beyond the injection of oil rents) and thereby generate increased demand. However, there is little evidence that this was happening. A small number of tightly knit corporate *"grupos"* (Boulton, Philips, Mendoza, Vollmer, Polar, etc.), most of them families, reaped enormous profits, while much of the working class continued to live in poverty. On the one hand, a World Bank study in 1973 found that gross industrial profits were 17 percent of sales and a whopping 31 percent of the value of fixed capital.[18] On the other hand, according to a study by the state planning agency, CORDIPLAN, 21 percent of Venezuelan workers were earning less than the minimum wage. Despite low official figures, the study found that unemployment in 1974 was 16 percent, with another 20 percent underemployed.[19]

With the benefits of economic expansion evidently narrowly shared, how was it that the economy managed to expand? According to economic historian Miguel Ignacio Purroy, "Only the supportive actions of the state made possible the strange coexistence of low productivity of capital and labor, low marginal income, and *at the same time* an extraordinarily high rate of profit."[20] By the end of the 1960s, competition from Middle East producers and falling oil prices were threatening the state's ability to continue financing this version of import substitution.

Although generally regarded as more conservative than his predecessors, COPEI's Rafael Caldera assumed the presidency in early 1969 without the same commitment to import substitution as AD. His administration (1969–1973) began to shift the role of the state from one that encouraged industrialization through the private sector to one that emphasized a more direct role in production. Caldera's *Plan IV* proposed significant expansion of state-owned steel works in Zulia and Guayana, as well as development of a public sector aluminum industry, and he deemphasized support for industrialization in the central zone where traditional industries, like textiles, were located. The large business interests grouped under FEDECAMARAS did not welcome this deviation from the policies of the 1960s; they turned to their traditional allies in the *adeco* "Old Guard" for support. However, not all elements of the bourgeoisie followed their lead. By 1973 the internal structure of Venezuelan capitalism had grown considerably more complex than it had been in 1958. This division became evident during the first presidency of Andrés Pérez.

As secretary general of AD after its defeat in 1968, Pérez was responsible for restructuring the *adeco* approach to campaigning. He accomplished this by placing more emphasis on fund raising and media and less on traditional mass meetings in preparation for the 1973 election. He forged closer links with some elites not so closely tied to the Old Guard and import substitution, with brash entrepreneurs (like the media whiz, Diego Arria), and with figures like Pedro Tinoco, a banker in disrepute for his loyalty to Pérez Jiménez during the last days of the dictatorship. When Andrés Pérez assumed the presidency, his closest advisers and key ministerial appointments were individuals linked to these sectors. When the petrodollars began cascading into the national treasury in 1974, these elites found that they had won more than anticipated when they threw in their lot with CAP.[21]

The oil bonanza enabled Pérez to play the part of a populist and to initiate grandiose development plans. Among his first actions were to decree a wage increase and to require employers to expand their work force by 10 percent. Foreign owners in a wide variety of enterprises, including major commercial outlets, were required to sell 80 percent of their stock to Venezuelan nationals. Within two years the government would nationalize the petroleum and iron ore industries.

The unbounded optimism of the era found expression in *Plan V,* developed under the guidance of Gumersindo Rodríguez, a former guerrilla leader. What distanced Rodríguez from the *adeco* Old Guard turned out not to be his guerrilla experience, however, but his ties to Pedro Tinoco. Tinoco enjoyed close links with Bethlehem Steel Corporation and Chase Manhattan Bank, and was appointed by CAP to head the Commission for the Integral Reform of Public Administration, CRIAP. CRIAP's mission was to "depoliticize" public administration, that is, put it in the hands of technocrats and distance it from influence by Congress and the political parties. In fact, by increasing the autonomy of the public administration, Tinoco and other economic elites close to Pérez would be able to more readily dispose of oil rents to favor their own projects. This alarmed not only certain political sectors, but also sectors of the bourgeoisie close to the *adeco* Old Guard, whose base now became Congress.[22]

Congress rejected CRIAP's key proposals—a result possible only because a sizable block of the *adeco* Old Guard broke party discipline. However, the legislature had already granted Pérez emergency powers

TABLE 5.2 Public Financing in the Manufacturing Sector, 1973 and 1977, Millions of Bolívars

Industries producing:	1973	1977
Nondurable consumer goods	40	189
Semidurable consumer goods	5	53
Durable consumer goods	5	23
Capital goods	18	205
Intermediate goods	142	1193
Total	210	1663

Source: Banco Central, *Informe Económico*, (Caracas, 1977).

to govern by decree. Riding the crest of a wave of popularity created by his early measures on wages and employment, CAP did not hesitate to use these powers to accomplish the "reform" indirectly, principally by putting the state-owned basic industries (oil, steel, aluminum, energy, etc.) under the control of the minister of investment, Carmelo Lauría (later secretary to the president), another banker with close links to the petroleum companies and foreign creditors. As it turned out, far from rationalizing administration of basic industries and state finances, the concentration of power accomplished early in CAP's administration contributed to several major scandals (described below) implicating close associates of the president and even the president himself.

Industrialization and New Forms of Dependence

Plan V contemplated nothing less than overnight transformation of Venezuela. The state planned to boost public investment 168 percent (after inflation) over *Plan IV*, tripling investment in the manufacturing sector alone.[23] Nearly 60 percent of public investment was to flow into basic industries—petrochemicals, steel, and aluminum, with the latter two sectors expected to lead Venezuela away from dependence upon oil exports (see Table 5.2.), and to produce inputs for domestic industries. Even after other economic sectors (such as nondurable goods) found their access to credits limited after 1975, public investment continued to flow nearly unabated to basic industries, like steel, aluminum, and motors.

Plan V set wildly unrealistic goals for basic industries. For example, the plan envisioned doubling steel production, with the SIDOR (Siderúrgico de Orinoco, the state steel corporation) plant in Guayana alone increasing production from 1.25 million to 5 million metric tons. With this increase and the addition of a new plant in Zulia, *Plan V* projected that by 1990 Venezuela would produce 15 million metric tons of steel. However, by 1984 Venezuela's steel output had barely reached 2.5 million tons. In that year SIDOR reported a net loss of Bs. 1.9 billion, mostly due to payments on its debt. Growth of the metallurgical sector was so

TABLE 5.3 Economic Growth in Venezuela and Other Nations, 1960-1970 and 1970-1982

| | Average annual growth rate (percent): | | | | | | | | |
| | GDP | | Agriculture | | Industry | | Manufacturing | | Other | |
	1	2	1	2	1	2	1	2	1	2
Venezuela	6.0	4.1	5.8	3.0	4.6	2.4	6.4	4.8	7.3	5.3
Other Latin American nations										
Chile	4.4	1.9	3.1	3.1	4.4	0.6	5.5	-0.4	4.6	2.7
Brazil[a]	5.4	7.6	--	4.5	--	8.2	--	7.8	--	7.7
Argentina	4.3	1.5	1.8	2.2	5.8	1.0	5.6	-0.2	3.8	1.7
Peru	4.9	3.0	3.7	0.7	5.0	3.3	5.7	2.5	5.3	3.4
Colombia	5.1	5.4	3.5	4.5	6.0	4.4	5.7	5.2	5.7	6.5
Other major Latin American oil exporters										
Mexico	7.6	6.4	4.5	3.4	9.4	7.2	10.1	6.8	7.3	6.5
Ecuador	--	8.1	--	2.9	--	11.3	--	9.9	--	8.4
Other middle-income oil exporters										
Nigeria	3.1	3.8	-0.4	-0.6	14.7	4.8	9.1	12.0	2.3	6.7
Algeria	4.3	6.6	0.1	3.9	11.6	7.0	7.8	10.9	-1.1	6.4

1 = rate for 1960-1970; 2 = rate for 1970-1982.
[a]Data for Brazil are for 1970-81.
Source: World Bank, *World Development Report, 1984* (New York: Oxford University Press, 1984).

far below projections that plans for expansion of steel production in Zulia were indefinitely postponed.[24]

None of this is to deny that the Venezuelan economy experienced significant growth and development of its productive capacity. Overall, the gross national product increased by 41 percent between 1968 and 1980, with manufacturing increasing by 47 percent. The fastest-growing sectors were intermediate and capital goods industries. Chemicals, plastics, and basic metals production constituted only 9.7 percent of manufacturing output in 1968; by 1980 they accounted for 21.8 percent. The percentage of manufacturing output constituted by mechanical goods (machinery, electrical equipment, transportation materials, etc.) rose from 9.3 percent in 1968 to 15 percent in 1978.[25]

Nonetheless, if measured against the performance of other oil exporters and other semi-industrialized nations in Latin America, this economic performance was not exceptional. Other major oil exporters (see Table 5.3) demonstrated even stronger growth. Venezuela's economy outperformed Chile and Argentina, but it did not match the industrial expansion of Brazil. The economic performance in targeted areas, such as the machinery and transport sector and chemicals, was not as impressive as that in the oil-importing countries of Argentina, Brazil, and Chile or the oil-exporting country of Mexico (see Table 5.4).

In the 1980s, aluminum emerged as a major growth sector and prospective area for export diversification, but the expansion took place within a context of deepening dependence upon foreign technology and

TABLE 5.4   Distribution of Manufacturing Value Added in Various
Sectors, Venezuela and Other Nations

		Percentage of manufacturing value added in various sectors Distribution in 1980[a]					Value added in manufacturing (millions of 1975 dollars)	
	A	B	C	D	E		1970	1980
Venezuela	25	7	8	9	51		3,419	5,718
			Other Latin American Nations					
Chile	15	5	16	11	53		1,881	2,107
Brazil	14	10	28	10	38		18,819	44,733
Argentina	12	11	27	13	37		10,693	12,637
Peru	27	14	10	11	38		2,911	4,048
Colombia[b]	32	15	12	12	29		1,800	3,293
			Other Major Latin American Oil Exporters					
Mexico	19	9	19	12	41		14,592	29,084
Ecuador	29	14	10	7	40		322	872
			Other Middle-Income Oil Exporters					
Nigeria[b]	25	18	13	13	31		1,191	3,598
Algeria[c]	24	16	22	14	34		1,068	3,125

[a]Manufacturing value added in: A = Food and agriculture; B = Textiles
and clothing; C = Machinery and transport equipment; D = Chemicals;
E = Other manufacturing.
[b]Data for 1979.
[c]Data for 1981.
Source: World Bank, *World Development Report 1984, 1985.* (New York:
Oxford University Press, 1984, 1985).

need to service a burgeoning debt, hardly what was envisioned under
Plan V. Venezuelan law mandates majority ownership for Venezuelan
capital in the basic industries sector, but private Venezuelan investors
are often fronts (*"testaferros"*) recruited by foreign investors to satisfy
the letter but not the spirit of the law. In 1988, the government proposed
obtaining credits to expand the industry by guaranteeing the loans with
future sales of aluminum and oil, raising fears that Venezuela was
returning control of natural resources to foreign capital.[26]

Bottlenecks Caused by Inequality

The vision of *Gran Venezuela* failed to materialize for several reasons.
Not least in importance, but often overlooked, are the limitations imposed
by wealth and income inequality, especially important factors in a small
market. The richest 5 percent of the population consumed the largest
percentage and the poorest 20 percent had the smallest percentage of
income among seven semiindustrialized Latin American nations, according to a 1970 study by the United Nations Economic Commission
on Latin America.[27] The infant mortality rate of 1973 of 53.7 per 1000
was higher than it was during the Pérez Jiménez dictatorship. During
the post-1973 boom, while the wealthy enjoyed trips to Europe and

Miami and luxury imports (liquor, luxury cars), an estimated 800,000 people still lived in the worst *ranchos* on Caracas hillsides.[28] Inequality has been exacerbated by an ineffective tax system. In 1983, a person earning $50,000 might expect to pay only $3,500 in income taxes. Even at this low rate, evasion is the rule, not the exception.[29]

Even before the onset of crisis, articles like "Full Coffers but Empty Pledges Irk Venezuelans" and "Venezuelan Oil Riches Fail to Trickle Down; Pessimism Widespread" began to appear in the North American press.[30] In 1980, official figures indicated that 43.2 percent of households suffered poverty, 6.7 percent extreme poverty. By 1983, these figures would rise to 74 percent and 15.7 percent, respectively. Official unemployment figures hovered between 7 percent and 10 percent; the CTV argued that if those who were underemployed or had stopped looking for work were included, the rate would be well over 50 percent.[31]

One economist summed up the relationship between inequality and other factors that blocked Venezuela's progress during the boom in this way:

> It is impossible to think of massive production for a consumer market so small and selective. It was necessary to install many different industries, but all in a tightly limited market. Imported equipment and technology were designed for much greater scales of production. As a consequence, the burden of fixed costs was disproportionately high, making products even more expensive and beyond the reach of the high proportion of the population with low income. High prices, small volumes of production, low productivity, and reduction of consumption all interacted with each other in a vicious circle.[32]

For these reasons, even though the expansion of basic industries was intended to provide an infrastructure for domestic industrialization, the basic industries have become increasingly oriented to export markets. These "national" industries are dependent on foreign financing, managerial expertise, technology, and inputs (capital and intermediate goods). Between 1971 and 1977, imports of consumer goods as a percentage of all imports fell from 26.4 percent to 10.8 percent; the percentage of imports composed of intermediate goods shot up to 56.8 percent. By 1980, 61.6 percent of imports consisted of intermediate goods. Unfortunately, although consumer goods accounted for a smaller *share* of imports, domestic production did not keep pace with demand, and in absolute terms imports of food and mass consumption goods increased.[33]

As implied by these data, industrialization in Venezuela was not necessarily reducing dependency. In many of the key sectors, firms were deeply indebted to foreign capital, which often retained managerial prerogatives, and they remained dependent upon transnational corporations for technology and marketing. A typical example is a new aluminum-smelting enterprise, Aluminio Alam S.A. (ALAMSA), slated to become operational in 1990. ALAMSA is to be majority-owned by the Corporación Venezolana de Guyana (CVG), the state holding company, but 70 percent of its $660 million financing comes from a West German company (Austria Metall) and from the French aluminum giant, Pechiney. The other 30 percent of financing was to come from the CVG (through one of its subsidiaries). Pechiney would recover most of its investment almost immediately in the form of payments for the technology it would provide to the new enterprise. Approximately $280 million of the CVG's investment would come from debt/equity swaps supervised by Chase Manhattan. Despite the CVG's majority ownership on paper, foreign investors would be heavily represented on the board of directors and top management of the company. Pechiney and Austria Metall would absorb 70 percent of production from the new plant, and half of the Venezuelan share of production is slated for export, so very little of the new production would be marketed internally.[34]

By the early 1980s, the limits of the development strategy adopted in 1974 were becoming clear. The industrialized world was in a deep recession, limiting the demand for oil, steel, aluminum, etc. Short-term loans, obtained at favorable terms in the 1970s, were coming due just as oil prices were descending. Yet imported capital goods and technology were still needed to maintain production and to complete projects, lest any benefit from earlier investments were to be foregone. In 1990, SIDOR announced that 3,000 workers would be laid off as part of its effort at "economic conversion," that is, reduction of product lines and more intensive exploitation of labor. Even with these changes, however, it is not clear that Venezuela can compete against other major exporters for a sufficient share of the world market to make its aluminum and steel industries profitable.[35] As a result, the government faces the prospect of an economic crisis in Guayana, just the region, as we shall see, where the working class is most militant and independent of control by *Acción Democrática*.

FOREIGN RELATIONS DURING BOOM AND BUST

The trajectory of Venezuela's foreign policy has tended to follow the path of the economy—innovative and nationalist during the boom, cautious and reactive during the bust. Relations with neighboring states, Central America, and the country's role within OPEC have become the most important issues in Venezuelan foreign policy. Nominally, the fundamental basis for hemispheric foreign policy has remained the

Betancourt Doctrine, calling for nonrecognition of de facto regimes and their exclusion from the Organization of American States (OAS). Since 1968, however, there has been a softening of both the doctrine and anticommunism in Venezuelan foreign policy.

Between 1958 and 1963, Betancourt broke or suspended relations with military regimes and, of course, Cuba. Leoni maintained these policies, but showed a more pragmatic approach to the dictatorships, choosing, for example, to recognize the military regime that came to power in 1964 in Brazil. Caldera, unencumbered by *adeco* doctrine, took an even more pragmatic line on relations with military regimes. As the guerrilla war wound to a close, Caldera also improved relations with Cuba, signing an antihijacking accord in 1973, which was followed by a cultural exchange.[36]

After assuming the presidency in February 1974, Andrés Pérez was determined to establish a new hemispheric image more consonant with his vision of *Gran Venezuela*. He reestablished the tourist trade with Cuba and convened a consultative meeting of foreign ministers from the OAS to discuss readmitting Cuba to the hemispheric body. This was blocked by the United States, but shortly afterwards Cuba and Venezuela renewed diplomatic relations.[37]

These policies earned CAP the enmity of the sizable Cuban exile community in Caracas, including former functionaries of the Batista government, some of whom held key posts within the "national security" apparatus. Anti-Castroites exploded a bomb aboard a Cuban civilian airliner in flight, resulting in seventy-three deaths. Several terrorists were captured. One of the plotters, Orlando Bosch, turned out to be an operative of the internal security police (DISIP) and remained on its payroll even after his arrest. Another, Luis Posada Carriles, bribed his way out of prison and in 1985 turned up in Nicaragua teaching his "skills" to the U.S.-backed contras. Bosch himself was released from prison in 1987, which temporarily soured relations with Cuba.[38]

During Pérez's first term, Venezuela was one of several nations (including Panama, Costa Rica, and Cuba) to aid the Sandinistas materially in their successful struggle to overthrow the U.S.-backed Somoza dictatorship. As an oil exporter, Venezuela, like Mexico, has been in a position to influence the regional struggle both by supplying Central American governments, including Nicaragua, with oil at a discount and favorable credit terms. (Venezuela also has an agreement with the Soviet Union under which it supplies Cuba with crude petroleum for refining while the USSR supplies Venezuelan customers in Europe, saving each nation transportation costs.) In 1983, Venezuela joined Panama, Mexico, and Colombia in forming the Contadora Group, a landmark effort on the part of Latin American nations to take a diplomatic initiative to resolve the Central American crisis, putting them at odds with U.S. intervention in the region.

AD and COPEI maintain close ties, respectively, to West Germany's Social Democratic and Christian Democratic parties, which can sometimes encourage positions at variance with U.S. perspectives on world events. However, Venezuela has been far from uncooperative with U.S. policy in Central America, especially since 1979. Herrera Campins shifted Venezuelan policy closer to the United States in order to support the military/civilian regime of fellow Christian Democrat José Napoleón Duarte in El Salvador. Lusinchi was less fervent about U.S. policy in El Salvador, and Venezuela remained in the Contadora Group, but the days of leadership on Central America were over. Otto Reich, a notorious architect of the Reagan administration's "low-intensity" war against Nicaragua, was sent to Caracas to serve as U.S. Ambassador. The Nicaraguan contras were allowed to open an office in Caracas, aided by several Venezuelan elites, notably the Cisneros family, whose vast media empire largely echoed U.S. propaganda on Central America.

Pérez has attempted in his second term to restore some semblance of independnce to hemispheric policy, mostly through symbolic gestures, such as inviting Fidel Castro to attend his inauguration. However, he cooperated actively with U.S. attempts to bring down Panama's General Manuel Noriega, a significant contribution since the Panama Defense Forces regularly trained with the Venezuelan military. Venezuela roundly condemned the subsequent U.S. invasion, but carried its opposition no further than words. The Pérez government also cooperated with the United States in financing the opposition (UNO) to the Sandinistas in the Nicaraguan elections of February 1990.[39] In 1990 Venezuelan troops took responsibility for the (partial) disarming of the contras after the victory of UNO's Violeta Chamorro. Caracas was the site for an effort to find a negotiated settlement of the Salvadoran civil war in May 1990.

Given Betancourt's alignment with U.S. policies, it is not surprising that Venezuela remained marginalized until very recently from the Non-Aligned Movement in the Third World. However, the movement's role in world politics has made it more difficult for any Third World state to appear as subservient to U.S. policy as did Venezuela in the 1960s. In his inaugural speech in February 1989, Pérez finally announced that Venezuela would trade its observer status for membership in the Non-Aligned Movement. On oil policy, Pérez responded to the 1990 crisis caused by Iraq's invasion of Kuwait by boosting production and exports, but he has remained a strong supporter of limiting production through quotas.

Venezuela's most volatile foreign policy issue is not Central America but the definition of its borders.[40] In the south, the ill-defined border with Brazil, an area inhabited mostly by indigenous tribes, has recently become a source of some tension as Brazilian miners and companies have begun operations in Venezuelan territory. However, even sharper disputes are with Guyana in the east over Esequibo, a sparsely populated, resource-rich region, and with Colombia over the gulf that provides access to Lake Maracaibo.

The dispute with Guyana is a legacy of the colonial era. Guyana was ceded by Spain to Holland in 1648, but the boundary between the two colonies was left unclear. When Venezuela declared its independence in 1810, it defined its eastern border according to the Spanish claim, at the Esequibo River. However, Holland included the area west of the Esequibo in territory ceded to Britain in 1814 (British Guyana). Britain recognized the Esequibo as part of Gran Colombia in 1824, but reasserted its claim in 1849.

In 1895, with Venezuela embroiled in civil war and European warships threatening its shores, Cipriano Castro agreed to a proposal by the United States to allow the dispute to be arbitrated by a commission composed of British, American, and Russian diplomats—but no Venezuelans. (The Russian diplomat was bribed by the British, it was later learned.) The result was the Award of 1899, which restored some of Venezuela's territory but established the border with the British Guyana well west of the Esequibo. In 1903 Castro renounced the settlement, and since that time Venezuela has maintained its claim, which has made for tense relations with now-independent Guyana.

Whatever its legal merits, the Venezuelan case has not evoked widespread support in the hemisphere, especially from Caribbean states, because Esequibo constitutes one-third of Guyana's national territory. The claim has done little to calm the nervousness of the smaller Caribbean states about Venezuelan pretensions in a region where it stands third only to Cuba and the United States as a political power, and second only to the United States as an economic power. Smaller nations like Trinidad and Tobago, Aruba, Barbados, and Curacao have been outlets for Venezuelan investment. For example, Venezuela acquired control over the Shell oil refinery in Curacao after the company announced plans to close the facility in the former Dutch colony in 1988. The move was welcomed by Curacao, but it gives Venezuela major leverage as the largest employer in the small island nation.

The conflict with Colombia revolves over how much of the Gulf of Venezuela can be claimed by either country as interior or territorial waters, a matter that determines rights of navigation and control over natural resources. These tensions and military prestige were factors inducing a small-scale arms race between Colombia and Venezuela in the 1970s. Tensions with Colombia have been further aggravated by smuggling, including drug trafficking, and illegal immigration. However, the civil unrest in Colombia has tempered Venezuela's eagerness to confront its neighbor over these issues. Venezuelan elites want neither a leftist revolutionary experiment nor a wider guerrilla war on their doorstep. Several agreements for cooperation between the two militaries have been reached. During the Lusinchi administration, there was discussion about building an oil pipeline from Colombia's southeastern fields through Venezuela to Zulia in order to replace a line in Colombia destroyed by guerrillas. However, it was attacked by those who felt it would logically lead to expansion of guerrilla operations into Venezuela, and the government backed away from the idea.

Military conflict with Colombia seems unlikely, but periodically tensions rise, as they did in 1988 when a Colombian warship sailed into the disputed waters north of Lake Maracaibo. Such incidents are often exploited for political gain by politicians, and the Venezuelan military finds it convenient to highlight these disputes as it seeks authorization for major military purchases. Any "weakness" in the government's position provides an opportunity to wave the flag before Venezuelan voters, as Pérez discovered when he suggested during the 1988 campaign that the government seek a long-term, negotiated solution to issues raised by the incursion of the Colombian warship.

Two troubling consequences of tensions with neighbors have been the militarization (on the Venezuelan side) of border regions and the subordination of local police to the military chain of command. Rather than shielding Venezuela from the problems that afflict Colombia, these policies seem to have opened conduits for transmitting them. There are signs of increased involvement of political and military elites in drug trafficking and human rights abuses, particularly in the region of Apure, where the high *llanos* meet the Colombian border (see Chapter 6).

CORRUPTION AND THE RISE OF A STATE BOURGEOISIE

Competition among Venezuelan capitalists for contracts, credits, and the financial accounts of institutes and public enterprises intensified the rivalry among elites. Controversies and scandals swirled around several major projects, exacerbating tensions between the Old Guard and several of CAP's key political advisers, including Pedro Tinoco, Gumersindo Rodríguez, Carmelo Lauría, Enrique Delfino, Gustavo Cisneros, Diego Arria, and others who became known (with Andrés Pérez) as the "Twelve Apostles."

An early battle erupted over government credits to expand national production of cement. Despite the fact that the combined capacity of existing cement enterprises was sufficient even for the ambitious expansion envisioned under *Plan V*, the government awarded a credit of Bs. 631 million to construct a new plant, Cementos La Vega, controlled by the Delfino family. This angered the Mendoza group, which had controlled 61 percent of national production (1974). Mendoza's influence was concentrated in the *adeco* Old Guard, particularly Minister of the Interior Luis Piñerúa Ordaz. When contracts for petrochemical projects were awarded to firms controlled by several "apostles," Piñerúa denounced the arrangements, alleging influence peddling and claiming that several of the firms awarded contracts were merely fronts for foreign capital.[41]

Similar divisions with economic and political elites sabotaged the government's goal of 95 percent national content in the value of the motor vehicles produced in Venezuela by 1985. The transnational automobile companies, each with allies among Venezuelan *grupos*, competed with one another for contracts to produce those truck and automobile models allocated to Venezuela within the framework of the Andean Pact, an economic integration project to which Caldera had committed the country after abrogating the Reciprocal Trade Agreement with the United States in 1971. When companies with established links to the traditional *grupos* lost out in the competition to other transnationals, they successfully applied political pressure to revise the contracts. These divisions contributed to the unraveling of the pact, never popular with the businesses that had most benefited from import substitution policies under Betancourt and Leoni.[42]

The scale of business deals made it possible for Venezuelan middlemen to earn commissions worth millions of dollars on a single contract or transaction. The scale of corruption correspondingly increased. Just before the 1978 election a scandal erupted over the murder of a lawyer with connections to powerful and wealthy politicians in AD. There were murky and tenuous links to Andrés Pérez, and the incident probably contributed to the party's defeat in the December elections. Pérez was later implicated in another scandal involving the purchase of a refrigerated container ship, the Sierra Nevada, at a price $8 million over its assessed value. After leaving office, he was officially censured by AD and escaped censure in Congress—which would have banned him from running again for president—by only one vote.[43]

Several embarrassing banking scandals revealed the complicity of private and public officials in other lucrative schemes. In 1978 the government was forced to take over the leading commercial bank, Banco Nacional del Discuento, a major depository of funds from public companies, institutes, and ministries. The bank's directors had deposited billions of bolívars into companies that were little more than skeleton corporations controlled by the directors themselves. Similar arrangements were revealed when the Herrera Campins government intervened to take over the Venezuelan Workers Bank, which is owned by the CTV, thereby implicating the national labor leadership in the system of corruption. In 1985, Lusinchi was forced to intervene in yet another major bank, Banco Comercial, to save it from insolvency. It was subsequently revealed that just before the intervention, the Central Bank and Interior Minister Octavio Lepage, a contender for the 1988 presidential nomination, had deposited huge sums in the bank. Conveniently, the Banco Comercial's president had already fled to Miami. There he invested US$332 million into two Florida banks, just before warrants for his arrest were issued. Kickbacks to the campaign funds of Lepage and other politicians were widely rumored.[44]

Several high officials in the government of Herrera Campins, including two defense ministers and the governor (who was at that time appointed) of the Federal District, were charged with corruption, but as usual the accused anticipated their indictments and fled the country. Several businessmen and politicians associated with the corruption in the administration of exchange rates (the RECADI scandal) during Lusinchi's presidency were charged and detained, but they were released in February 1990 when the highly politicized Supreme Court annulled the arrest warrants on a technicality. AD created a special disciplinary tribunal that expelled some of the officials from the party, but they were subsequently reinstated by the National Executive Committee, where the ex-president's supporters retained a majority.

In June 1990, the Venezuelan court charged with investigating corruption issued judgments in connection with the diversion of public funds to AD officials who used them to purchase twenty jeeps for the 1988 campaign. The court found that the purchase was supervised by Lusinchi's interior minister, José Angel Ciliberto, with the apparent knowledge and approval of the president himself. In an unprecedented move, the court ordered the jailing of Ciliberto, whose power in the past administration was second only to Lusinchi himself. The court also found grounds to jail the ex-president, but deferred a final decision on whether such an order would violate his congressional immunity (as Senator for Life) to the Supreme Court.

As a result, a vicious internal war has broken out within AD ranks, and it is not clear whether the party can close them again. Lusinchi's supporters, who felt that President Pérez had not protected his party brethren, struck back with a series of charges against members of Pérez's cabinet, which led to the resignation of the minister of transportation in July 1990. Piñerúa Ordaz led a third faction and was expected to seek the 1993 presidential nomination, campaigning as a reformer who would cleanse the party of corruption—although he himself operated a far-from-clean campaign when he was the party's (unsuccessful) candidate in the 1978 election. COPEI faced a similar crisis as former president Caldera threatened to run an independent campaign if Eduardo Fernández, the party's secretary general and its presidential candidate in 1988, captures the nomination for 1993, as seems highly likely.

The cases against Ciliberto and Lusinchi are potentially significant, but the Venezuelan public has little confidence that they will be seen through to the end. The common retort of the man and woman on the street to the journalist's question, "Do you think anything will come of this?" is, "*Aquí no ha pasado nada*," "Nothing has happened here." As if to confirm this cynicism, Gonzalo Barrios, the nonagenarian honorary President for Life of AD, defended Ciliberto's refusal to surrender to authorities on grounds that "justice in Venezuela does not merit any respect."[45] It was as if Barrios was attempting to measure just how much hypocrisy the system is capable of enduring. (Shortly afterwards, Ciliberto escaped to Orlando, Florida.)

Corruption has spread to all levels of society. For example, a job as a toll taker on the main highway between the airport at Maquetía and Caracas is known to be a political plum because toll takers can easily skim off sums of money far in excess of their meagre salaries— provided, of course, that the appropriate shares are passed up to supervisors.

Tensions Between the Private and Public Sectors

The private sector has seized on political corruption as a weapon in its ideological offensive to force the state to retreat from the economy— a trend consistent with the general tendency toward "neoliberalism" on the continent in the 1980s. Neoliberals argue that Venezuelan democracy is threatened by a powerful state and that its economy can only be rationalized by exposing it to international market forces and by privatizing public enterprises and services.

Indeed, the state does exercise an enormous influence on the economy. Public foundations and enterprises exercise considerable autonomy in regard to financial matters (e.g., acquisition of debt). Between 1969 and 1977, public investment came to surpass private investment in the economy, reaching a peak in 1977 at 61.2 percent (falling back to 54 percent in 1984). Expenditures by state enterprises alone rose from 23 percent of all public spending in 1960 to 40 percent in 1970 and 52 percent in 1975.[46] State enterprises, decentralized institutes and foundations, and special funds—all controlled by public managers—together accounted for 72 percent of all public spending in 1975. By 1981, the public sector included 66 autonomous institutes, 167 state enterprises,

53 "mixed" enterprises (joint state and private ownership), and 104 miscellaneous authorities (e.g., cultural foundations). In 1982, state enterprises other than those in petroleum were responsible for 7.2 percent of the gross national product (29.4 percent if petroleum is included) and for 10 percent of wages and salaries paid in the national economy.[47]

Much of the public sector has operated at a significant loss, which provides fodder for neoliberal critics who prefer to turn more of the economy over to the private market. However, the performance of public entities varies greatly according to the quality of management and purpose. Some, like the PDVSA, are highly efficient and rational. Some, like the Agricultural Marketing Corporation or the National Coffee Fund, are intended to subsidize private producers and operate at a loss in the first place. Others, like the state telephone company, have generated profits but offer notoriously poor service. Others that are intended to be financially solvent, like the state airline, Venezolana Internacional de Aviación (VIASA), suffer such stupendous and consistent losses, that "if a Martian visited the earth, she might ask whether they really have profit as their goal."[48]

However, the weight of the state sector does not mean that Venezuela's economy can be called "socialist." Although the state owns basic industries and much of the economic infrastructure, the private bourgeoisie profits from commissions, contracts, and downstream economic activities. The crucial role of the state as the collector and distributor of oil rents and the historical weakness of Venezuela's bourgeoisie has resulted in a capitalist economy with the following special charateristics.[49]

- Late development of the financial and industrial infrastructure. More than 80 percent of the industrial factories in the country in 1979 were founded after 1960; only thirteen of thirty-one banks existing in 1983 operated in 1950.
- An extraordinarily high degree of concentration of ownership in the private sector. Of Venezuela's forty-five largest private, nationally owned enterprises (i.e., not owned by the state or foreign capital), thirty-nine were owned by a small coterie of families and economic groups; only six were listed on the public stock exchange. Most private firms had never undergone a transition of control and were closely held by about thirty-five major families and groups. These groups fiercely rival one another over some matters (e.g., the conflicts over cement and automobile expansion, described above), but they suppress competition by keeping business within the family whenever possible.
- Heavy dependence on foreign managerial talent. According to a 1982 study, 56 percent of the members of the Association of

Venezuelan Executives and 70 percent of executives of 109 ran-
domly selected industrial firms had been born outside of the
country.

Just as they did when Betancourt made them the target of his
invective in the 1930s, Venezuelan capitalists have gravitated toward
financial speculation and commerce, not productive investment. The 1982
survey of private, Venezuelan-owned industries showed that 60 percent
of their working capital was secured from loans, only 19 percent from
their own portfolios. The ratio of borrowed capital to actual investment
was 2.25 to 1, with most of the loans coming from state-financed banks
and funds.[50] State enterprises are required to make purchases from
domestic firms, adding to the monopolistic, uncompetitive economic
environment. During the oil boom years of 1976 to 1982, gross profits
rose from 21.6 percent of the total gross national product to 44.1 percent,
a profit ratio that one knowledgeable Venezuelan businessman estimates
is grossly underestimated.[51]
    The Venezuelan bourgeoisie cannot embrace neoliberalism whole-
heartedly because the private sector remains highly dependent upon
state subsidies, purchases, and protection from foreign competition.
Venezuelan capitalists complain of a too-powerful state, but they seek
to preserve their own particular access points to power when it is
threatened by depoliticization. Privatization is also resisted by the unions,
which fear unemployment; by some politicians, to whom patronage is
the lifeblood of the system; and by the left, which is philosophically
opposed to neoliberalism. Yet under pressure from the International
Monetary Fund and from sectors of the bourgeosie eager to acquire
state assets, Pérez, after returning to office in 1989, committed his
government to neoliberal economic policies.
    In compliance with conditions demanded by the IMF, the Pérez
government lifted restrictions on profit repatriations (previously, 20
percent over LIBOR, the London Interbank Offered Rate) and requirements
for technology transfers, drastically reduced tariff rates to a maximum
of 50 percent, and announced plans to hive off sixty-four public enterprises—hotels, textile firms, metallurgical industries, etc.—to the private
sector, with more to follow.[52] In contrast to the policies of his first
government, in his second administration Pérez has lifted many restrictions, such as content requirements in local production, and welcomed
foreign capital into areas formerly reserved by law for national capital,
for example, utilities. Telecommunications, electricity, and water have
been slated for privatization. While public services are often poor and
getting worse, critics fear that without a strong and effective system of
regulation similar to that exercised over utility monopolies in developed

countries, the poor and working class will soon find themselves excluded from services.

In his first two years, Pérez moved more slowly on these plans than suited COPEI and the most fervent neoliberals, but what seems to be in doubt is not privatization but its pace and form. Some party leaders continue to criticize Pérez's policies, but for AD in particular, much of the criticism seems to be solely for public consumption. The parties have not challenged the administration in Congress, nor has AD attempted to assert party discipline over Pérez. The president's closest economic advisers have been drawn from outside the party, particularly from the well-funded Instituto de Estudios Superiores de Administración (IESA), known for its close connections to the international banking community.

Between 1958 and 1980, Venezuelan politics seemed a four-cornered game among business elites, the CTV, the parties, and the managers of state enterprises. After 1980, the private sector launched an ideological campaign to strengthen, if not reassert, its hegemony. This campaign gathered momentum throughout the decade and has neared its moment of triumph since the 1988 elections. Under CAP I (Pérez's first administration), the public sector reached the peak of its influence over the economy. With CAP II, for the first time in fifty-five years, the state began to retreat to a more traditional role within the economy and society. Even a new round of oil price hikes and production increases after the August 1990 Iraqi invasion of Kuwait did not deter Pérez from his new economic course.

Neoliberalism by Default?

Although they invariably campaigned on a promise to improve the quality of life, every president since 1978 has instead implemented austerity, rationalizing it as an inevitable response to trends outside of their control. Herrera Campins promised to shift priorities from heavy industries to production for human necessities, but rather than increase production of food, he radically reduced subsidies to the agricultural sector, resulting in huge price increases in sugar, coffee, corn flour, rice, milk, and animal feed. Upon taking office, Lusinchi boosted the minimum wage and increased the transportation subsidy for low-income users, but before the end of his first year (1984) he removed dairy subsidies, resulting in a doubling of milk prices. Lusinchi had hoped to revive the spirit of the Pact of Punto Fijo through a new social pact among government, employers, and the unions. However, he was unable or unwilling to make effective its most important component, the tripartite Cost, Price, and Salary Board, composed of representatives of FEDE-

CAMARAS, the CTV, and the government. Despite CTV protests, real wages fell below their 1974 levels.[53]

President Pérez has attempted to portray the austerity package announced in February 1988 and his neoliberal approach to economic reform as the only ways to correct past "mistakes." But these policies pose a serious legitimation problem for Pérez. The Venezuelan people may not understand the economic theory of ground rent, but they understand after fifty-five years of struggle over oil that petroleum income was supposed to be sown in a way that benefited the entire nation. As oil revenues flow through state coffers into foreign banks, and as "excess" workers are fired from the government jobs and from enterprises to be privatized, the contradiction between neoliberalism and this nationalism becomes more apparent.

The Venezuelan left has accused the government of reversing the most significant historical achievement of AD, the nationalization of oil in 1976, by permitting the oil companies to return to production through marketing and joint production agreements with the PDVSA. Bernard Mommer, the country's leading expert on oil and an adviser to the minister of energy and mines, defends the PDVSA's policy on grounds that it is necessary to distinguish between the policies of the country as a landlord and its aspirations to become an effective producer capable of extending its operations into the international economy and developing products and services important to the overall development of the domestic economy. As long as the state maintains ownership of the reserves and control over pricing and levels of production, he argues, it is in a position to associate with foreign capital without contradicting the basic principles embodied in nationalization of 1976.[54]

President Pérez is unlikely to defend the PDVSA on these grounds, however. To do so he would have to acknowledge that much of the income that Venezuela earns from oil consists of rent and has little to do with oil's value as "natural capital" or costs of production, the traditional way that Venezuelan nationalists have conceived their most important source of capital. Equating the value of oil with its international price flies in the face of the most controversial part of the agreement that Pérez negotiated with the IMF—that Venezuela will raise its fuel prices to international levels. It is true that these prices, particularly for gasoline, are far below those charged in other countries, but they are, according to Mommer, high enough to cover the cost of production and an average profit for the PDVSA.[55] Higher prices mean, therefore, that the Venezuelan state is renouncing a natural comparative advantage, agreeing to extract a rent from itself in order to pay its debt to the banks.

Such concepts may not be the stuff of everyday conversation on the streets, but Venezuelans seem to understand that higher prices at the gas pump are a way to extract more economic sacrifices from them, not a "reasonable" adjustment of a price well below the real "value" of oil. Prices at the gasoline pump and transportation fares have become the flash point for conflict between the government and the people, especially since the urban riots of February 1989 were touched off by a hike in the latter. In 1990 the government was forced several times by outbreaks of violence to postpone modest increases of gas prices, but it finally managed to impose the first of a monthly series of rises in July. However, the government's victory, renounced by Pérez's own party, did little to enhance the legitimacy of the system.

At the start of his first presidency, Carlos Andrés Pérez had warned that if Venezuela failed to invest income from the oil boom effectively, "everything will have been nothing more than a dream that one generation of Venezuelans will have lived, only to have our children wake from this dream into a poverty stricken and ruined country."[56] In 1990, as the real income per family fell to the level of 1964, this prophecy seemed to have been borne out, but the problem was not that oil itself had run out. In 1987, new discoveries doubled proven reserves, which reached 55 billion barrels, fourth largest in the world. The price of oil remained, even at its nadir, high enough to generate considerable rent for the economy. However, no longer could oil earnings, even after the surge of prices after the 1990 Persian Gulf crisis, be expected to satisfy simultaneously demands generated by the greed of the bourgeoisie and international banks, the patronage-driven party system, the media-driven rate of consumption, the basic needs of the popular sectors, and the required level of investment to sustain economic expansion. The question for Venezuela has been: Which of these sets of demands should take priority? So far, popular needs have been the last priority. *"La noche postpetrolera,"* "the postpetroleum night," should more properly be called *"la noche neoliberal."*

WOMEN, WORK, AND POPULATION GROWTH

The social and cultural tendencies that were eroding traditional Venezuela continued to manifest themselves in "Saudi Venezuela." Some trends, like the penetration of the media by foreign influences, simply became more entrenched. Others, like incorporation of women and immigrants in the work force, accelerated. Between 1971 and 1982, the total work force expanded from just under 3 million to 4.35 million workers, with almost all new jobs added outside of agriculture. The greatest increases were again in services, especially in commerce and finances, as befits a rent-based, consumer-oriented economy. Employment in commerce and finance grew from 378,844 to 1,018,008; by 1982, 50.4 percent of the work force was employed in these two sectors of the economy alone.[57]

The work force was also expanding as a result of rapid population expansion. The gap between the birth rate and death rate in Venezuela was the widest among those for seven Latin American countries classified in the World Bank study as "upper middle income." Between 1960 and 1980, Venezuela had by far the highest population growth rate of any Latin American nation and of any of the twenty-two countries classified as "upper middle income" by the World Bank. Its average annual growth rate of 3.8 percent between 1960 and 1970 far exceeded the 3.5 percent rate for the two next highest nations (Mexico and Israel).[58]

As a Catholic nation, Venezuela shares a religious inheritance that limits the effectiveness of family planning. However, Venezuela is also a nation with a considerable African inheritance, a strong secular tradition in politics, and a consumer-oriented media that presents images of middle-class women in the developed world. In 1981 it was reported that 49 percent of Venezuelan married women of childbearing years use contraception, a rate exceeded only by Costa Rica and Panama among Latin American countries. Abortion remains illegal, but widely practiced.[59]

Between 1971 and 1981, the number of women in the work force doubled, from 676,064 to 1,260,978 (from 22.6 to 29.1 percent of all employees). Some women have entered manufacturing and construction, but more have entered clerical and technical occupations. Women are often vulnerable to sexual as well as economic exploitation, a problem most acute for maids, waitresses, and female "*buhoneros*," that is, street vendors. Many *buhoneros* (male and female) are Colombians and are even more vulnerable to harassment from the local police and the National Guard. Women are usually in the leadership of new organizations that have been formed by *buhoneros* to defend against extortion and harassment (often sexual) from police and the National Guard and to demand construction of markets or the right to continue to sell on the street.[60]

Women often emerge as leaders of other grassroots organizations as well, particularly neighborhood associations. As food purchases alone have risen from 30 percent to 80 percent of the family budget between 1984 and 1988, these organizations have become necessary means of survival in many barrios. Referring to one community's reaction when a child was denied medical care for lack of money, a barrio leader described how it spurred the founding of a neighborhood association. "On other occasions we only felt anger, but this time we organized and went from house to house, and from a neighborhood where 90 to 100 families earn less than 3,000 bolívars ($81) per month, in two days we collected what was necessary."[61] This sense of accomplishment led the organizers to form an association capable of addressing other needs in the community, including ones with political implications.

Some women's networks have formed to address the special concerns of women as employees, notably the *Círculos Femeninos Populares* (Popular Feminist Circles), which held its first national congress in 1987, and *Red Todas Junta* (Everyone Together Network). These groups have been working to insert women's rights (e.g., maternity leave, equal pay for equal work) into the Labor Code, which is currently in the process of being revised. However, women continue to face formidable obstacles to achieving these goals. Middle-class families, lacking many of the appliances that lighten housework in mass-consumer societies, rely upon low-paid domestic labor from the barrios. An attitude of contempt toward the women who hold these jobs is common even among those whose political ideology and activity formally includes a commitment to feminist ideals. In the barrios women encounter resistance from men who prohibit their wives from attending educational and organizing courses organized by neighborhood associations.[62] Of course, machismo remains a serious cultural obstacle.

Women and Politics

Women are beginning to press for more influence in the key arena of Venezuelan society, the party system. Women first gained the right to vote in municipal elections in 1944 and achieved full suffrage in 1946. Women played an important role in the mobilization politics of the 1930s and 1940s; today they account for 50 percent of party membership. Yet from 1968 to 1978 only 6 percent of congressional deputies were women. In 1983, the entire Senate was composed of men. The percentage of women elected to municipal councils has also been low (6.1 percent in 1973 and 14 percent in 1978), but in 1984, the first year in which local elections were conducted separately from national contests, the percentage of women elected as representatives jumped to 21.5 percent. This suggests that loosening the grip of the central party bureaucracies on local politics could result in increased success for women.[63]

The modest advances that women have made in electoral politics in recent years were achieved in part by the efforts of Mercedes Pulido de Briceño, appointed by Herrera Campins in 1980 as minister of state for the Participation and Development of Women in recognition of the United Nations declaration of the 1980s as the "Decade of the Woman." As a result of her leadership and support from women's organizations, the Civil Code was reformed to increase women's rights in 1982. In December of that year, Congress formally declared Venezuela's adherence to the 1979 U.N. convention, calling for the elimination of all forms of discrimination against women. However, the superficiality of male politicians' commitment to women's rights was demonstrated when the Ministry for Women was downgraded to the General Sectoral Office for the Promotion of Women within the Ministry of the Family.[64]

In 1988, a new organization, United Women Leaders, was created to protest the small number of women placed on electoral *planchas* by the parties. They successfully increased the percentage of women on AD and COPEI slates from 2.5 percent to 15 percent, although women continued to occupy places far down the lists. In the general election, women captured twenty of 201 seats in the House of Deputies and three of forty-five elected seats in the Senate.[65]

Unfortunately, the most publicized female politician has been the controversial Blanca Ibañez, President Lusinchi's private secretary and rumored mistress, who was accused of corruption and of using her position to harass the president's wife, who had filed for divorce. Ibañez cultivated a populist image by delivering speeches in the barrios as the personal representative of Lusinchi, inducing the media to draw comparisons between her and Eva Perón. In 1988, Ibañez was included on AD's preliminary list of congressional candidates from Caracas for the December elections, but she was among several candidates dropped at the insistence of Piñerúa. In 1989, she was indicted for corruption, but some feel that she had been singled out. Haydee Castillo, a *copeyano* deputy, has commented, "Discrimination will no longer exist when they let women be as inept as the men."[66]

THE CHALLENGE OF IMMIGRATION

Another major source of labor during the oil boom period was massive immigration from other Latin American and Caribbean countries, especially Colombia. In his first administration, Andrés Pérez mandated limits on the number of foreign-born workers to 25 percent in larger enterprises, a measure that was largely ineffective. Between 1971 and 1981, despite a slight decline (to 323,192) in the number of European-born residents, the total number of foreign-born residents in Venezuela increased from just under 600,000 to 1,039,106. Among 653,850 Latin Americans counted, over 491,000 were Colombian, and a majority (59 percent) were women. It has been estimated that an additional 700,000 to 900,000 illegal aliens, most from Colombia, have entered the country.[67]

With the onset of economic crisis, the Venezuelan government came under pressure from labor unions and merchants (unhappy about competition from *buhoneros*) to enforce immigration laws more effectively, but manufacturers, especially in areas like textiles, exerted pressure in the opposite direction. The government struck a compromise by offering an amnesty to illegal aliens who registered with immigration officials. Approximately 300,000 workers registered in 1980. Subsequently, tens of thousands of Colombians were forcibly repatriated, and many others voluntarily returned. According to a 1985 study, however, many immigrants chose to stay because they had already improved their economic position since leaving their homeland. Others have little choice. The Caracas valley is dotted with the cardboard and zinc shanties of Colombian women who braved great hardships to emigrate, but now find themselves abandoned by their male partners, trapped with their children in poverty, unwelcome aliens with few prospects of returning to their native land. Overall, the study concluded that despite economic decline and government policy, the Colombian population in Venezuela has continued to increase.[68]

Cultural Penetration and the Threat to Indigenous Peoples

Given the economic crisis and high rates of unemployment, immigrants are often scapegoated and perceived as a threat to the country's national identity, but, as in earlier decades, a much greater threat to Venezuelan culture comes from the cultural penetration of North American mass media. A study in January 1983 of one week of programming on the popular, privately owned network (controlled by the Cisneros family) showed that of 123 programs covering 121 hours, 83 were of foreign origin. Of these, 85.5 percent were cartoons and television series from the United States.[69]

Economic concentration and foreign cultural penetration are linked. In 1983 the Cisneros family owned five major radio stations, a television production company and one of the two national networks, three advertising agencies, two electronics assembly factories, six companies related to computers, and the major videotape distribution chain in the country. These enterprises rely upon association with foreign, especially North American, media corporations, for programming, technology, and so on. The state-run media are little better. Hence, foreign production pervades film, television, recording, video, etc. This has especially important consequences for a country where a typical child will spend only 8,000 hours in school, but 16,000 watching television. Dr. Arnaldo Cogorno, Venezuela's most distinguished child psychiatrist, comments, "In this country TV is utilized egotistically in favor of a small minority of national and international interests, whose priorities are violence, competition, and consumerism."[70]

The values and culture of the United States are reaching far into the Venezuelan hinterland. The CVG and its foreign partners are driving deep into the Amazonian frontier to find and mine additional deposits of bauxite, iron ore, and gold. As in Brazil, the Indians, like the Yanomani, who have for centuries escaped the domination of the European and creole elites, now face prospectors searching for gold, gunmen hired by ranchers who want their land for cattle, soldiers, police, and land speculators, all of whom seem to follow in the wake of the transnational corporations. The Catholic clergy have become more sensitive to the cultural traditions of the Indians and eager to help them preserve their way of life. However, the Indians are understandably suspicious of the Catholic missionaries, who tend to be European or creole in origin and have enjoyed a privileged relationship to the national state for centuries. This has opened opportunities for fundamentalist Protestant sects ("New Tribes"). The latter are much favored by the new conquistadors, who find the evangelicals more cooperative in pacifying the Indians, in contrast to Catholic missionaries who are encouraging them to assert their rights and defend their culture.[71]

Typical of the Indian peoples threatened by Venezuela's drive into the interior are the Panare, who are threatened by the CVG's bauxite expansion program. Under Venezuelan law, the indigenous tribes are entitled to ownership of the lands they presently occupy. The CVG, however, has defined Panare lands as "empty," and decreed that two little *pueblos* be moved to make room for bauxite mining. The CVG defends its policy on grounds that the Indians will be compensated and that the national interest demands access to the region's minerals.

Paul Henley, an anthropologist who has studied the Panare, acknowledges that Venezuela may need access to the areas mineral wealth, but he warns that merely moving the Panare to another area of the country and paying them will not guarantee their survival. "Until Venezuelan society has more to offer the Panare than a miserable existence amidst the ranks of the rural poor," he writes, "one can only hope that the efforts of the CVG and other government agencies will be directed not towards the assimilation of the Panare, but rather towards consolidating the material base of their social and economic self-sufficiency."[72]

The Panare and other tribes have suddenly attracted the attention of the world because of the threat posed to the global ecosystem by the destruction of the tropical rain forests. Unfortunately, most Venezuelans do not yet realize how much they share in common with these earliest inhabitants of their land. Seventy-seven years after the first gusher burst in Zulia, and fifteen years after the extraordinary oil boom seemed to place the dream of order and progress within their reach, economic self-sufficiency remains elusive not just for the indigenous population, but for the majority of Venezuelans.

6

Testing the Limits
of Venezuelan Democracy

Populism in Venezuela was based on a political project to modernize the economy and society, a project that required lifting the standard of living of the working class and peasantry. Populist politics at least ensured that some benefits of the oil boom were passed to those at the bottom of the social order.[1] Now neoliberal intellectuals are attacking populism as the root cause of the economic crisis. Their economic "solutions" are technocratic and market oriented; their political views on the state are reinforced by recent tendencies in Eastern Europe.[2] An alternative critique of the populism, or more specifically of the role of the political parties, comes from grassroots social movements. For them, the challenge is to defend the democratic gains that, however attenuated, were consolidated after the 1958 popular struggle against the dictatorship, while at the same time promoting reforms to free them of the suffocating influence of the traditional political parties.

"PARTIDOCRACIA" AND PARTICIPATION

The pervasive influence of political parties in Venezuelan society is a legacy of their role in the struggle for electoral democracy and the social transformation of the country after 1935. All of the leftist parties can trace their origins back to the PCV or AD, both of which adopted democratic centralism because of the experience of their founders (including Betancourt) with Communist parties in exile, which was reinforced by several periods of clandestineness and repression between 1920 and 1970. COPEI adopted a similar structure. The three largest parties have all operated in a highly disciplined, hierarchical style—"verticalist," as some call it. After 1958, this highly centralized mode of operation was adopted to the politics of patronage and corruption.

In December 1989, the typical Venezuelan voter went to the polls to cast two votes on a colorful, but confusing paper ballot. Over one of thirty-four party seals displaying the picture and name of twenty-six different candidates, most voters marked a choice for president—the *"voto grande."* Over one of the smaller seals of seventy parties, most voters also marked their choice for the Congress—the *"voto pequeño."* The large and small seals are presented next to one another on the same ballot, discouraging crossover voting. A reform implemented in 1989 gave voters the *option* of expressing a preference for candidates on lists in state and local elections only, but such voting is discouraged by the convenience of casting a single vote for a party slate, called a *"plancha."* With this sole and partial exception, local voters exercise little control over who represents them. Nor do party cadre exercise much influence. Who appears on the *planchas* and in what order is usually determined by bargaining at higher levels, by a small group of leaders who form each party's *"cogollo"* ("heart of lettuce").[3]

The president is chosen by a simple plurality. Each of twenty-one states and the Federal District is allocated two senators. (Ex-presidents become senators for life.) The party receiving a plurality receives one seat; unless its vote is double that of its closest competitor, the latter wins the second. States and territories (and the Federal District, which includes Caracas) are represented in the House of Deputies in proportion to their population. The number of seats won by each party is determined proportionally, but according to a formula weighted toward the larger parties. However, smaller parties may also win seats if their national vote (i.e., their combined vote in all of the states) exceeds a "quotient" determined by a complex formula.

Elections in Venezuela are pervasive, used to select officials of municipalities, state legislatures, unions, universities, professional associations, student associations, neighborhood associations, etc. After a presidential candidate is chosen, the political world is afflicted by a period of intense intraparty competition, called *"planchitis,"* as factions within the parties battle and deal for places on the ballot in legislative races. It is not unusual for parties to reward faithful service with a place on a party list, even when the individual is unknown to the constituency involved. Such officials, especially common in unions, are popularly known as *paracaídas*, that is, "parachutists."

In response to neoliberal criticism and signs of growing popular alienation from politics, the Lusinchi administration created the Commission for Political Reform (COPRE). The commission's report on electoral reform echoed the views of the largest network of *Associaciones de Vecinos* (neighborhood associations, AVs), the Federation of Urban Communities Associations (FACUR), which has called for single-member district representation at the state and municipal level. COPEI and AD initially expressed general support for the goals of COPRE, but they have hesitated to implement any changes that would weaken the power of the central party bureaucracies or threaten their hegemony over the smaller parties. So far the only reforms actually implemented have been limited to direct election of governors, separation of the legislative and presidential ballot, and giving voters the right to indicate preferences among candidates on lists. After the elections for governor in December 1989 resulted in opposition parties winning control of several key states, AD blocked the next projected step in the reform, the decentralization of fiscal powers to the elected governors. The chairman of COPRE, Carlos Blanco, joined AD in 1989, thus depriving the commission of much of its reputation for independence.

The crucial legislative decisions in Venezuelan politics are not made by Congress, but by a handful of powerful party leaders that compose the national directorates of each party, the *cogollos*, who determine the fate of political careers of their followers. The widespread and usually accurate perception among the population is that whether a scandal is investigated, a reform enacted, or a bill made a law is largely a decision made by the *cogollos*, rather than by their elected representatives. When one party has a congressional majority, as did AD from 1984 to 1988, party discipline gives it nearly complete control over the legislative process. Often, however, the *cogollos* of AD and COPEI need to form alliances with one another or with smaller parties to control Congress or important social organizations, like labor unions. The negotiations rarely involve ideological or programmatic issues, but patronage or power-sharing in other arenas. For example, after losing the 1968 presidential election, AD abandoned its hostile opposition to President Caldera in exchange for COPEI's help in repelling MEP's challenge within the labor movement.

The degree of penetration of the party system into society is remarkable. One study estimates that party members constitute 25 to 30 percent of the population, equivalent to well over 50 percent of the population over fifteen years of age.[4] But these statistics are deceptive. Many "members" carry a card only to secure employment, and some wisely carry more than one. However, there are enough party activists to staff impressive "get out the vote" efforts on election day. Local party leaders keep lists of those who owe political favors or have indicated a favorable attitude in surveys. As many as 500 names are provided to teams of party cadre who then scour their communities to gather and herd supporters to the polls.[5]

Whereas the party cadre were once foot soldiers in the struggle, between 1935 to 1958, for democracy, they are today the competitors for spoils within the populist system. As Domingo Alberto Rangel, a cynical *adeco* intellectual, stated:

> The activists who convoke or attend assemblies and undertake other routine tasks for the organization reap the benefits of power. . . . [They] are peasants who obtain credits from the Agricultural Bank or land from the National Agrarian Institute, barrio residents who are able to get an apartment from INAVI [the housing agency], those who get work in state industries, and middle class professionals who find themselves on the list of appointments to jobs in the Administration.[6]

The reward for political service may also be a financial loan from an associate of a candidate, an assurance that the police will not ask questions about contraband, the ability to use a questionable receipt to exchange bolívars at a favorable rate, etc. "In many cases," wrote Rangel, "people are able to maintain their honesty. But in others, they lose contact with today's Venezuela, degrade their souls . . . to do what they must."[7]

Within each party, groups and candidates constantly seek to position themselves for the next election, producing an unseemly, confusing battle of factions, constantly shifting and changing as leaders rise and fall. Even the split between AD and MEP in 1968 was more the result of a rivalry between two "*caudillos*," Betancourt and Prieto Figueroa, than a struggle for the soul of the AD. The tension within AD between Carlos Andrés Pérez's so-called "Twelve Apostles" and the party's Old Guard was ostensibly around the issue of corruption, but more fundamental were generational differences and the conflicts among economic elites over access to oil rents (see Chapter 5). During the second Pérez presidency, factions in each party raised issues about cleansing and democratizing the party organizations, but the real issues seemed to revolve around patronage and power, not principles.

Competition within the parties for the presidential nomination begins almost immediately after one presidential election is concluded. The position of secretary general is a coveted power base for potential candidates because it gives them a powerful grip on the party apparatus. However, there are other power bases from which to launch candidacies. This is particularly true for whichever party—that is, COPEI or AD—controls the executive. The incumbent interior minister, as the second most important official within a state with enormous material resources, is almost always a formidable contender for his party's nomination, as are ex-presidents. Within AD, the support of the powerful Labor Bureau, tied to the Confederation of Venezuelan Workers (CTV), has proven decisive in recent contests for the nomination.

The struggles among "precandidates" for the presidential nomination can be bitter. In 1988, Caldera refused to campaign for Fernández after loosing the nomination to his former protege, and he denounced Fernández's announcement of his candidacy the day after his loss to Pérez. Followers of Fernández, incensed that Caldera refused to close ranks during the campaign, jostled his supporters and verbally abused Caldera himself outside of COPEI headquarters shortly after the election. The recriminations within AD over charges of corruption threaten to escalate and burst the bounds of party solidarity. However, leaders of rival factions know that an open split means almost certain defeat in the general elections, and a poor showing in the general election is costly in very material ways to all factions.

At all levels, then, party activists tend to place partisanship above the welfare of the constituents. Cadre of the president's party or of parties allied with the presidential party try to mute social and economic conflict, while cadre of opposition parties are likely to fan discontent in order to embarrass the government. This is particularly noticeable in the CTV. When AD controls the presidency, strike activity tends to be lower than when it is out of power. However, in the era of austerity, leaders of unions, cooperatives, neighborhood associations, and so on are finding it more difficult to reconcile popular demands with the loyalty to their party.

POLITICAL DEVELOPMENTS IN THE ERA OF ECONOMIC CRISIS

For a brief while after the 1983 elections, it appeared as though AD might regain the political dominance it had achieved during the *trienio*. There was talk of a "PRI"-vatization of Venezuelan politics, an allusion to the one-party dominance of the Institutionalized Revolutionary Party in Mexico. However, in 1988, AD lost the congressional majorities it had achieved in 1983. Although he lost the 1988 presidential race, Fernández ran considerably better than Caldera did in 1983 (see Table 6.1). As of 1990 AD had no obvious candidate of imposing stature poised to run in 1992, while Fernández and several other prominent *copeyanos* were positioned to pose formidable candidacies.

Perhaps the most important phenomenon of the 1988 election was evidence of growing alienation among the electorate, signified by a jump in the abstention rate. The abstention rate was only 3.5 percent in 1973, but it rose above 12 percent in 1978 and 1983, and then soared above 18 percent in 1988.[8] With null and void votes (a traditional method of protest), over 20 percent of the electorate did not vote in 1988. Voters also seemed to be registering discontent with party rule by an un-

TABLE 6.1   Election Results, Major Parties and Candidates, Percentages, 1958-1988

Parties and types of votes	Electoral Years						
	1958	1963	1968	1973	1978	1983	1988
AD							
Presidential	49.2	32.8	27.5	46.5	43.3	56.7	52.9
Congressional	49.4	32.7	25.6	42.8	39.7	49.9	43.8
COPEI							
Presidential	15.2	20.2	28.7	33.8	45.2	34.5	40.2
Congressional	15.2	20.8	24.0	29.1	39.7	28.7	31.4
LEFT[a]							
Presidential	3.2	--	19.3[b]	8.9	7.8	7.5	3.1
Congressional	6.2	--	15.8[b]	12.4	13.5	11.0	14.9
OTHER							
Presidential	30.7	45.3	28.0	8.9	7.8	1.1	2.7
Congressional	26.8	43.6	30.5	3.1	6.3		8.1
Percentage not voting among all eligible voters	7.9	9.16	5.6	3.5	12.4	12.7	18.2

[a] Includes PCV, MAS, MEP, MIR, CAUSA R, Liga Socialista.
[b] For 1968, the vote for MEP (17.4 percent for president, 12.9 for congress, was included in the left total, as it is for other years. Michelena and Sonntag, from which this data is derived, categorizes MEP among "other" parties.
Sources: For 1958 to 1978, José Agustín Silva Michelena and Heinz Sonntag, *El proceso electoral de 1978, su perspectiva histórica estructural* (Caracas: Editorial Ateneo, 1979), p. 73.   For the 1983 elections, *The Daily Journal* (Caracas), October 31, 1988.   For 1988 elections, *Revista SIC,* 52 (January-February 1989):4-5, 14-15.   Totals may not equal 100 due to rounding.

precedented level of crossover voting; the gap between the congressional and presidential vote of the two largest parties rose from 13.5 percent in 1983 to 21.2 percent in 1988. In the December 1989 state and local elections, the first time that voters directly chose the governors of the states, the rate of abstention reached 55 percent and was most pronounced in Caracas where it reached 68.7 percent. Of course, rates of abstention and crossover voting are typically higher in the United States, but in the Venezuelan context, with mandatory voting and a ballot that discourages ticket-splitting, such behavior on the part of the electorate has been widely interpreted as evidence of discontent with the party system.[9]

Contributing to low voter confidence in government is the vacuous and lengthy campaign, which lasts more than two years. In the 1988 general elections, both candidates attempted to appeal to the electorate in a populist style, blasting corruption and projecting an image of political invincibility. Fernández launched a media campaign identifying himself as *"El Tigre,"* and taking to the streets of Caracas on a motorcycle to attract the votes of the expanding corps of cyclists. For his part, Andrés Pérez barnstormed the country in a white suit, waving his arms before assembled multitudes in the style of an evangelical preacher. In more demure settings, especially before business groups, the candidates tended to speak more of difficult economic times and hint—Fernández more than Pérez—at neoliberal solutions. Fernández even suggested that Venezuela's underdevelopment was "our own fault for having too much populist government."[10] Yet six months later Fernández praised a general strike called to protest austerity measures announced by Pérez.

Confidence in the system requires that the Supreme Electoral Council (CSE) enjoy an untarnished reputation. The CSE determines what position parties occupy on the ballot, settles disputes for control of party machinery when these arise, determines whether parties are in violation of laws regulating media or spending, etc. The massive increase in media campaigning has forced the council to deal with the highly ambiguous and politically charged question of whether extensive official government propaganda, on privately and government-owned media alike, is designed to inform or, in violation of campaign laws, to favor the fortunes of the incumbent party's candidates. Of course, there is no mistaking the partisan nature of the barrage of television commercials, newsreels, and print ads on the part of government, but the CSE has few means of enforcement at its disposal.

The major parties generally evade the law against foreign participation in campaigns and find ways to hire North American media wizards like David Doak and Bob Shrum, David Garth, and Joe Napolitan. Charges and countercharges of violations of campaign laws have become more shrill, politicizing the atmosphere in which the CSE carries out its business. With a strained budget and few powers to investigate or punish offenders, the CSE thus appears to the public as no more than another arena for the sordid competition among the parties. In 1988 and 1989, for the first time since the dictatorship, there were serious questions raised about whether the count in legislative races was conducted fairly.[11]

Besides corruption, constant reports of wheeling and dealing among political elites have taken their toll on popular confidence in democracy. Smaller parties, including those on the left, routinely charge one another with accepting contributions or making deals for bureaucratic spoils in exchange for coordinating their electoral strategy with either AD or COPEI—for example, to join a formal coalition or to run candidates just for the sake of drawing votes away from the other major party.[12] Some newspapers, notably the chain controlled by the powerful Capriles Group, have been known to put their editorial endorsement—and favorable coverage—up for grabs to the party offering the most places on its *planchas* to candidates favored by the group. On the other hand, parties can apply considerable leverage on the commercial media because the government is their largest single source of advertising revenue.[13]

By any standard, the amount of money spent on Venezuelan elections is extraordinary. In 1988, the two major parties are conservatively estimated to have spent nearly $69 million each on the campaign, and some estimates double that amount.[14] Such money cannot be raised from ordinary party members; it comes from the powerful and wealthy economic groups that contribute to both parties regardless of their preference. The system reached its nadir as both parties published full-page ads with photographs of prominent politicians sharing cocktails with notorious international drug traffickers.

The Left and Other Small Parties

The voters have shown little confidence that the smaller parties can manage the system any better than AD or COPEI. In 1988, the MEP elected only two deputies, the PCV just one; their joint presidential candidate received less than 1 percent of the vote. The MIR split several times and finally submerged itself into MAS. The centrist URD found itself reduced to two deputies. Meanwhile, a new rightist force emerged— anticorruption parties with a protestant evangelical tint. One, the New Generation party, largely urban based, won the fourth-largest amount of votes. New Generation and two other recently formed conservative parties have formed a legislative coalition (ten deputies, one senator), the "Emerging Right," in Congress.

The most significant leftist parties today are MAS and CAUSA R (Radical Cause, with the "R" printed backwards in the party logo), both of which split from the PCV around 1970. In 1988, CAUSA R won three seats in Congress and emerged for the first time as a significant electoral force outside of Guayana. In 1989, its leader, Andrés Velásquez, stunned AD by winning the governorship of the state, and he is expected to run (for the second time) for president in 1993. Still, in each election CAUSA R garnered only approximately 2 percent of the national vote. Its most important base remains the industrial working class of Guayana. However, on July 27, 1990, the party held an open forum in Caracas, "Alternatives for a New Kind of Government," and attracted over 800 participants. Just two days earlier, in the same location, MAS staged a well-publicized debate between two candidates for secretary general of the party, and only 20 people attended.

While CAUSA R is generating new interest, MAS remains capable of attracting the votes of 10 percent of the electorate, making it easily the largest electoral force on the left. It was founded in 1968, mostly by young Communists, many of whom had been guerrilla leaders, disenchanted with the Soviet invasion of Czechoslovakia and attracted to the Eurocommunist movement. In contrast to the PCV, which has its own small labor confederation, MAS decided that a more fruitful strategy to win working-class support was to accumulate power within the CTV. While MAS has developed some influence in the labor movement, its firmest base is among Venezuelan intellectuals. MAS has played an important role in Congress as a critic of the main parties, instigating investigations of corruption and human rights abuses. In 1988, a MAS deputy played a key role in ensuring the safety of three survivors of an Army massacre (see "The Role of the Military and Human Rights Conditions," below) and insisting upon a congressional investigation of the incident. MAS has not been immune from practicing the politics of patronage, but it has also shown itself capable of self-criticism and open to vigorous debate. To some, MAS represents a new form of pragmatic leftism capable of adjusting to changing circumstances in Latin America.[15]

In 1988, MAS deliberately focused on Congress to the detriment of the presidential campaign of its titular leader, Teodoro Petkoff, the former Communist guerrilla leader. Petkoff received only 2.7 percent of the national vote. However, MAS elected three senators and eighteen deputies, gaining 10.2 percent of the *voto pequeño*. The party ran well in state and local elections in the traditional industrial belt west of Caracas. Since neither COPEI nor AD gained a majority in the election, MAS positioned itself to exercise some political power. But the electoral prospects of the left are limited by popular skepticism about parties in general. Although leftist politicians and union leaders seem to be more honest than their centrist counterparts, they are often accused by grass-roots leaders in neighborhood associations and unions of practicing co-optive politics in the same style as COPEI and AD.[16] Unfortunately, there is ample justification for this charge.

THE ROLE OF THE MILITARY AND HUMAN RIGHTS CONDITIONS

Although the parties remain the key political actors in Venezuelan politics, for the first time in thirty years there have been stirrings of discontent within the military establishment. As recently as May 1988, the Jesuit *Revista SIC* could still assert that in Venezuela the armed forces had not been implicated in massive human rights abuses and still accepted civilian authority.[17] However, on October 26, tanks and armored personnel carriers rumbled through the streets of downtown Caracas for the first time in decades. The government subsequently "explained" that the movement had been in response to a prankster's telephone call alleging that an assault on the presidential palace, Miraflores, was underway. This explanation was greeted with widespread skepticism. *Revista SIC* speculated that the most likely reasons behind the movement were dissatisfaction of some within the military with the deterioration of the economic situation of lower-ranking officers, interference of the parties in high-level promotions, and the lack of military influence in the policy-making process.[18] The likelihood of an actual coup is low, but speculation about the role of the military has reentered public discourse.

Four days after the tanks rumbled in Caracas, the media were filled with news that the Venezuelan military and national security police (DISIP) had killed sixteen Colombian guerrillas trying to cross the Apure River into the Venezuelan *llanos*, allegedly to kidnap and hold ranchers for ransom. The next day, however, Venezuelans were shocked to learn that two survivors of the "battle" had made their way back to the small town of Amparo telling a different story. They were not guerrillas, nor even Colombians, but unarmed Venezuelan fishermen who had been ambushed. The military and DISIP denied any wrongdoing, and when Lusinchi backed their story, riots broke out in several major cities, including on the campus of the UCV in Caracas.

The military had indeed been implicated in a serious crime, but instead of moving to assert civilian oversight, President Lusinchi cooperated with military authorities to impede a full investigation. A MAS deputy, Walter Márquez, organized a congressional investigation and concluded that the massacre was connected to an extortion scheme in which high officials in the military and DISIP offered "protection" to area ranches from the "threat" of guerrillas. Despite the constitutional provision of congressional immunity, Márquez has been threatened with prosecution for pursuing the case; the two survivors had to flee temporarily into Mexico because of threats. Since returning to Venezuela, they have remained under the protective custody of the Catholic church. Meanwhile, a military court claimed jurisdiction and released those officers accused in the case for "lack of evidence." In summer 1990, it was still unclear whether there would be any prosecutions.[19]

There are other troubling signs of growing independence of the "security" forces from civilian control. The National Guard, DISIP, the Judicial Technical Police (PTJ, comparable to the U.S. Federal Bureau of Investigation), and the military all have been suspected of complicity in smuggling, including drug trafficking, in areas near the Colombian border that have been militarized. Retired military officers have acquired land in the Apure region, forcing smaller cultivators and ranchers off desirable land, which may have been an underlying factor in the Amparo massacre.[20] Along the border with Brazil, the military has tolerated the expansion of illegal mining and ranching activities in the La Nublina rain forest and cooperated with the forced removal of indigenous people from areas under development. Since 1975 local officials in Guayana have been authorized to use troops to deal with labor disputes, and the National Guard has been used to break several strikes. Ironically, in the one area of the country (Anzoátegui) where a guerrilla *foco* has operated, the military has been ineffective at bringing the small band under control.[21]

The military has been implicated in several major scandals, including the purchase of defective amphibious craft, which led to the drowning deaths of several soldiers in Lake Valencia. Two defense ministers under Herrera Campins fled the country to avoid prosecution. In 1988, José Vicente Rangel, a leftist deputy, relying on documents brought to light as a result of the Pentagon procurement scandal in the United States, produced evidence linking the high command and Lusinchi to the purchase of defective and obsolete aircraft and tanks for $200 million over their true value, estimated at $535 million. AD successfully squelched an investigation by Congress, asserting that the matter was under the jurisdiction of the military courts and that full disclosure of the agreement would jeopardize national security.[22]

Despite a contracting economy and government budget, military expenditures tripled during the 1980s, reaching $1.38 billion, 3.6 percent of the gross national product, in 1987. One disgruntled general complained that the officer corps was being expanded well beyond a size rational to its organization. With 50,000 men under arms in ten brigades and five divisions, Venezuela has 103 active brigadier generals and thirty generals of division. In contrast, Brazil, with an army five times as large, had only 116 generals altogether. Nonetheless, many ambitious officers reach a high rank but are retired without having satisfied their aspirations for command, while junior officers are promoted over more senior ones for apparently partisan reasons. At retirement ceremonies in 1988, one retiring general handed President Lusinchi a card that read, "My family and I will always remember you for having cut short my career," for which he was detained two days at the Ministry of Defense.[23]

The military does not appear keen to grasp control of government at present. When widespread rioting broke out in Caracas on February 27, 1989, the high command responded to thinly disguised calls from some quarters for a coup with a clear statement of support for civilian authority. "In a moment in which the faithfulness of the military . . . was vital to its survival, the Armed Forces reacted as a fundamental (and founding) ally of the political system installed in Venezuela after 1958," commented Arturo Sosa, editorial director of *Revista SIC*.[24] The military chief of staff, Gen. Italo del Valle Alliegro, practiced at the art of public relations, astutely seized on the riots to present the military as the chief bulwark of democracy, and since his retirement has increasingly sounded like he will be a presidential candidate for 1993. But many remember him not as the savior of democracy, but as the commander of an army that committed many human rights abuses, including disappearances and indiscriminate killings of civilians during the disorders.

The riots, the mistrust of populism, and a sense of growing social anarchy are producing a political climate more conducive to military involvement in government. The danger is not so much a coup, but a drift toward a regime, as in neighboring Colombia, where civilians control the government but the military exercises great authority beyond their control.

Human Rights Conditions

Admirers of the Venezuelan model see human rights as one area where Venezuela has proved itself superior to the experience of Cuba, which has been criticized by Americas Watch and Amnesty International for restricting freedom of expression, association, and privacy rights and for inadequate judicial processes. In the area of free speech, Venezuela continues to show a remarkable degree of pluralism and independence in its printed media, but journalists and newspapers are vulnerable to threats by the government, the largest commercial advertiser in the country. Journalists are notoriously underpaid and subject to intimidation by their employers, but they have a strong *gremio* (professional association) and union which vigorously defend press freedoms. These rights are increasingly abused, and journalists have occasionally been jailed or physically threatened for carrying out their duties.

While Venezuela may be able to boast of a more pluralistic media, it does not compare so favorably to Cuba in the use of extrajudicial violence, resort to which has become extensive and is growing. According to Amnesty International's 1987 report:

> Many people were arrested in connection with anti-government demonstrations: most were released but several were sent for trial before military tribunals. Other long-standing political prisoners remained on trial before military tribunals whose procedures were extremely protracted. There were new reports of killings by police in circumstances that strongly suggested they were extrajudicial executions. One military cadet died apparently as a result of torture.[25]

Among the hundreds arrested, thirty-four were held for several months, accused of involvement with the *Bandera Roja* guerrilla group, but Amnesty notes that they were "trade unionists, students, community leaders and

Clergy, students, and others protest the muzzling of local media in Mérida in 1987 (photo by Luis Trujillo)

people who had been charged with politically motivated crimes years before but then released." Eight were still being held for trial in 1988.[26] Concern with the deteriorating human rights situation has led to the emergence of the Support Network for Peace and Justice, in which the church plays a crucial role.[27]

Amnesty estimated that in 1987 1 million people were detained in Caracas alone under the notorious Law against Vagrancy and Delinquency. Many were beaten, and hundreds were shipped without trial to a penal colony in the Amazonian Territory. In 1986, five bodies were found in a well in Maracaibo; a subsequent investigation by Congress revealed that they were among at least forty-six who were known to have died in police custody. Vigilante groups, often operating with the tacit consent of the government and police, have sprung up in barrios in recent years. Ostensibly they offer security against criminals, but they also threaten grassroots organizers. In March 1988, the minister of justice resigned in order to avoid an investigation into charges that he had created an extrajudicial antidrug force which was placed at the disposal of some politicians to harass their political and personal opponents.

In May of 1987, forty-six religious clergy paid for a two-page advertisement to denounce the human rights situation under the headline, "We can't be silent anymore," which earned them the interior minister's denunciation as foreign agitators. After the February 27, 1989, riots, Amnesty International sent a telegram to President Pérez expressing concern over reports of "serious violations of human rights during the disturbances which occurred in recent weeks," including reports of civilians killed during house-to-house searches and mistreatment of detainees. The Catholic church has formed a special human rights commission, and the Archbishop of Caracas designated Arturo Sosa to investigate the cases of hundreds of persons alleged to have either disappeared or been unjustly imprisoned in the wake of the riots.[28]

Román Escobar Salóm, the fiscal general (something like the attorney general in the U.S. system) proclaimed in May 1990 that a state of law no longer prevailed in Venezuela. This statement may be something of an exaggeration from a politician with aspirations to the presidency himself, but for many of Venezuela's poor who have suffered unjust imprisonment while major officials implicated in corruption remain free, the statement rings true.

NEW SOCIAL MOVEMENTS

Underlying the deteriorating human rights situation is the crisis facing the political party system. In the postpetroleum era, there are fewer material resources available for the parties to co-opt social movements. Venezuela's elites must decide whether to respond to this political challenge with more democracy or with repression. The record is not encouraging so far. On January 23, 1988, the Venezuelan bishops, on the anniversary of the fall of Pérez Jiménez, published a denunciation of the parties for trying "to manipulate all expression of social life."[29] Parties have used legal and material resources to co-opt or to defeat grassroots organizations founded to address grievances. A struggle over housing in El Carmen, a community in the north of Barquisimeto, Venezuela's fourth-largest city with 600,000 inhabitants, illustrates the difficulties faced by grassroots organizers.[30]

El Carmen: A Case Study of Local Conflict

Migrants in Barquisimeto came from rural areas seeking jobs in construction, services, and industry. Lacking access to housing in the city, they built their homes on public, unclaimed land in villages like El Carmen. Unfortunately, the same economic processes that were generating jobs were also making land in outlying areas more valuable to speculators and investors. When the oil boom commenced in 1974, the Pérez administration supplied plentiful credit for industrial expansion, and El Carmen, strategically located near a rail line, found itself the target of a concerted drive to relocate its population in favor of an industrial park.

The government had hoped to lure the residents into a nearby public housing project. However, even during prosperous times public housing remained well beyond the reach of the average Venezuelan worker, who in 1980 needed a deposit of 20 thousand bolívars ($4,650) to secure a mortgage for even the least-expensive apartment. The government offered to forgive the down payment, but few residents wanted to trade in their self-constructed homes for a rented or mortgaged residence where they could not keep their chickens or catch their own fresh rainwater. At one stage of the struggle, community leaders offered to move into the high-rise housing project if the government would concede full ownership in exchange for their existing homes. The government refused, fearing that the concession would generate a wider demand for free housing.

In 1981, a small stream that empties the foothills around Barquisimeto, spilled its banks and flooded into the community, leaving 200 families homeless and many other residences severely damaged. A nearby brewery quickly received state credits to repair damages and to reinforce the stream bank near its warehouse, but the local community received nothing. At this point, some local university students and Catholic clergy helped them to organize a neighborhood association and a Christian base community. The new neighborhood association carried out a census to determine the actual number of homeless and where each family stood in relationship to a law granting any Venezuelan ownership of vacant public land after occupying it for ten years. Most residents of El Carmen either qualified or were close to qualifying for ownership. In June of 1981, the association organized a series of actions, including a one-day takeover of the city center, in order to press their demands.

The government responded that it had already relocated approximately 150 families from El Carmen and other affected barrios. However, the relocation sites were far removed from jobs and transportation, and conditions in the new settlements were primitive. Each family was provided a tiny (7 by 13 meters) plot of land and a prefabricated zinc shack measuring 6 by 3 meters. Venezuelans call such shacks, which are devoid of floors, sanitary facilities, or even windows, *"hornos de zinc"* (zinc ovens), because the sun turns them into hot boxes during the day. Three children died in the summer of 1981 from diseases aggravated by lack of sanitation and medical attention in the camps around Barquisimeto. Journalists who attempted to publicize conditions of the *damnificados* were threatened with prosecution for "slandering"

"*Hornos de zinc*," San Felix, Ciudad Guayana (photo courtesy of *El Pueblo de Guayana*)

government officials. The National Guard was deployed to cordon off the communities and keep journalists out.

As long as one fiercely combative resident remained its leader, the association resisted co-optation, but after she died of cancer, the parties gained the upper hand. Some of the leaders of the association were offered jobs, housing, or other benefits if they would give up the struggle or induce the community to accept government proposals. Many residents of El Carmen feared that they would be left with nothing if they refused the government's offers to relocate—better a free *horno de zinc* or a mortgaged apartment than no place to live at all.

Growth of the Neighborhood Association Movement

Experiences like that in El Carmen proved that neighborhood associations could not expect to survive without coalescing into a national movement. Middle-class citizens realized this early and created the Federation of Urban Community Associations (FACUR), which emerged in 1971 in Caracas in the wake of several struggles to limit encroachment by speculators and developers into residential areas. In 1978, as a result of reform of the municipal laws, FACUR's fifty member AVs were officially recognized as representatives before municipal councils.

AD sought to co-opt FACUR, and it appeared that it had succeeded when the federation accepted a $60,000 annual subsidy from the government and the federation's president successfully ran for Congress in

1978 on an *adeco plancha*. By 1982, AD could boast of control over 250 associations. These party-affiliated AVs are often patronage machines intended to do little more than mobilize votes at election time. COPEI once hoped to create a Christian Democratic movement of neighborhood associations as a counterweight to AD's dominance of the labor movements. The Herrera Campins government used the state-financed FUNDOCOMUN ("Common Foundation") to funnel money and resources to favored associations. By 1982, COPEI claimed to have organized 100 associations. But the neighborhood association movement has proved less malleable than the parties expected.[31]

FACUR's middle-class constituency, educated and skilled in making its voice heard, was not so vulnerable to co-optation as were the residents of El Carmen. Disenchantment with the parties led FACUR to renounce its affiliation with AD in 1982.[32] COPEI also found it difficult to co-opt the movement it fostered. Many community organizers trained by church-affiliated groups proved resistant to party control and committed to the new philosophy that the church must show a "preferential option for the poor." Organizations like *Fe y Alegría* (Faith and Happiness) have lost much of their paternalistic character and sought to encourage barrio residents to organize independent cooperatives, neighborhood councils, youth organizations, etc.

At times, there has been tension between associations in middle-class *urbanizaciones* and those in the barrios, particularly when middle-class groups have sought to contain the spread of the latter into their neighborhoods. However, the post-1983 economic crisis has hit the middle class hard. Many are concerned with falling back into the ranks of the poor. They have become more willing to participate in broader popular struggles. One example was the May 1989 boycott of bakeries, organized by FACUR, to protest the failure of the government to regulate the price of bread effectively.

The economic crisis and unplanned urban growth have propelled more organizing. One study estimates that there were already 600 AVs in Caracas alone in 1984.[33] The AVs and elected neighborhood councils (*Juntas de Vecinos*) in the barrios often exist for very specific purposes, for example, cultural activities or environmental defense. Others represent neighborhoods before municipal councils, for which official recognition is necessary. While this makes the latter more dependent on the parties, AVs formed for limited, specific purposes (nutrition, health, music, crime prevention, sports, transportation, etc.) need fewer resources and do not require official recognition to survive. Some AVs have organized successful grassroots struggles over issues significant beyond their specific locality. For example, residents of Petare and La Pastora, two working-class neighborhoods in Caracas, prevented the bulldozer and wrecking ball

Cultural event organized by a neighborhood association in Caracas (photo by author)

from eliminating these neighborhoods, which contain the last vestiges of the city's colonial architecture.

Most Venezuelans still lack any experience with independent organizing. One survey of barrio residents in 1989 found that nearly 52 percent could recall no neighborhood struggles. Whereas 25 percent could remember using "*la palanca*" (someone's political pull) to deal with a problem, only about 4 percent could remember turning to neighbors for help.[34] Still, the neighborhood association movement is clearly growing in importance. In 1989, Carlos Andrés Pérez asked FACUR and other neighborhood associations to take the lead in fighting hoarding and speculation—although AD simultaneously launched a major new effort to bring them under its hegemony.[35] However, leaders associated with parties will find it difficult to keep the confidence of residents unless they respond effectively to the deteriorating quality of life, and there is little to suggest that either major party is prepared to reorient its priorities toward popular needs.

Bitter Coffee

In rural areas, where AD continues to dominate the Venezuelan Peasants Federation (FCV), there are fewer signs of effective resistance to *partidocracia;* nonetheless, underlying tensions are visible. Venezuela

TABLE 6.2 Distribution of Landholdings, 1988

Size of parcel in hectares	Number of parcels	% of all parcels	Number of hectares	% of all hectares
Less than 20	209,072	73.19	1,308,209	4.18
500 or more	11,392	2.98	21,823,892	69.77

Source: Ministerio de Fomento, V Censo Agropecuario (Caracas, 1988).

continues, after fifty years of promises and thirty years of "land reform," to be characterized by an unequal pattern of land tenancy (see Table 6.2). Agricultural labor's share of agricultural income fell in the 1960s, and between 1974 and 1985 it plummeted further, from 45.78 to 35.35 percent. The Lusinchi administration announced that it would make agriculture an investment priority, and indeed its policies seemed to produce an "agricultural miracle." However, the increases in production registered under Lusinchi seem to have resulted from more extensive than intensive use of land, that is, from putting more land into production rather than from higher productivity on land already cultivated. As usual, small producers received little from the government largesse. Credits went disproportionately to large-scale enterprises producing cereals, beef, and dairy products, and industrial inputs, while the traditional sector, where a majority of Venezuela's 800,000 peasants are found, was starved for credit.[36]

Traditional areas of agriculture, like coffee, have been hit hardest by the economic crisis and have begun to exert pressure on the government and the FCV. Once the backbone of the economy and of the traditional social structure, coffee is now dominated by smaller producers. The overvalued bolívar made it difficult for Venezuelan producers to compete with Colombia, Brazil, and Central American exporters. Unlike many other coffee-producing states, Venezuela's superior beans have been allocated not to exports but to the domestic market, ultimately reaching the myriad soda fountains and sidewalk bakeries introduced by European immigrants who brought their espresso machines to the country after World War II.

FONCAFE (National Coffee Fund), a state agency with a legal monopoly over purchases, was established by the first Pérez government to subsidize the coffee sector. During the boom, FONCAFE had little difficulty meeting its obligations, essentially transferring rent generated by the oil boom to growers. However, by 1986, the 30 bolívars per quintal (100 kilograms) paid by the fund through officially recognized cooperatives was far below the 70 bolívars needed by producers to cover costs. FONCAFE claimed inadequate funds to meet its obligations, but the problems were not due merely to the fall in oil prices. In 1985,

FONCAFE officials were accused of defrauding the country of 80 million bolívars in 1984 and 1985 alone through manipulation of currency exchange rates. In 1987, producers in one cooperative in the state of Lara, angered that a local agency of FONCAFE had purchased new FAX and TELEX machines while they went unpaid, decided to act.[37]

The cooperative organized a demonstration of 3,000 producers in Barquisimeto to support its demand that FONCAFE pay in accordance with real costs. One group of peasants from the area of Tocuyo in western Lara organized an independent audit that accused FONCAFE of paying 158.5 million bolívars to its own employees, but only distributing 20.3 million bolívars to the growers. In March 1988, peasants seized an important bridge near the town of Guárico because FONCAFE had not yet paid for a harvest deposited the previous December. The peasants refused to move until driven from the bridge by tear gas.[38]

As of March 1989, the coffee growers of Lara had managed to force FONCAFE to pay only one-third of what they were owed, despite a Supreme Court ruling that under the constitution they were entitled to full payment. Nonetheless, they had shaken the local and state political structure by organizing demonstrations independently of the leadership of the political parties. The protests spread to the Andes.[39] In Lara, a state legislature controlled by AD repudiated the policy of the government, forcing the resignation of Lusinchi's minister of agriculture.[40] With direct election of governors, this type of strain on *partidocracia* is likely to grow more intense.

STUDENTS, ENVIRONMENTALISTS, AND VIOLENCE IN THE ANDES

Mérida, a picturesque city of 200,000 in the shadow of the 16,000-foot Pico Bolívar and its glacier, is the capital of the state by the same name and home to the University of the Andes (ULA), oldest in the country. Mérida had long been a *copeyano* stronghold, but AD broke through to take control of the state and city governments in the wake of Lusinchi's impressive landslide in 1983. The new *adeco* government proceeded to cooperate with Lusinchi's priorities for development—agro-industry and tourism. Conflict over the government's development priorities, environmental concerns, abuses in human rights, and cuts in education combined to generate discontent and several violent incidents. In the summer of 1988, several government and university buildings were burned in the worst disturbances. Although the immediate catalysts were specific to Mérida, the underlying causes were not so different from those leading to the national social explosion of February 1989.

For the working class, the ability to send their children for a university education and an opportunity to escape the *ranchos* was a powerful legitimizing force in a system that failed them in so many other ways. The university system could never keep up with demand, but during the oil bonanza, the *Gran Mariscal de Ayacucho* program provided funds for tens of thousands to study abroad, thus relieving pressure on the system. Even before the crisis, only six of every 100 students beginning a university program were able to complete their degrees.[41] With the collapse of oil prices and the devaluation of the bolívar, the opportunities to study abroad virtually disappeared; the number of applicants far exceeded available places in the university system. In 1990, those accepted into the Central University in Caracas could anticipate a two-year wait before they could begin classes. Many students are finding it impossible to meet living expenses. Resentment was also developing among professors, who had to go on strike for four months in 1986 to collect (only part of) their back pay.[42]

In Mérida, resentment toward the *adeco* government first erupted in March 1987, after police failed to arrest a politically prominent lawyer who had killed a student for defecating in front of his house. In retaliation, students marched on the lawyer's home and burned it down, triggering widespread rioting and a military occupation of the city. Although residents and students have often been alienated from one another, the city's population aligned itself with the spontaneous revolt. Two more rounds of violence—in one case following the killing of a student and a worker by police in the neighboring state of Trujillo—followed.

The tense atmosphere worsened after Mérida's central market was destroyed by an arsonist on May 31. The very next day, the market, including a part untouched by the flames, was bulldozed down by the government, fueling widespread suspicions that the local *adeco* government had authored the crime to drive reluctant merchants into the new, concrete, six-floor market constructed on the outskirts of town. The government saw the new market as a way to increase the tourist trade, a high priority of the Lusinchi government's plan to reactivate the economy. But the new market held little attraction for local residents. Merchants did not want to relocate and pay rent for a facility considerably removed from their steady customers in town. Peasants were accustomed to vending their wares weekly in the old market, and few could afford to utilize the new one. Many residents had long-standing, close relationships with the mountain people through the market, which was their most immediate tie with the surrounding countryside. In the midst of rapid modernization, the market served as the collective memory of the city.

Rector of the University of the Andes, Mérida, leading a protest over human rights abuses, in this case the killing of a student by police in the neighboring state of Trujillo, 1987 (photo by Luis Trujillo)

Although there is no real proof that the government was involved in the arson, the fact that almost everyone *believed* it culpable reveals much about crisis of confidence in Venezuelan democracy.[43] Local neighborhood groups and cultural organizations began to press the government to rebuild the market. This struggle became intertwined with their response to another threat to the quality of life in Mérida, the contamination of the Mucujun River, which flows through spectacular green, flowering meadows (*páramos*) north of the city and provides its water supply.

The immediate threat to the Mucujun came from the construction of hotels, use of chemical fertilizers, and greater concentration of livestock, all encouraged by the generous credits and subsidies provided by the government to spur rural development and generate an "agricultural miracle." With its eye exclusively on minimizing costs, the government failed to include water treatment facilities in its plans. Aroused residents, professors, religious organizers, and students in Mérida founded a grassroots environmental movement. They found allies among some peasants whose own small plots were threatened by pollution or who were being threatened with eviction to make way for modern farms and ranches. The coalition won a temporary suspension of any new

Mérida's old market falls victim to arson, the bulldozer, and greed (photo by Luis Trujillo)

agricultural development in the region, but the struggle to make the ban permanent led to continued friction between residents and authorities in 1988.

Just as in the case of housing in El Carmen, leaders of Mérida's social movements have found it difficult to maintain unity and independence. The ban on new farms had the unintended effect of preventing peasants already displaced by development from moving onto new lands. Large landowners, with thinly disguised support from the government, deftly exploited the situation by encouraging these peasants to demonstrate against the environmentalists, causing tensions to rise and attitudes to polarize. This played into the hands of extremist elements among students and contributed to violence that has rocked the community several times since 1986. The most serious incident occurred on July 13, 1988, when extremist elements converted a peaceful takeover of the city center, organized to demand a permanent ban on development in the Mucujun, into several days of major rioting, including the burning of several university buildings. Although the immediate causes were very different, the incident foreshadowed the social explosion that rocked the county nineteen months later—that is, the growing alienation of people from their elected leaders and lack of confidence in the parties to articulate their demands.

A woman and her daughter milking a cow, Andes (photo by Mayela Iribarreu)

The price of a more responsive political system would be one in which elites are less capable of overcoming grassroots resistance to economic austerity and development plans. However, some concessions involve considerably higher costs for elites. Nowhere is this situation more evident than in the geographical and economic area where the Venezuelan state has staked the future of the country's economic development—in the new industrial zone of Guayana.

THE NEW UNIONISM MOVEMENT

The CTV estimates that one-third of the urban work force is unionized, but according to the Ministry of Labor, only about 15 percent of the work force was covered by some form of union contract in 1978. However, 75 percent of workers in oil and mining are organized, as are 55 percent of workers in manufacturing, construction, and utilities. Although the smaller confederations are strong in a few sectors, the system of electoral competition established by the economic and political pacts of 1957 and 1958 has generally discouraged parties from founding their own confederations parallel to the CTV. The CTV is estimated to have 1 million members, while three smaller confederations together claim a total of 170,000 members.[44]

On the surface, the Venezuelan labor movement is extraordinarily democratic. At the June 1985 meeting of the International Labor Organization in Geneva, Juan José Delpino, president of the Confederation of Venezuelan Workers (CTV), proclaimed:

> In Venezuela there exists a democratic regime that guarantees the free play of ideas and freedom of organization for different political tendencies. By the same token, Venezuela . . . has recognized and respected the right of workers to join unions that correspond to their political sympathies. . . . The state provides each union organization with economic resources so that they can function without compromise or under pressure.[45]

In contrast, José Arrieta, labor correspondent for *Revista SIC*, describes the CTV as an organization wracked by "corruption, trafficking of influence, absence of internal democracy, mutual deception and patronage, oppression of adversaries."[46]

After the end of the guerrilla war and the defeat of the *mepista* challenge to *adeco* hegemony in 1968, the leftist parties (especially MAS, MIR, and the PCV) saw the goal of controlling the union movement as simply a shift in the class struggle from armed struggle to a peaceful and legal means. The left identified itself with a class-oriented type of unionism, an alternative to the philosophy espoused by AD, which has officially dropped socialism as its ultimate objective. However, the difference between *adeco* and *copeyano* leaders and leftist leaders has usually been considerably narrower than official ideology suggests. The rhetoric of class struggle by leftist leaders often obscures the rather economistic and materialistic ("*reinvindicalista*") goals of their actions, as well as their own susceptibility to co-optation by management.[47]

A new type of labor tendency emerged in the 1970s, partly as a result of a bitter struggle that pitted the leftist Central United Venezuelan Workers Confederation (CUTV), which had gained the upper hand in the textile sector, against employers, the CTV, and the state. The CUTV had negotiated a very favorable contract in 1977, while the oil economy was booming, but the Pérez government was attempting to retreat from the protectionism implemented by the *adeco* Old Guard in the 1960s. In 1978, the textile industry began to experience pressure on its high rate of profit as it faced competition from imports, including goods smuggled from Colombia, and a domestic recession. By discharging workers, the owners sought to weaken the unions, to replace many Venezuelan workers with lower-paid Colombians, to roll back provisions of the 1977 contract, and to pressure the government to maintain subsidies and protection to the industry.

To discharge workers, the employers needed the support of the Labor Ministry, which they received because AD and the CTV were eager to see the unions returned to "responsible" leadership. Despite the firings, the workers stood by their unions. Unhealthy and unsafe working conditions in the plants had impressed workers with the need for effective union representation. The government consequently stepped up the pressure. In 1978, some of the CUTV leadership was jailed on charges of having collaborated with a guerrilla *foco* alleged to have been operating in the nearby mountains. Few independent observers took the charge seriously, but the *adeco* and *copeyano* leaders of the CTV echoed it and refused to extend solidarity to the jailed labor leaders.

Throughout 1980, there were waves of additional firings targeting supporters of the leftist union leadership. Finally, in 1980, textile workers from one plant, where 36 percent of the workers suffered from respiratory or auditory problems, took over the main cathedral on the Plaza Bolívar in Caracas, touching off a strike in Valencia, capital of the state of Aragua, the key textile center in the country. The Labor Ministry declared the strike illegal, but workers persisted. After a union demonstration was violently attacked by police on August 13, workers in the entire state staged an unprecedented general strike throughout Aragua, producing major concessions from owners and managers.

The employers' concessions included a promise to reinstate workers dismissed without just cause. Unfortunately, the leftist leaders of the textile union, primarily motivated by the desire to inflict a mortifying political defeat on the CTV, pressed for complete capitulation, rejecting the offer on the relatively narrow question of whether fired union leaders would be incorporated before or after the signing of an agreement. This was a serious miscalculation. The owners signed a similar agreement with a CTV-affiliated, parallel union without any commitment at all to reinstate workers loyal to the CUTV. Workers who remained loyal to the CUTV were fired in droves. The strike and the leftist unions were crushed.

In the aftermath, some leftist leaders undertook a self-criticism and concluded that the defeat of the textile strike was due to a lack of union democracy and to the elevation of partisan interests in the name of "class unionism." The *"tendencia classista"* had in common with *adeco* and *copeyano* leaders a tendency to put political goals ahead of worker democracy. Both were committed to a form of vanguardism that contributed, in the left's case, to the textile strike defeat.[48] As this critique was going forward it was enriched by new experiences in Guayana, the new industrial heartland. The result has been *el nuevo sindicalismo*, the "new unionism" movement.

New Unionism in Guayana

In 1961, Ciudad Guayana was little more than a series of blueprints and maps in the briefcases of North American and Venezuelan urban planners. Despite the fact that the city's population of 143,000 (1971) was well below the 200,000 projected by planners, its social infrastructure lagged far behind the pace of industrial expansion. According to the 1971 census, Ciudad Guayana had the highest proportion of *ranchos* (shanties), the highest rate of inflation, and the most notoriously inadequate social services of all major cities.[49] And things have gotten worse in the postpetroleum era. In 1988, 30,980 cases of malaria (probably an underestimate) were recorded in Guayana.[50] Workers were now confronting problems that seemed to have been eliminated during the *trienio*.

In the face of declining oil revenues, the Venezuelan state and AD are counting on the mining and metallurgical industries of Guayana to generate new export earnings. Success requires that Venezuela bring costs in line with producers in developed countries (see Chapter 5). Unfortunately for Venezuelan workers, management has sought to lower costs not by streamlining bureaucracy or eliminating corruption and favoritism, but by keeping wages low and compromising health and safety in the workplace. For local leaders of the two main parties, competition to control unions is part of the national game of politics. For traditional labor officials, mostly *adecos*, maintaining control of unions means access to material rewards customarily used to co-opt the labor bureaucracy. Thus, maintaining hegemony over labor in Guayana is a political priority for AD and an economic priority for the state and public managers.

The traditional leftist parties were active and successful in the 1970s in wresting control of several major unions in mining, steel, aluminum, ports, and transportation from AD and COPEI. However, for many of the same reasons that resulted in the defeat of the textile workers, the centrist parties were able to counterattack effectively, utilizing a combination of repression and material incentives. Many labor leaders from leftist parties were co-opted by the lucrative offers that managers and CTV officials dangled during the era of the oil bonanza. However, militants of a number of smaller leftist parties, rooted mostly either in leftist Christian organizations or splinters from the PCV, MAS, MIR, and MEP, began in the late 1970s to practice a more democratic form of unionism.

CAUSA R has been the most successful of these parties. Its activists concentrated first on smaller, ancillary industries, winning a number of conflicts by emphasizing demands that were concrete and capable of generating solidarity from other workers. They made it a practice to keep workers accurately informed of their strengths and weaknesses, using their newspaper as an educational and organizing tool, emphasizing information over ideological proselytizing. Their first success came in 1978 when they organized a successful work action by bus drivers who are hired by the CVG to transport workers on the two-hour trip (each way) to and from their jobs in Matanzas, the industrial zone of Ciudad Guayana. The drivers were forced to work long hours for poor pay, generating conditions that were not only unjust but unsafe for the passengers. This made it easier to generate support for the struggle of the transport workers among employees of SIDOR and other industries in Matanzas. A newspaper, *Matancero*, kept workers informed of developments and of the choices they faced. For most, this was a completely new form of unonism. It gave birth to the movement known as *"Matanceros."*[51]

Other leftist groups were gaining ground in other industries, notably in the aluminum sector, mining, and shipping. However, the greatest shock to the *adecos* came when a leftist coalition, headed by CAUSA R's Andrés Velásquez and Tello Benítez, swept to victory in SUTISS (the United Workers in Steel and Similar Industries) in SIDOR, the very centerpiece of Venezuelan industrial development with its (then) 12,000 industrial workers. The CTV leadership and AD correctly concluded that the struggle for control of SUTISS and other mining and metallurgical industries was strategic in nature. They were determined to regain control regardless of legal niceties.

The *adeco* counterattack included outright repression, selective firings, concessions, and co-optation. Gradually and slowly, AD by 1981 managed to regain control of most of Guayana's unions. However, the sheer size of SIDOR, the need for an effective union in a plant with dangerous working conditions, and resistance of the CAUSA R leaders to co-optation proved too much for AD to overcome. The workers might vote for AD in general elections or even to carry an *adeco* membership card to keep their jobs, but in secret voting they were determined to defend the integrity of their union as long as their leaders kept faith with them. AD would have to resort to more extreme tactics. In October 1981, the CTV, through its affiliated federations (FETRAMETAL and FETRABOLIVAR), "intervened" and replaced the elected leadership of SUTISS with their own officials, charging that CAUSA R was exploiting negotiations for a new contract for political gain. Velásquez, Benítez, and other *Matancero* leaders were fired shortly afterwards.

The CTV also claimed that the leftist leadership of SUTISS was deliberately stonewalling negotiations in order to "subvert" the viability of Venezuela's nascent steel industry. In fact, the key issue stalling negotiations was the union's demand that the workweek be shortened from 48 to 40 hours. Management saw the extended workweek as necessary to keep the industry with competitors abroad. The union argued that productivity had already risen, from 23 hours per metric ton of liquid steel to 16 hours per ton. This was still far below Japanese and German standards. Union leaders blamed corruption and managerial inefficiency for the gap in productivity and pointed out that without the extraordinary burden of debt repayment, SIDOR would turn a healthy profit.

After the intervention, FETRAMETAL chief José Mollegas negotiated a contract containing a wage and benefit increase, but failing to shorten the workweek or to address poor health and safety conditions in the plant, two of the most salient issues to the workers. However, an overconfident Mollegas decided to submit the contract to the members, and the ratification vote became a de facto referendum on the intervention itself. The CTV released the "news" of a smashing victory before the votes had even been counted, but the membership shocked AD by following the instructions of their ousted leaders and abstaining in massive proportions. The result, widely reported in the media, was a humiliating defeat, but Mollegas moved ahead with the agreement. After the contract was signed, it was revealed that FETRAMETAL and FE-TRABOLIVAR demanded $460,000 from SIDOR as payment for their services in resolving the conflict. Mollegas publicly acknowledged the arrangement and explained that this was a "completely normal" way of conducting collective bargaining negotiations in Venezuela. (Unions are entitled by law to recover the costs of the negotiating process from management.)

In August 1987, after Velásquez and Benítez lost several legal battles to win reinstatement as employees of SIDOR and thereby regain eligibility to run again for union office, and after a turnover of thousands of SIDOR employees (either as a result of politically motivated firings or normal attrition), Mollegas felt confident enough to hold elections, but he cautioned, "If the workers make another mistake, we will not hesitate to correct it once again." Despite the threat, and without Velásquez and Benítez on their *plancha*, the *Matanceros* won an overwhelming victory and regained leadership of the SIDOR workers, now numbering 17,000.[52]

One year later, after difficult negotiations, the new leadership reached a new agreement with management. The new contract failed to provide for a reduced workweek, which attracted criticism from other leftist groups. Some critics argue that CAUSA R, although uncorrupted, had failed to *consult* rather than merely to *inform* workers during negotiations. However, CAUSA R does not appear to have lost the confidence of the working class in Guayana. In the December 1988 elections, the party made major gains in the state of Bolívar, entitling it to send three deputies to the National Congress. In late 1989, CAUSA R strengthened its grip on the SUTISS leadership in new union elections in which AD lost its place as the second party to MAS. Then, Velásquez was elected governor of the state of Bolívar in December 1989.

The CTV Bureaucracy

The working class provided indispensable support for AD's rise to power and in the struggle for electoral democracy.[53] More and more, however, *adeco* domination of the CTV has come to rest on its ability to use the Labor Ministry to manipulate elections and the collective bargaining process. By forming parallel unions and controlling myriad smaller unions, each of which are entitled to one vote in electing officers of regional and national federations, AD is able to manipulate the system of indirect elections to ensure domination of the federations and the CTV. Thus, for example, the SUTISS union, the largest in the country, is entitled to no more representation in regional or industry federations or in the CTV than a union with a few dozen workers.

In the 1960s and 1970s the state provided the CTV with 90 percent of its funds. Although this subsidy would slip to 43 percent by the 1980s, the difference was made good by CTV economic investments, including those generated by the CTV-owned Venezuelan Workers Bank (BTV). The CTV has moved from financial dependence to status as an economic empire, and the result has been a new style of co-option.[54] When the Herrera Campins government took over the BTV to prevent its insolvency it revealed massive corruption, indicating that the CTV leadership was running the "bank of the workers" not much differently than the rapacious bourgeoisie runs the commercial banks. (The BTV was returned to CTV control by Lusinchi in 1985.)

Corruption has become endemic in the CTV. Common forms include kickbacks to union leaders under the guise of compensation for negotiating expenses, collaboration between union leaders and management to pad payrolls with checks for phony employees and are apparently widespread. Some practices are legal, but highly compromising. Cooperative labor leaders can expect future employment in managerial positions, like personnel director, after years of faithful service. This sometimes results in former labor leaders "negotiating" contracts with their own handpicked successors in the unions. Some regional labor leaders in Guayana owned a consumer finance company (METALCREDITO) that extended credit liberally to workers and then had management attach their wages when they fell behind in payments.[55]

Unions are a linchpin in the party patronage system. In 1988, for example, the aluminum enterprise CORALUM reneged on a promise to hire construction workers as part of its permanent work force once they completed work on a new production line for permanent employment on the line itself. The construction workers union was controlled by COPEI, and neither the exiting union leadership nor management, both closely linked to AD, wished to integrate members of a union controlled by COPEI into the work force. Hundreds of workers were discharged under the pretext of slack demand—even as the company pressed ahead with expansion plans.[56]

Despite Venezuela's reputation as a democratic nation where labor rights are respected, strike action is highly restricted. To carry out a strike, union leaders must complete a cumbersome, detailed, and time-consuming series of procedures overseen at each step by the highly politicized Ministry of Labor. Between 1959 and 1982, only ninety-six of 2,341 recorded strikes were recognized as legal.[57] In the case of the textile workers struggle, the CTV failed to defend the right to strike of a sister union affiliated with another confederation. In 1984, the CTV failed to support one of its own unions even after the latter had won an unprecedented Supreme Court ruling in favor of the right to strike, raising questions not only about labor rights but also about the viability of constitutional rights in general in Venezuela.

Deterioration of Constitutional Labor Rights

The dispute originally broke out in June 1984 between workers and the management of HEVENSA (Hornos Eléctricos de Venezuela). HEVENSA is a small firm with only 200 employees producing silicon manganese and ferro-silicate, two alloys without which SIDOR cannot operate. The dispute concerned worker discontent over violations of their contract and hazardous working conditions, which included handling dangerous substances in 120 degree heat. Scrupulously following provisions of the labor laws, the workers, independently of any political organization or party, organized an assembly and replaced the company-controlled union leadership with a new set of officers.[58]

The ousted leadership had been cronies of a former leftist labor leader, Pedro Marcano, subsequently hired by the Mexican and Chilean management of the firm to a lucrative job as personnel director. Marcano responded to the worker initiative by firing the new leaders and, with the help of the National Guard and SIDOR, bussing in scab workers to maintain production. The workers countered with legal action that eventually resulted in a Supreme Court ruling, the first of its kind, declaring that the firings violated constitutional protection of the right to strike. Instead of accepting the ruling, HEVENSA threw up a cordon of National Guardsmen and private guards around the plant to greet

National Guard troops protect strike-breakers, industrial zone of Matanzas, Ciudad Guayana, 1987 (photo courtesy of *El Pueblo de Guayana*)

returning workers. The issue had been clearly framed: Could HEVENSA defy the constitutional right to strike without an effective labor response?

Instead of supporting the workers, the CTV and the Labor Ministry labelled the dispute "political" and, as in the case of the struggles in SIDOR and the textile industry, said that the left was not seeking to represent workers but to subvert the country's economy. In contrast, the judge whose ruling was upheld by the Supreme Court specified, "I firmly believe that it has no political tint and that we are dealing instead with a just petition of the workers." The CTV offered no material support for the struggle. Instead of demanding that the workers be reinstated, CTV leaders suggested that they submit their grievances to arbitration—a course that probably would have produced a cash settlement without reinstatement. After one more year of struggle, by which time only thirty of 108 workers who had participated in the original strike remained, the remaining workers accepted a settlement for severance pay well below what they had lost while on strike. The company had won.[59]

Strains Between AD and the CTV

There are signs that the prolonged economic crisis is creating strains in alliance between the parties and the CTV. Neither Lusinchi nor Andrés Pérez has implemented policies consistent with what the Labor Bureau expected when it provided critical support for their drive to the *adeco* presidential nomination. Abandonment of import substitution has generated economic hardship for workers in traditional industries, like textiles, bottling, etc. The work force in the critical oil industry has remained relatively docile, but the drive to increase nontraditional exports has increased tensions in Guayana.

Relations between Delpino, the president of the CTV, and Lusinchi grew steadily worse during the latter's term. The split became public at the nationally televised IX Congress of the CTV in 1985, where, with the president seated on the same stage, Delpino attacked the government's economic policies, particularly the terms of a debt rescheduling package. CTV demands for an across the board wage increase were deferred, as the labor leadership stepped up the volume but not the pressure on the government in Lusinchi's last two years. However, the announcement by Andrés Pérez, in February 1989, of his austerity program and the subsequent rioting seems to have opened a new chapter in labor relations.

An extraordinary Congress of the CTV was convened on May 1, 1989. Attacks upon the government were launched by all political tendencies within the confederation. Perhaps even more important, the adeco-dominated Congress issued a proclamation of independence from party control. To demonstrate commitment to this new position, Delpino and the CTV called for and organized a 98 percent successful twelve-hour general strike on May 18, 1989. The CTV even sought and received the active support of the smaller labor confederations and dissidents, like Velásquez. No concrete demands were posed or achieved, but the general strike was unprecedented in the post-1958 era and has been followed by an upsurge in further activity.[60]

In 1990, the government decreed a boost in wages, skewed toward lower-income workers, but well below the 80 percent jump in consumer prices registered during the previous year. Tripartite negotiations among government, the CTV, and FEDECAMARAS were underway concerning adjustments in unemployment, social security, and other benefits, which have soared as a result of higher unemployment and inflation. Resolution of some issues would necessitate major changes in the 1936 labor law, and as a result, the discussions have gradually expanded to encompass a comprehensive reconsideration of the labor relations system.

Unemployment was officially estimated at 10.9 percent in July 1990, but other sources have constantly estimated the real rate at well over 20 percent. Employment in the "informal sector" was 40.8 percent, a good indication that the latter estimates are much closer to reality. The government feared that 160,000 of the 6.9 million employees in the work force might be laid-off in the aftermath of the expiration of the dismissal freeze in effect between the February 1989 riots and the end of the year. The minister of labor admitted, "We cannot take measures to prevent the continuation of layoffs."[61] The CTV has shown a willingness to negotiate and cooperate with Pérez's administration to promote "concertation" among social sectors, but the severe crisis afflicting its members has also induced an unprecedented degree of militancy shown by CTV leaders toward an *adeco* government. The labor leadership seems to recognize that it ignores the deteriorating situation of its constituency only at grave risk to its own legitimacy.

In 1990, much of the labor movement was engaged in a debate about a proposal, advanced by Rafael Caldera, to replace Venezuela's forty-five-year-old labor law. Caldera's law offers some important tangible benefits for workers, such as doubling severance pay for unjustified dismissals and paid maternity leave for women. FEDECAMARAS has opposed the new law, partly on the basis of these provisions and partly on other grounds, including the claim that it lays the basis for tying wages to inflation—that is, indexing. (Actually, the proposed law only says that presidentially decreed wages should take inflation into account.) But the proposal also has several key provisions that are resisted by the CTV. Perhaps the most important one would allow workers to take money out of their retirement funds, which under the present system are all deposited in the CTV-controlled Venezuelan Workers Bank and are a major source of capital for the labor bureaucracy's economic empire. Many labor leaders also complain that although severance pay is doubled, the law allows employers much wider latitude in dismissing workers without approval of the Labor Ministry. Finally, the *nuevo sindicalismo* leaders have complained that the new law, in addition to making it easier to fire workers, does nothing to promote union democracy and leaves untouched the system of indirect elections through which AD continues to dominate the CTV. In July 1990, the law was still being debated in Congress, its future uncertain.[62]

CONCLUSION

Labor unrest and the "new unionism" are being generated by the same forces that have stimulated other grassroots movements among women, environmentalists, neighborhood residents, peasants, and others. These social movements remain embryonic, but they are clearly growing. What remains in question is whether Venezuela's parties and elites can adopt to increased grassroots militancy. Certainly their response to rank-and-file challenges in the labor movement is not encouraging. But there is a new sense of urgency to reform the system Venezuelans have come to know as *partidocracia*. This was brought into sharp relief by the violent outburst that shook the country during the week of February 27, 1989.

7

February 27, 1989: The Day the Mountains Tumbled

Each evening, at rush hour, tens of thousands of Venezuelans exit the Metro station at Catia and join a queue for the jeep trucks that will return them to their *ranchos* in dozens of barrios perched high above the valley floor in western Caracas. Most have spent their ten-hour workday in the oil-fueled, service-oriented economy, waiting on tables, cleaning office buildings, cleaning and cooking in middle-class homes, selling clothing, making juice in a *Fuente de Soda*, and so on. They wait for an hour, inching forward while tired workers ahead pile onto wooden benches bolted to the sides of the small trucks. The jeeps disappear one after another into the *cerros* covered by crude brick-and-mortar homes piled onto one another, each with a single, bare light bulb shining through the twilight in glassless windows. The barrios get progressively poorer as one ascends the steep mountain roads. As quickly as one jeep departs, another emerges from the cool smog that settles into Caracas every weekday evening.

Twice daily, most working-class *Caraqueños* suffer this commuter endurance test, paying two or three fares each way. Not long ago, the hardships of life in the barrio were made bearable by the hope of a better life for their children, but few share that hope today. In the summer of 1988, most workers were earning far less than when Carlos Andrés Pérez, "*el gocho*" of the Andes, was president the first time. In the next six months, the cost of living would rise another 30 percent while their salaries would remain the same. This reality of falling real wages was being brought home in higher prices for basic commodities and, for the first time in their lifetime, food shortages. Transportation fares had doubled in only five years. Much of the talk on the queues for jeeps was about unemployment and the soaring cost of living.

189

THE RETURN OF CARLOS ANDRÉS PÉREZ

In December 1988, three-quarters of Venezuela's people waited on another type of line—to elect a president and Congress. Despite the bitterness of the campaign, the exercise was peaceful. Most of the electorate apparently thought that Carlos Andrés Pérez, the man who had nationalized the oil industry and presided over the oil bonanza, was the candidate best qualified to restore prosperity and stand up to the international banks for them.

It had been rumored that Pérez would announce during his inaugural speech on February 16, 1989, his intention to align Venezuela more closely with those Latin American nations pressing for concessions on the debt. On this occasion, Fidel Castro would come to Venezuela for the first time in thirty years, a signal perhaps that the new Venezuelan president intended to pursue more nationalistic policies than his predecessor. The United States seemed unconcerned; it sent its lightly regarded vice-president to an inauguration that would be attended by the heads of state of virtually every major country in the hemisphere.

Much about the inauguration ceremony at Caracas's grand Teresa Carreño Theater, across from the gleaming towers of the Hilton Hotel, smacked of power and wealth rather than of democracy or economic crisis.[1] One by one, foreign dignitaries and prominent national politicians filed past rows of cadets at strict attention in their multicolored uniforms, sabres drawn. The murmur of the crowd grew to a growl of thunder as Fidel Castro entered and took his seat. The anticlimactic tone was restored by Interior Minister Octavio Lepage as he intoned the obligatory rehearsal of the glory of the antidictatorial struggle—history as a morality play. The name of Rómulo Betancourt elicited the mandatory acclamation, including polite applause from Fidel.

Finally, at 10:30 A.M., Lusinchi passed the presidential sash to Carlos Andrés Pérez. During the first part of his speech, Pérez discussed international affairs, then he addressed the problem of the debt. "If we do not innovate, we will perish. Utopias lead to bankruptcy. The onerous debt cannot be paid under intolerable conditions." Peru's García stirred. He had innovated, now he was about to perish. The new president offered no further elaboration of how he would "innovate." A journalist later commented:

> In his grand moment of triumph, in front of this constellation of notables, with the fixed attention of an entire country intoxicated by the illusion of change, it would have been in bad taste, politically inconvenient, to have announced the ugly "measures." The raising of prices. The freezing

of salaries. The sacrifices. The burdens. The accord with the IMF. This would come later.[2]

Later the austerity package was announced. The exchange rate would be unified and allowed to float freely, and the scandal-ridden foreign exchange agency, RECADI, would be eliminated. Trade policy would be rationalized—that is, import taxes lowered and simplified. Interest rates would be allowed to rise to market levels after years of controls, an effort to attract foreign investment and to keep more Venezuelan money in national banks. Pérez promised to continue to subsidize mortgages and agricultural loans, but the era of cheap credit for other sectors was over. The fiscal deficit would be cut by freezing public employment, instituting a sales tax, and eliminating certain personal income tax deductions, but business would be allowed greater depreciation rates for active investments. Payments on the external debt would be suspended until September 30, and negotiations for a new US$4.5 billion bridge load would commence. Actually, negotiations were already well underway, and the package of measures were part of understandings already reached.

Some new social measures, including infant day-care centers and increased food programs in the schools, were announced. But with family incomes falling, fewer children were in school anyway. Barrio children were being jettisoned from the educational system into the informal economy, or worse into the streets. Subsidies and regulation of prices for eighteen basic foods and transportation were announced, but the state agency responsible for regulating prices under Lusinchi had virtually ceased to function. Many of the products to be regulated had already disappeared from the grocery shelves, and many residents suspected that merchants were hoarding these products in anticipation of higher prices. What good were regulated prices for goods that no one could find?

The minimum salary would be raised for the poorest urban and rural workers and for the lowest-paid public employees, but there would be no across-the-board increase, as demanded by the CTV—even though the labor movement had been crucial to Pérez's victory in the bitter struggle for the AD nomination. The wage hike recovered for workers approximately what they had lost from the explosive inflation of the last six months of 1988 and early 1989, but real wages were far below their level at the start of Lusinchi's term. By 1990, they would have plunged to the level they were at in 1964.

Additional increases in the cost of living were built into the new measures, including a 50 percent increase in utility prices and a 30 percent raise in transport fares. Gasoline prices were to double, to be followed by two more increases in subsequent years. This was the part of the package that lit the fuse for the social explosion of February 27. Surely, observed some North American reporters afterwards, Venezuelans have been spoiled by the lowest prices on fuel in the world and hardly realize how expensive transportation is in the rest of the world.[3] Obviously, none of these observers had ever ridden a jeep from Catia to a working-class barrio.

THE "27 DE FEBRERO"

Owners of Caracas's buses and *por puestos* (vans), most of whom operate their own vehicles, were unhappy that they were to be allowed an increase of only 30 percent in their fares, while gasoline prices were to double. Their attempt to double fares and refusal to accept 50 percent student discount cards on the morning of Monday, February 27, 1989, proved to be the catalyst for the riots.

The first outbreaks of violence were reported in Guarenas, just outside the Federal District in the state of Miranda. Just how the spark jumped so rapidly to the center of Caracas is not clear, but trouble in the capital began near the central bus station in Nuevo Circo. There, in response to the refusal of drivers to honor their discount cards, a number of students began hurling rocks at passing busses. Soon they were joined by other angry commuters who seized the streets and began to burn some of the vehicles. As though the entire valley had been soaked with gasoline, the violence spread through the Caracas valley and then up the mountainsides into the barrios. Streets were barricaded; buses, automobiles, and vans were burned; stores were looted. As the news spread, nineteen other cities exploded.

Stores where the critical needs of life—clothing, food, tools—were stocked were immediate targets. The people next turned their anger against the shops where just beyond their reach, behind glass, were kept so many of the goods—stereos, appliances, liquor—dangled before their eyes on television. In the barrios themselves, many merchants threw their stores open to the crowds, who usually respected the buildings; looting was sometimes done in shifts, overseen by sympathetic police. However, little respect was shown for merchants and department stores in upper-class, entertainment, and tourist districts or whenever a crowd confirmed that a warehouse or store contained products hoarded in anticipation of price increases.[4]

In Caracas, the Metropolitan Police proved incapable of stemming the rebellion. Many shared with rioters the same conditions of life in the barrios. (In fact, a police strike broke out just a few months later.) Even the National Guard seemed to take the side of the rioters in some instances. Although in some areas police and guardsmen fired on crowds, on the first two days their main purpose seemed to be to regulate rather than to prevent looting. By the end of Tuesday, things seemed to have run their course. Yet at this point Andrés Pérez announced the suspension of constitutional rights (which lasted two months) and a state of siege. However, he combined a carrot with the stick, announcing additional wage increases on the next day. The United States, alarmed at the scale of the explosion in its showcase democracy in South America, announced an emergency bridge loan of $2 billion and promised additional aid. Most people retreated to their homes to put away the food and necessities they had seized and to converse about how these events compared with the last days of Pérez Jiménez or the most intense days of civil war. The emergency seemed to have subsided.

However, the violence was not over. Small bands of delinquents, drug traffickers, and extremists roamed the city, fanning fires figuratively and literally.[5] Smaller shops and restaurants were attacked and set afire. Criminal elements that debased life in the barrio roamed the street without fear of reprisal. On Wednesday, 10,000 troops entered the city and conducted massive sweeps through neighborhoods, confiscating goods whether or not there was reason to believe they had been obtained through looting and arresting tens of thousands. Included in the roundup were community organizers, including several Jesuit priests whose pastoral work had put them at odds with views of police and military officials.

This was the phase of wild rumors about military coups and massacres, and it was also a phase of retribution for some military and police officials. There were reports of snipers and casualties, especially in the massive 23 de enero housing block, renowned for its populist militancy since the days of Pérez Jiménez. It is likely that the military did take casualties from snipers in some neighborhoods; however, there are also well-documented cases in which automatic weapons and light artillery were fired indiscriminately into residential buildings. Many parents would tell of teenagers deliberately shot by soldiers or security police during the "restoration of order."[6]

By the time the violence ended on March 5, no one could doubt the ferocity of the official response. Medical personnel told one reporter that they estimated 1,000 to 1,500 deaths in Caracas alone; even conservative independent estimates placed the number of dead far above the 287 mentioned by the government.[7]

POLITICAL AFTERMATH OF THE RIOTS

President Pérez responded to the violence with political skill. Rather than blame the rioting on guerrillas or leftist extremists, Pérez acknowledged that the rioting was a social response to the austerity measures. He also attempted to restrain the military and security forces, particularly where prominent critics, including educators and clergy, were being abused by overzealous officials. (However, he responded indignantly to a letter of concern from Amnesty International and refused to lift the state of siege for two months.) Later, Pérez announced a four-month freeze on dismissals in response to demands from the CTV. Hence, the riots yielded some immediate concessions for the people, but even as he blasted the banks, Pérez sent representatives of the government to complete final arrangements for the loans along lines already negotiated.[8]

Pérez's temperate response (in contrast to the belligerence of Lusinchi to lesser incidents) was motivated in part by his hope to secure the future cooperation of the CTV, the church, and neighborhood associations in his plan to restructure the economy through *concertación* (concertation).[9] By mid-1990, this had not materialized. The remainder of 1989 saw the extraordinary National Congress of the CTV and the general strike of May 18. The first anniversary of the disturbances were marked by mass demonstrations protesting the dismissal of 60,000 workers after the expiration (in December 1989) of the hiring freeze. Food riots erupted in seven cities, including Caracas. Inflation reached 81 percent in 1989, surpassing by one point the level at which President Pérez had promised to go into voluntary exile. (He didn't.)

Some commentators believe that Pérez's populist campaign rhetoric contributed to the February 27 violence but see the austerity measures announced in February as inescapable, given the debt and the fiscal mess that CAP inherited from Lusinchi. Such an analysis makes sense only if one accepts that there is no way to shift the burden of sacrifice to the rich who exported in the last decade nearly as much money (US$30 billion) as the country owes its foreign creditors (US$32 billion).[10] This may well be an insuperable obstacle, but it is a political one, not an economic one, and it calls into question the character of democracy in Venezuela. The economic package announced by Pérez did not even contemplate a serious tax reform, and the efforts at *concertación* have so far produced little of benefit to workers, whose real wages continue to slip.[11]

If ever a people's rising expectations were being frustrated, Venezuela would seem to be the textbook case. Beginning with Black Friday in 1983, Venezuelans began to suffer directly the consequences of economic mismanagement of the oil boom. For the first time since Gómez, hunger and malnutrition became a reality for hundreds of thousands. Drastic cuts in social services resulted in deteriorating conditions in health and the outbreak of diseases thought to have been long eliminated (e.g., tens of thousands of malaria cases). As jobs, educational opportunities,

and social benefits disappeared, people were faced with increased competition for those that remained. Parents could no longer be optimistic
that their sacrifices would permit their sons and daughters to escape
the *ranchos*.

The middle class—teachers, public employees, technicians, etc.—
has begun to see the looming barrios as its destiny. In contrast, the
view from the barrios high above Caracas is of a glittering valley where
they are permitted to work, but not to share in the wealth. This view
is a daily reminder that the sacrifices demanded from the poor are
substantially greater than those demanded from the rich in *la noche
postpetrolera*. The mass media continue to dangle the luxuries associated
with the era of prosperity before their eyes, and the rich seem to grow
more corrupt and venal with each illegal dollar obtained from RECADI,
sales commissions, or embezzlement. While barrio residents were subjected to abuse by security forces and local gangs, efforts to crackdown
on corruption were met with cries about "judicial uncertainty" when
prominent politicians and businessmen were touched.[12]

The course of political events since February 27 are disturbing. So
far the only type of political action that has effectively wrested concessions
from the government has been violent. The February 27 revolt itself
forced the government to postpone implementation of the austerity plan.
The failure of the government to deliver on its promise to deliver milk
to poor communities at affordable prices led to violence (in May 1990)
and to the decision to import additional supplies. Repeated violent
incidents in June and July resulted in the government postponing gasoline
price hikes. Given the government's response to violence as opposed to
peaceful and legal protest, what are people to conclude?[13]

Revista SIC, the Jesuit journal, charges the nation's politicians with
"abusing the demonstrated loyalty of the Venezuelan people to the
democratic party system." According to the editors, "The party leadership
believed that it could make the client pay without handing over the
goods, that is to say, that it could radically reduce the standards of
living of the population without threatening political stability and without
additional social conflict." To those politicians, like Gonzalo Barrios,
who charge that popular reactions are being orchestrated by "professional
agitators," they respond, "Dr. Barrios himself should remember how
this was used by General López Contreras in 1936 to neutralize the
activities of the self-proclaimed Democratic Left to which, along with
Rómulo Betancourt, Rómulo Gallegos, Luis Beltrán Prieto, Raúl Leoni
. . . etc., belonged. When he tries to defend the established order,
historical memory fails, and historical, intellectual and even political
lucidity is lost."[14]

Military and students battle in Mérida, 1987 (photo by Luis Trujillo)

One peaceful response that bears watching is the experiment underway in the state of Bolívar where the leftist governor, CAUSA R's Andrés Velásquez, has launched an ambitious anticorruption drive based on mobilizing the population. CAUSA R's recent success has depended upon a perception that the party offers something different from the traditional leftist parties, which, like AD and COPEI, have always subordinated unions, neighborhood associations, and other social organizations to their electoral interests. If Velásquez can succeed in maintaining the confidence of the people of his state, he and CAUSA R may be able to muster the same kind of challenge that Ignacio "Lula" da Silva and the Workers Party have mounted in Brazil.

There is a point of convergence in the critique of Venezuelan democracy offered by the neoliberals and the new left. The latter would have little to quarrel with the diagnosis offered by the conservative think tank, VenEconomy:

> Soldiers in the streets. Gasoline prices about to rise. AD on the ropes, while COPEI fumbles for a coherent position. The CTV out of touch with the country's work force and demanding a return to the past. Corruption rewarded and decency punished. Rumors of a possible coup, and hasty assurances by various politicians that there is no danger of a coup, and that everyone loses in a coup. What's happening in Venezuela? Is there really danger of a coup? Not really. But Venezuela's democracy is in urgent

need of a curative. There are cracks running all through the system, and its institutional foundations are crumbling.[15]

It is too soon to write off the power of AD and COPEI, but such circumstances create openings both for popular democrats, like Velásquez, and conservative mavericks, like former General Italo del Valle Alliegro, to contest their grip on the presidency. Venezuelans need only look to recent elections in Brazil and Peru for examples of the latter type of result.

CONCLUSION

The invasion of Kuwait by Iraq in August 1990 touched off a dramatic new hike in crude oil prices. Prices soared to $40 a barrel within weeks, before falling off again to $30 by late November. Just as importantly for Venezuela, the crisis provided an opportunity to drastically increase production. For a brief moment, the government of Pérez expressed sympathy for Iraq's position. After all, Kuwait had been systematically violating OPEC production quotas, and the social and economic structure of Venezuela more closely approximated Iraq than the small emirate. However, the force of U.S. hegemonic power in the hemisphere and the opportunity to gain some economic relief quickly shifted Venezuelan policy. After perfunctory consultation with Saudi Arabia and other OPEC producers, Venezuela announced that it would cooperate in expanding production to meet the shortfall in world supplies caused by the implementation of United Nations sanctions against Iraq and occupied Kuwait.

As might be expected, the sudden rise in oil prices was welcome news to the politically and economically troubled nation, but President Pérez soon made it clear that his embrace of an austere program of economic readjustment, designed to satisfy the conditions laid down by the International Monetary Fund, remained firm. In fact, despite expectations that the Gulf crisis would generate an additional US$2 billion in export earnings, the government admitted it would fall $800 million short on debt obligations due in November 1990.[16] Some additional funds would be spent to ease the plight of the poorest sectors, but within a month of the outbreak of the Persian Gulf crisis, it had become clear that any improvement in economic conditions for the majority of families would have to wait several more years of what Venezuelans bitterly call the "*Pérez truca*" ("Pérez trick").

February 27 will probably stand out in Venezuelan history as an event similar to the massacre of students in the Plaza of Tlalteleco in Mexico City in 1968, that is, as a turning point in which the hegemony of the governing elite can no longer be taken for granted, as the beginning of a longer term historical process of change. Even if AD were to return to its popular roots and offer a more humane and just approach to economic reform, the level of repression may very well grow and threaten the democratic gains made between 1935 and 1958. With the enormous resources of the media and the power of the international banks and corporations behind them, proponents of the neoliberal project have enormous advantages over proponents of the alternative, democratizing project of the new social movements.

Against this pessimism there are those who hold out hope. At a recent forum organized by CAUSA R in Caracas, Matias Camunas, a priest from the working-class barrios of Petare issued this proclamation:

> We cannot design from above a way out of this corrupt system in which people are routinely jailed for standing up for their rights. . . . But with solidarity it is possible to save lives and create conditions for the people themselves to find a way out and solutions to problems. . . . Never will one party, including CAUSA R, be the protagonist of change. We are in a time of new forms of struggle that require new ideas. The people will develop the way out, free of political chiefs, free of the verticalism that characterizes the so-called left in this country."[17]

Only the people can restore lustre to Venezuela's tarnished democracy.

Acronyms

AD	Acción Democrática
ALAMSA	Aluminio Alam S.A.
ARDI	Revolutionary Group of the Left
AVs	Associaciones de Vecinos (Neighborhood Associations)
BTV	Venezuelan Workers Bank
CAP	Carlos Andrés Pérez
COPEI	Independent Political Organizing Committee
COPRE	Commission for Political Reform
CRIAP	Integral Reform of Public Administration
CSE	Supreme Electoral Council
CTV	Confederation of Venezuelan Workers
CUTV	Central United Venezuelan Workers Confederation
DISIP	internal security police
FACUR	Federation of Urban Communities Associations
FALN	Armed Forces of National Liberation
FCV	Venezuelan Peasants Federation
FEDECAMARAS	Federación de Cámaras de Comercio e Industria (Federation of Chambers of Commerce and Industry)
FEV	Federation of Venezuelan Students
FLN	National Liberation Front
FONCAFE	National Coffee Fund
GNP	gross national product
HEVENSA	Hornos Eléctricos de Venezuela, Sociedad Anónima (Electric Ovens of Venezuela S.A.)
IBEC	International Basic Economy Corporation

IESA	Instituto de Estudios Superiores de Administration (Institute of Advanced Studies of Administration)
IMF	International Monetary Fund
JOC	Young Catholic Workers
LIBOR	London Interbank Offered Rate
MAS	Movement for Socialism
MEP	Movimiento Electoral del Puebo (People's Electoral Movement)
MIR	Left Revolutionary Movement
OPEC	Organization of Petroleum Exporting Countries
ORVE	Organization for Venezuela
PCV	Venezuelan Communist Party
PDN	Democratic Nationalist Party
PDVSA	Petroleos de Venezuela, Sociedad Anómina (Petroleum of Venezuela S.A.)
PRV	Venezuelan Revolutionary Party
PTJ	Judicial Technical Police
SIDOR	Siderúrgico de Orinoco (Orinoco Steel)
SUTISS	United Workers in Steel and Similar Industries
UCV	Central University of Venezuela
ULA	University of the Andes
URD	Democratic Republican Union
VIASA	Venezolana Internacional de Aviación, Sociedad Anómina (Venezuelan International Airlines, S.A.)

Notes

CHAPTER 1

1. *El petróleo, un encuentro con nuestro destino* (Caracas: Central Information Office, 1975), pp. 25–26.

2. See Charles Ameringer, "The Foreign Policy of Venezuelan Democracy," in *Venezuela: The Democratic Experience*, ed. John Martz and David Myers (New York: Praeger, 1977), pp. 335–358. The *Report of the Bipartisan Commission on Central America* (Washington, D.C.: U.S. Government Printing Office, 1984), p. 95, cited Venezuela as an "enlightened model" of combining counterinsurgency tactics with political reform. President Vinicio Cerezo of Guatemala, a Christian Democrat, remarked shortly after assuming office that in his country, "Out of violence and repression can come democracy . . . such as happened in Venezuela." See "Excluding Reformists from Power," in *The Central American Crisis*, ed. Kenneth Coleman and George Herring (Wilmington, Del.: Scholarly Resources, 1985), p. 90.

3. See Daniel H. Levine, *Conflict and Political Change in Venezuela* (Princeton: Princeton University Press, 1973), and "Venezuela Since 1958," in *The Breakdown of Democratic Regimes: Latin America*, ed. Juan J. Linz and Alfred Stepan (Baltimore: Johns Hopkins University Press, 1978), pp. 82–109. Charles Anderson, *Politics and Economic Change in Latin America* (Princeton, N.J.: Van Nostrand Company, 1967), pp. 281–289, 310–363. Duarte's remark is reported by Terry Karl, "After La Palma: Christian Democracy, U.S. Policy, and the Prospects for Democratization in El Salvador," *World Policy Journal*, 2 (Summer 1985):309.

4. Cited in Janet Kelly de Escobar, "Las empresas del estado: Del lugar común al sentido común," in *El caso Venezuela, una ilusión de armonía*, ed. Moisés Naím and Ramón Piñango (Caracas: Instituto de Estudios Superiores de Administración, 1985), pp. 131–132.

5. *El Nacional* (Caracas), July 6, 1988.

6. Asdrubal Baptista, "Venezuela, 1975–1981, la cuestión salarial," *Revista SIC*, XLV (December 1982):449–451. On the correlation between oil income and wages, see Norelis Betancourt and Arturo Sosa A., *Realidad social de Venezuela* (Caracas: Centro Gumilla, Curso de Formación Sociopolítica 6, 1985), p. 19. On public total employment, see Héctor Valecillos, "La dinámica de la población y

201

del empleo en la Venezuela del siglo XX," in *El caso Venezuela*, ed. Naím and Piñango, p. 66. Kelly, "Las empresas del estado," p. 135. On the role of parties and the state, see Jennifer L. McCoy, "Labor and the State in a Party-Mediated Democracy: Institutional Change in Venezuela," *Latin America Research Review*, 24 (No. 2, 1989):35–67.

7. Fabricio Ojeda, *El Nacional* (Caracas), March 1, 1989. *El País* (Buenos Aires), March 6, 1989, quoted unofficial estimates of 800. Julie Skurski, an anthropologist from the University of Chicago, cited medical personnel who estimated 1,000 to 1,500 dead in Caracas alone. See Skurski, "Bloody Riots Hit Caracas" and "The Streets Are Quiet but the Crisis Goes On," *The Guardian* (New York), March 16 and April 5, 1989.

8. M. Sanoja and I. Vargas, *Antiguas formaciones y modos de producción venezolanos* (Caracas: Monte Avila, 1974), passim.

9. Federico Brito Figueroa, *História económica y social de Venezuela, Tomo I* (Caracas: Universidad Central de Venezuela, 1975), pp. 156–157. On slavery, see John V. Lombardi, *The Decline and Abolition of Negro Slavery in Venezuela 1820–1854* (Westport, Conn.: Greenwood Publishing, 1971).

10. Visitors to Venezuela are blessed by the existence of a 900-page *Guide to Venezuela*, revised edition, by Janice Bauman and Leni Young (Caracas: Ernesto Armitano, 1987), available in English or Spanish.

11. Susan Berglund and Humberto Hernández Calimán, *Los de Afuera: Un estudio analítico del proceso migratorio en Venezuela, 1936–1985* (Caracas: Centro de Estudio de Pastoral y Asistencia Migratoria, 1985), passim.

12. Bertha Brito, *Los medios de comunicación en Venezuela* (Caracas: Centro Gumilla, Curso de Formación Sociopolítica 26, 1984), pp. 22–23. Quote from Carmelo Vilda, *Proceso de la cultura en Venezuela, III (1935–1985)* (Caracas: Centro Gumilla, Curso de Formación Sociopolítica 31, 1984), p. 32.

13. Actually, Uruguay, where only 72 percent of the population is Catholic, is probably the "least Catholic" Latin American country. Catholic News Service, "Countries with a Catholic Majority," *St. Louis Review*, June 30, 1989.

14. Figures on clergy and impact of the church's new role are from Alberto Micheo, *Estudio histórico de la iglesia Venezolana* (Caracas: Centro Gumilla, Christianismo Hoy no. 1, n.d.), pp. 34–42. For the Caracas survey, see José Virtuoso, "Desafíos pastorales en los sectores urbano-populares," *Revista SIC*, 52 (March 1989):78–81. On the history of the church in Venezuela, see Daniel Levine, *Religion and Politics in Latin America: The Catholic Church in Venezuela and Colombia* (Princeton: Princeton University Press, 1981).

15. *Economic and Social Progress in Latin America* (Washington, D.C.: Inter-American Development Bank, 1988), p. 540.

16. For adaptation of Marx's theory of rent to oil, see Bernard Mommer, *La cuestión petrolera* (Caracas: Fondo Editorial Tropykos, 1988), forthcoming in English as *The Petroleum Question* (Boulder, Colo.: International Research Center for Energy and Economic Development), which has greatly influenced my own views. Ground rent is that portion of surplus value rendered by capitalist tenants to landlords. Differential rent results from differences in productivity arising out of natural variations (e.g., fertility) or improvements made by tenants. Absolute

rent (recognized by Marx, not Ricardo) is defined as the rent extracted by landlords, as a result of their monopoly power, from the least profitable land put into production. Industrial capital is in conflict with landed capital over distribution of differential rent, but absolute rent produces a more antagonistic struggle because it necessarily drives up the cost of production. With the establishment of host countries' right to set reference prices in the 1960s, and with nationalization, the landlord states radically improved their position to collect not only differential rent but also absolute rent. The Organization of Petroleum Exporting Countries (OPEC) must be understood essentially as an instrument of landlord states to maximize absolute rent.

17. The key sources in English on the history of the Venezuelan oil industry are Edwin Lieuwen, *Petroleum in Venezuela: A History* (Berkeley: University of California Press, 1954); Franklin Tugwell *The Politics of Oil in Venezuela* (Palo Alto, Calif.: Stanford University Press, 1975); and Rómulo Betancourt, *Venezuela: Oil and Politics*, trans. Everett Bauman (Boston: Houghton-Mifflin Co., 1979). In Spanish, see Mommer, *La cuestión petrolera;* Angel Márquez, ed., *El imperialismo petrolero y la revolución venezolana, tomo 2, las ganancias extraordinarias y la soberanía nacional* (Caracas: Editorial Ruptura, 1977); Luis Pedro España N., *Democracia y renta petrolera* (Caracas: Universidad Católica Andrés Bello, 1989).

18. More kind to Gómez is B. S. McBeth, *Juan Vicente Gómez and the Oil Companies in Venezuela, 1908–1935* (Cambridge: Cambridge University Press, 1983). While perceptive about the objective limitations that any government would have faced, McBeth's analysis fails to recognize that even within these limits, the class biases and corruption of the regime were factors in weakening Venezuela's initial response to the arrival of the companies.

19. The classic expression of this consciousness is Rómulo Betancourt, *Plan de Barranquilla,* written in 1931 and reproduced in Arturo Sosa and Eloi Lengrand, *Del garibaldismo estudiantil a la izquierda criolla: Los orígenes marxistas del proyecto de A.D. (1928–1935)* (Caracas: Ediciones Centauro, 1981), pp. 455–468.

20. Naím and Piñango, ed., *El caso Venezuela.* Aníbal Romero, *La miseria del populismo: Mitos y realidades de la democracia en Venezuela* (Caracas: Ediciones Centauro, 1987). Alfredo Castro, ed., *1984: ¿A dónde va Venezuela?* (Caracas: Editorial Planeta, 1984).

21. Robert Bottome, José Antonio Gil Yepes, and John Sweeney, *Economic Outlook for Venezuela, 1987–1992, Update* (Caracas: VenEconomy, February 1988), p. 21.

CHAPTER 2

1. Arturo Sosa A., S.J., *Colonia y emancipación en Venezuela (1498–1830)* (Caracas: Centro Gumilla, Curso de Formación Sociopolítica 2, 1978), pp. 2–3.

2. Concise histories of Venezuela in English include John V. Lombardi, *Venezuela, the Search for Order, the Dream of Progress* (New York: Oxford University Press, 1982) and Judith Ewell, *Venezuela: A Century of Change* (Stanford, Calif.: Stanford University Press, 1984). Federico Brito Figueroa's four-volume *Historia económica y social de Venezuela* (Caracas: Universidad Central de Venezuela, 1975) provides a comprehensive social and economic history of the country.

3. Sosa, *Colonia y emancipación*, p. 16.

4. Daniel Levine, *Religion and Politics in Latin America* (Princeton: Princeton University Press, 1989), pp. 58–59.

5. Sosa, *Colonia y emancipación*, pp. 20–39. See also Brito Figueroa, *Historia económica y social*, I, pp. 159–288. For a brief summary of the independence war and Bolívar's role, see Benjamin Keen and Mark Wasserman, *A History of Latin America*, 3rd edition (Boston: Houghton Mifflin, 1988), pp. 157–161.

6. The key source on slavery in Venezuela is John V. Lombardi, *The Decline and Abolition of Negro Slavery in Venezuela 1820–1854* (Westport, Conn.: Greenwood Publishing, 1971). All estimates of population figures are suspect, but figures are given in Miguel Izard, *Series estadísticas para la historia de Venezuela* (Mérida: Universidad de los Andes, 1970), p. 9. The estimate of slaves is taken from Lombardi, *Negro Slavery in Venezuela*, p. 35, who cites Alexander von Humboldt, *Viaje a las regiones equinocciales del nuevo continente* . . ., 2nd edition (Caracas: Ediciones de Ministerio de Educación, 1956).

7. María Gabriela Troconis, *Venezuela republicana, siglo XIX* (Caracas: Centro Gumilla, Curso de Formación Sociopolítica 3, 1988), pp. 4–9.

8. Robert L. Gilmore, *Caudilloism and Militarism in Venezuela, 1810–1910* (Athens: University of Ohio Press, 1964), p. 47.

9. Ibid., p. 71.

10. Robert Paul Matthews, *Violencia rural en Venezuela, 1840–1858: Antecedentes socio-económicos de la guerra federal* (Caracas: Monte Avila Editores, 1977), pp. 39–60.

11. John V. Lombardi, "The Patterns of Venezuela's Past," in *Venezuela, The Democratic Experience*, ed. John Martz and David Myers (New York: Praeger, 1977), p. 11.

12. Bolívar quote is translated from his letter to Sr. Coronel Patricia Campbell, August 5, 1829, in *Simón Bolívar, Documento: Los orígenes de la dependencia neocolonial* (Bogatá: Frente de Estudios Sociales, n.d.) p. 216. Ali Primera, "Canción Bolivariana," from the album *Abrebrecha* (Caracas: Promus, cigarron, 50020, n.d.).

13. Troconis, *Venezuela republicana*, pp. 18–19.

14. Ramón Valoz, *Economía y finanzas de Venezuela desde 1830 hasta 1944* (Caracas: Impresores Unidos, 1945), cited in Luis Ugalde, *Venezuela republicana, siglo XIX* (Caracas: Centro Gumilla, Curso de Formación Sociopolítica 3, 1978), p. 7. This work is an update of Troconis, *Venezuela republicana*.

15. Ugalde, *Venezuela republicana, siglo XIX*, pp. 29–30. Matthews, *Violencia rural en Venezuela*, pp. 39–60.

16. Ugalde, *Venezuela republicana, siglo XIX*, p. 29. Izard, *Series estadísticas*, p. 213.

17. For example, see Eveling Bravo and Napoleon Franceschi, *Problemas de historia de Venezuela contemporánea* (Valencia: Vadell Hermanos, 1980), pp. 151–179.

18. Ibid., p. 157. Troconis, *Venezuela republicana*, p. 31.

19. Quoted in Ugalde, *Venezuela republicana, siglo XIX*, p. 31.

20. Troconis, *Venezuela republicana*, pp. 36–40.

21. Susan Berglund, "Las bases sociales y económicas de las leyes de inmigración venezolanas, 1831–1935," *Boletín de la Academia Nacional de la Historia*, 65 (No. 260, 1982):951–962.

22. Troconis, *Venezuela republicana*, pp. 44. Quote from Ewell, *Venezuela: A Century of Change*, p. 20.

23. This section draws heavily on Ewell, *Venezuela: A Century of Change*, pp. 31–35, and Carmelo Vilda, *Proceso de la cultura de Venezuela, I y II* (Caracas: Centro Gumilla, Curso de Formación Sociopolítica 29 and 30, 1983).

24. Calculated from data in Brito Figueroa, *Historia económica y social de Venezuela, I*, p. 296.

25. Izard, *Series estadísticas*, pp. 213–214.

26. Emelio Pacheco, *De Castro a López Contreras* (Caracas: Editorial Domingo Fuentes, 1984), pp. 16–25.

27. Manuel Caballero, "El hombre Gómez: Un retrato enemigo," in *Juan Vicente Gómez y su época*, ed. Elías Pino Iturrieta (Caracas: Monte Avila Editores, 1988), pp. 11–23. Rosalba Méndez, "¿Gómez, un periodo histórico?" in ibid., pp. 33–34. Ramón Velásquez, *La caída de liberalismo amarillo: Tiempo y drama de Antonio Paredes*, 2nd edition (Caracas: Talleres Cromotip, 1973) and his prologues to *El pensamiento político venezolano del siglo XX: Documentos para estudio*, volume 1, *El pensamiento político de la restauración liberal*, and volume 2–A, *La oposición a la dictadura de Cipriano Castro* (Caracas: Congreso de la República, 1983). Domingo Alberto Rangel, *Los Andinos al Poder* (Mérida: Talleres Gráficos Universitarios, 1965).

28. Pacheco, *De Castro a López Contreras*, p. 22.

29. Ibid., pp. 20–21. Ewell, *Venezuela: A Century of Change*, p. 39.

30. Izard, *Series estadísticas*, pp. 168, 184–185, 213–214.

31. For a description of events, see Velásquez, *Pensamiento político*, volume 2–A, xxii–xxxi; Bravo and Franceschi, *Problemas de historia*, pp. 236–238, 250.

32. Rómulo Betancourt, *Venezuela: Oil and Politics*, trans. Everett Bauman (Boston: Houghton Mifflin, 1979), p. 12.

33. Ibid, p. 9.

34. Angel Zeims, "Un ejército de alcance nacional," pp. 121–131 in *Juan Vicente Gómez y su época*, ed. Pino Iturrieta.

35. "Alocución en el Campo de Carabobo," in *El pensamiento político, 7, Los pensadores positivistas y el gomecismo* (Caracas: Congreso de la República, 1973), pp. 403–404.

36. Pacheco, pp. 44–47; Irene Rodríguez Gallad, "Perfil de la economía venezolana durante el régimen gomecista," in *Juan Vicente Gómez y su época*, ed. Pino Iturrieta, p. 87.

37. See Arturo Sosa A., S.J., *La filosofía política del Gomecismo: Estudio del pensamiento de Laureano Vallenilla Lanz* (Barquisimeto: Centro Gumilla, 1974).

38. Cited in Caballero, "El hombre Gómez," p. 20.

39. Ramón J. Velásquez, *Confidencias imaginarias de Juan Vicente Gómez* (Caracas: Ediciones Centauro, 1981), quoted by Bautista Urbaneja, "El sistema politica gomecista," in *Juan Vicente Gómez y su época*, ed. Pino Iturrieta, p. 58. See also Caballero, "El hombre Gómez," pp. 11–23, and Pacheco, *De Castro a*

López Contreras, pp. 20–48, on the construction of the centralized state and army and on the dominance of the Andinos. Also, Domingo Alberto Rangel, *Los andinos en el poder* (Mérida: Talleres Gráphicos, 1966).

40. Izard, *Series estadísticas*, p. 200.

41. *El pensamiento político, 6, Los pensadores positivistas*, pp. 191–193.

42. Caballero, "El hombre Gómez," p. 19. Méndez, "¿Gómez, un periodo historico?" p. 29.

43. Angel Márquez, ed., *El imperialismo petrolero y la revolución venezolana, tomo 2, Las ganancias extraordinarias y la soberanía nacional* (Caracas: Editorial Ruptura, 1977).

44. See Bernard Mommer, *La cuestión petrolera* (Caracas: Editorial Tropykos, 1986), pp. 61–73.

45. Ibid., pp. 73–84. Bravo and Franceschi, *Problemas de historia*, pp. 264–267, quote on p. 265.

46. Alberto Adriani, *Labor venezolanista* (Caracas: Academia Nacional de Ciencias Económicas, 1984), pp. 187–297.

47. This phrase was popularized by Pietri, a distinguished novelist and prominent spokesperson for Venezuelan business interests, in 1936. See his book, first published in 1949, *De una a otra Venezuela* (Caracas: Monte Avila Editores, 1977). On economic elites, see Ewell, *Venezuela: A Century of Change*, p. 51.

48. For the complete text, see Arturo Sosa A. and Eloi Lengrand, *Del garibaldismo estudiantil a la izquierda criolla: Los orígenes marxistas del proyecto de A.D. (1928–1935)* (Caracas: Ediciones Centauro, 1981), pp. 498–501. This work constitutes an important revisionist study of how Marxism influenced the thought of Betancourt.

CHAPTER 3

1. The most complete biography of Betancourt is Robert Alexander's sympathetic *Rómulo Betancourt and the Transformation of Venezuela* (New Brunswick, N.J.: Transaction Books, 1982).

2. Ibid., p. 37.

3. The phrase was used by Betancourt in an article in *Trabajo*, San José, Costa Rica, February 17, 1934. This theme is explored by Arturo Sosa and Eloi Lengrand in *Del garibaldismo estudiantil a la izquierda criolla: Los orígenes marxistas del proyecto de A.D. (1928–1935)* (Caracas: Ediciones Centauro, 1981), especially p. 114.

4. Quoted in Alexander, *Rómulo Betancourt*, p. 44. Other major works on AD tend to accept Betancourt's account at face value as well. For example, see John Martz's influential *Acción Democrática: Evolution of a Modern Political Party in Venezuela* (Princeton: Princeton University Press, 1966), especially p. 25.

5. The key sources on Betancourt during this period are Sosa and Lengrand, *Del garibaldismo estudiantil* and Alejandro Gómez, *Rómulo Betancourt y el Partido Comunista de Costa Rica: 1931–1935* (Caracas: Universidad Central de Venezuela, 1985).

6. Gómez, *Rómulo Betancourt y el Partido Comunista de Costa Rica*, p. 11.

7. Sosa and Lengrand, *Del garibaldismo estudiantil*, p. 122.

8. Alexander, *Rómulo Betancourt*, p. 64.

9. Excerpted from "Declaración hecha por las señoras A. de Muñoz Ruida y L. de Negretti sobre los sucesos ocurridos en la hacienda 'San Henrique'," *El Universal*, reprinted in *El pensamiento político del siglo XX: El debate político en 1936* (Caracas: Congreso de La República, 1983), pp. 121–126.

10. Kevin Singh, "Oil Politics in Venezuela during the López Contreras Administration," *Journal of Latin American Studies*, 21 (February 1989):89–95.

11. See John Duncan Powell, *Political Mobilization of the Venezuelan Peasant* (Cambridge: Harvard University Press, 1971), pp. 1–99.

12. About one-fourth of these essays are collected in Betancourt, *Problemas Venezolanas* (Santiago: Imprenta y Editorial Futuro, 1940). However, many important essays of the period are not included, for example, a column effusively praising Adriani in *Ahora*, August 12, 1937.

13. Especially representative is his column in *Ahora*, May 21, 1939.

14. *Ahora*, February 9, July 19 and 25, 1937; February 11, March 19, October 1, 1938; August 12, 1939.

15. *Ahora*, September 20, 1938; August 24 and 31, 1939.

16. For the evolution of Betancourt's views, contrast the article in *Ahora* on January 18, 1937, with those on February 11, 1937, February 2, 1938, and August 24, 1938. Also, Steven Ellner, *Los partidos políticos y su disputa por el control del movimiento sindical en Venezuela, 1936–1948* (Caracas: Universidad Andres Bello, 1980), pp. 54–94.

17. On import substitution, see *Ahora*, October 3, 1938, and January 18, 1939. On the Venezuelan bourgeoisie, see *Ahora*, January 25 and March 21, 1939.

18. See the defense of a peasant league's struggle in Aragua, in *Ahora*, July 18, 1938. See also *Ahora*, September 11, 1939, on parcelization; January 7, 1939, on *ejidos;* January 18, 1939, on the need for tariff protection and credits to agriculture.

19. See Betancourt's commentaries on various strikes in *Ahora*, May 23, August 8, September 20 and 21, November 16 and 26, 1938; September 21, 1939. In every case Betancourt focuses not on the issues or what is needed to force concessions from employers but on the desirability of the state intervention to resolve the dispute.

20. See *Ahora*, February 11, August 5, and December 10, 1938.

21. *Ahora*, March 23, 1939.

22. See Fernando Henrique Cardoso and Enzo Faletto, *Dependency and Development in Latin America*, trans. Marjory Mattingly Urquidi (Berkeley: University of California, 1979), where they discuss the idea of "associated dependent development."

23. On the competition between the AD and its bourgeois opposition see Alexander, *Rómulo Betancourt*, pp. 229–234, 248–250, and Rómulo Betancourt, *Venezuela, Oil and Politics*, trans. Everett Bauman (Boston: Houghton Mifflin Company, 1979), pp. 109–123, 235–249. One Communist who maintained a friendship with Betancourt despite the latter's anticommunist stance is Juan

Bautista Fuenmayor; see his *1928–1948, Veinte años de política* (Madrid: Editorial Mediterráneo, n.d.), pp. 271–355, and *Historia de la Venezuela política contemporánea, 1899–1969,* IV (Caracas, 1976). Arturo Sosa A. provides a useful, brief summary from a nonpartisan point of view in *Democracia y dictadura en la Venezuela del siglo XX* (Caracas: Centro Gumilla, Curso de Formación Sociopolítica 5, 1979), pp. 22–25. Perhaps the best account of the conflict is to be found in Andrés Stambouli, *Crisis política: Venezuela, 1945–1948* (Caracas: Editorial Ateneo, 1980), pp. 41–84.

24. A summary of the *trienio* record can be found in Alexander, *Rómulo Betancourt,* pp. 224–279.

25. A valuable study of the relationship between the peasant movement and urban reformers is Powell, *Political Mobilization of the Venezuelan Peasant.* Figures on union organizing, based on Ministry of Labor data, are presented on page 79.

26. Alexander, *Rómulo Betancourt,* pp. 224–279.

27. Betancourt, *Venezuela, Oil and Politics,* pp. 163–164. Any interpretation of the *trienio* involves a walk through a political and historical minefield, but even radical North American scholarship tends to accept the *trienio* regime as a revolutionary era. See, for example, James Petras, Morris Morley, and James Smith, *The Nationalization of Venezuelan Oil* (New York: Praeger, 1977). Recent Venezuelan historiography challenges this interpretation. See, for example, Sosa and Lengrand, *Del garibaldimo estudiantil;* Mommer, *La cuestión petrolera;* and Manuel Rodríguez Campos, *Venezuela 1948–1958, El proceso económico y social de la dictadura* (Caracas: Alianza Gráfica Editorial, 1983), which despite the title discusses the era extensively.

28. Samuel Moncada, "La contratación colectiva en la industria petrolera, 1945–1946," p. 357 in Alberto J. Pla et al., *Clase obrera: Partidos y sindicatos en Venezuela* (Caracas: Ediciones Centauro, 1982).

29. This is the main theme of Ellner, *Los partidos políticos.* See also Charles Bergquist's *Labor in Latin America: Comparative Essays on Chile, Argentina, Venezuela, and Colombia* (Stanford, Calif.: Stanford University Press, 1986), pp. 191–273.

30. Wanda M. Jablonski, "Report on Venezuela," *New York Journal of Commerce* (September 20, 1948), p. 3.

31. *Papers Relating to the Foreign Relations of the United States* (Washington, D.C.: Department of State, 1948), p. 776.

32. Ellner, *Los partidos políticos,* pp. 112–120, 136–144.

33. See Arturo Sosa A., *Pensamiento educativo de Acción Democrática: raíces e ideas básicas (1936–1948)* (Caracas: Central de Reflexión y Planificación Política, 1984); on opposition tactics during the *trienio,* see Stambouli, *Crisis política,* pp. 41–84.

34. Stambouli, *Crisis política,* pp. 41–84.

35. Stambouli, *Crisis política,* pp. 59–84.

36. Quoted, ibid., p. 80.

37. See Winfield J. Burggraaff, *The Venezuelan Armed Forces in Politics, 1935–1959* (Columbia: University of Missouri Press, 1972), pp. 79–111.

38. This interpretation is close to that of Rodríguez Campos in *Venezuela, 1948–1958;* however, neither he nor any other scholar has provided a definitive

account of the military conspiracy or how Pérez Jiménez consolidated power. Stambouli, in *Crisis política*, pp. 70–86, emphasizes the destabilization caused by AD's mobilization of mass support during the *trienio*. Sosa, in *Democracia y dictadura*, p. 25, hypothesizes that the military conspirators of 1945 aspired to political power never conceded to them by AD, a view that finds some support in Burggraaff, *The Venezuelan Armed Forces*, pp. 52–111, who stresses the influence of Cold War international politics on the military. On the attitude of State Department officials in Washington and Caracas, see Stephen G. Rabe, *The Road to OPEC, United States Relations with OPEC, 1919–1976* (Austin: University of Texas Press, 1982), pp. 112–116.

39. Rodríguez Campos, *Venezuela, 1948–1958*, p. 194. A few progressive capitalists, notably Eugenio Mendoza, who would emerge as leader of the business community again in 1958, were more friendly to the regime. See Terry Karl, "Petroleum and Political Pacts: The Transition to Democracy in Venezuela," *Latin American Research Review*, 22, (No. 1 1987):74.

40. For example, see Peter Odell, *Oil and World Power*, 7th edition (New York: Penguin Books, 1983), p. 76; Karl, in "Petroleum and Political Pacts," p. 75, claims that the companies feared nationalization.

41. See Bernard Mommer and Asdrúbal Baptista, "La capacidad de absorción de capital en el pensamiento económico Venezolano," (Proyecto PDVSA-IESA, mimeo, 1985). An exception among Venezuelan nationalists was Salvador De la Plaza, an independent communist thinker whose ideas were not widely embraced by the party. See, for example, *El petróleo en la vida venezolana* (unpublished manuscript, University of the Andes, Mérida, circa 1964).

42. See John J. Johnson, *Political Change in Latin America: The Emergence of the Middle Sectors* (Stanford, Calif.: Stanford University Press, 1958).

43. See Daniel C. Hellinger, "Populism and Nationalism in Venezuela: New Perspectives on Acción Democrática," *Latin American Perspectives*, 11 (Fall 1984):33–59. Another exception is that of Cárdenas and the PRI in Mexico.

44. Miguel Izard, *Series estadísticas para la historia de Venezuela* (Mérida: Universidad de los Andes, 1970), pp. 216–217.

45. According to Betancourt in *Ahora* (February 2, 1939).

46. See *Petróleo, renta del suelo e historia* (Mérida: CORPOANDES, 1983), pp. 25–34.

47. Besides Betancourt, *Venezuela, Oil and Politics*, the most authoritative source on *adeco* oil policy is Juan Pablo Peréz Alfonzo, *Petróleo y dependencia* (Caracas: Sintesis Dosmil, 1971). For a critique of AD's 50/50 policy, see Mommer, *La cuestión petrolera*, pp. 84–96; Angel Márquez, ed., *El imperialismo petrolero y la revolución venezolana, tomo II, las ganancias extraordinarias y la soberanía nacional*, (Caracas: Editorial Ruptura, 1977), pp. 183–232; Dorothea Mommer, *El estado venezolano y la industria petrolera* (Caracas: Universidad Central de Venezuela, 1974). I have reviewed much of this literature in "Populism and Nationalism in Venezuela."

48. Dorothea Mommer, *El estado venezolano*, pp. 29–33, and Bernard Mommer, *La cuestión petrolera*, pp. 84–96.

49. Márquez, *Las ganancias*, pp. 183–232.

50. Mommer, *La cuestión petrolera,* pp. 93–94. See also "Creole in Operation," *Fortune* (February 1949), pp. 180–183.

51. Mommer, *La cuestión petrolera,* pp. 93–94.

52. Luis Pedro España, *Venezuela y su petróleo, I* (Caracas: Curso de Formacíon Sociopolítica 10, 1988), p. 25.

53. Arturo Uslar Pietri, *De una a otra Venezuela,* (Caracas: Monte Avila Editores, third printing, 1972), p. 63.

54. The views of Betancourt, Uslar Pietri, and Pérez Alfonso are analyzed in España, *Venezuela y su petróleo,* and in Ramón Espinasa and Bernardo Mommer, "De una a otra Venezuela," *Revista SIC,* 50 (December 1987):477–481.

55. The compromising attitudes of the leftist politicians emerged early. On January 23, 1936, an *Ahora* editorial acknowledged that López Contreras had failed to concede enough to workers in his imposed settlement. However, it also argued, "Nevertheless, this decision ought to be obeyed because through it the Venezuelan worker may be able, invoking the authority of law, to demand and achieve more significant conquests." On February 14, an *Ahora* editorial explicitly repudiated using the strike as an instrument of political struggle.

56. Héctor Lucena, *El movimiento obrero petrolero, proceso de formación y desarrollo* (Caracas: Ediciones Centauro, 1982), pp. 196–223. See reports of communiques from the Frente Sindical de Trabajadores in *Ahora,* February 1 and 6, 1936, for examples of labor leaders' discontent with the Labor Law.

57. The best description of AD and Communist competition is Ellner, *Los partidos políticos.* See his detailed account of the 1944 Congress and careful research on the impact of Medina's dissolution of unions and *adeco* policy during the *trienio* on pp. 59–144.

58. This model is more fully spelled out in Cardoso and Faletto, *Dependency and Development in Latin America.*

59. Antonio Gramsci, *The Prison Notebooks and Other Writings,* trans. and ed. Quintin Hoare and Geoffery Nowell Smith (New York: International Publishers, 1971), p. 16.

60. Sosa, *Democracia y dictadura,* p. 25.

61. To summarize cultural trends, I have relied heavily on Carmelo Vilda, *Proceso de la cultura en Venezuela, III* (Caracas: Centro Gumilla, 1984). Data and descriptions of change are from this pamphlet unless otherwise indicated. The 1988 rate of urbanization is from the World Bank, *World Development Report 1988* (New York: Oxford University Press, 1989), Table 1. For a history rich with cultural commentary, see Judith Ewell, *Venezuela: A Century of Change* (Stanford, Calif.: Stanford University Press, 1984).

62. World Bank, *World Development Report 1984,* (New York: Oxford University Press), p. 262. Earlier data from Rodríguez Campos, *Venezuela 1948–1958,* p. 166.

63. Juan Liscano, *Venezuela Moderna* (Caracas: Fundación Eugenio Mendoza, 1976), quoted in Vilda, *Proceso de la cultura,* p. 3.

64. Vilda, *Proceso de la cultura,* pp. 16–18.

65. Daniel F. Sullivan, "Advertising in Venezuela," *Venezuela Newsletter* (June 15, 1947):2. Sullivan was director of Advertising for the New York-based Spool Cotton Company.

66. Vilda, *Proceso de la cultura.*

67. Ibid., pp. 10–11. An *adeco* account of the role of intellectuals, including Gallegos, within AD is *Acción Democrática y la cultura* (Caracas: Ediciones Centauro, 1977). Less partisan interpretations are Juan Liscano, *Rómulo Gallegos y su tiempo* (Caracas: Monte Avila Editores, 1980) and Harrison Sabin Howard, *Rómulo Gallegos y la revolución burguesa en Venezuela* (Caracas: Monte Avila Editores, 1977).

68. Mario Briceño Iragorri, *Mensaje sin Destino* (Caracas: Monte Avila, 1980), p. 80, quoted in Vilda, *Proceso de la cultura,* pp. 9–10.

69. Vilda, *Proceso de la cultura,* p. 10.

70. Ibid., pp. 28–30.

71. Ibid., pp. 26–28.

CHAPTER 4

1. There is a large corpus of highly partisan memoirs. The most important are Juan Bautista Fuenmayor, *1928–1948, Veinte años de política* (Madrid: Editorial Mediterráneo, n.d.) and his more extensive *Historia de la Venezuela política contemporánea, 1899–1969* (Caracas, various volumes and years); Rómulo Betancourt, *Venezuela, Oil and Politics,* trans. Everett Bauman (Boston: Houghton Mifflin Company, 1979).

2. See Wilfred Burggraaff, *The Venezuelan Armed Forces in Politics, 1935–1959* (Columbia: University of Missouri Press, 1972), pp. 118–127. The circumstantial evidence that implicates Pérez Jiménez in the murder of Carlos Delgado Chalbaud is summarized by Betancourt in *Venezuela, Oil and Politics,* pp. 252–255. Burggraaff finds more room for doubt than Betancourt in this regard.

3. Andrés Stambouli, *Crisis Política: Venezuela, 1945–1948* (Caracas: Editorial Ateneo, 1980), pp. 94–95.

4. Ibid., pp. 94–96. Betancourt, *Venezuela, Oil and Politics,* pp. 261–263.

5. See, for example, David Blank, *Politics in Venezuela* (Boston: Little, Brown, 1973), pp. 125–158 and John Martz, *Acción Democrática* (Princeton: Princeton University Press, 1966), pp. 193–223.

6. See Stambouli, *Crisis política;* Manuel Rogríguez Campos, *Venezuela, 1948–1958* (Caracas: Alianza Gráfica Editorial, 1983); and Arturo Sosa A., *Democracia y dictadura en la Venezuela del siglo XX* (Caracas: Centro Gumilla, Curso de Formación Sociopolítica 5, 1979).

7. See Federico Brito Figueroa, *Historia económica y social de Venezuela III,* (Caracas: Universidad Central de Venezuela, 1975), pp. 816–819. Carmelo Vilda, *Proceso de la cultura de Venezuela, 1935–85* (Caracas: Centro Gumilla, Curso de Formación Sociopolítica 31, 1984), pp. 7–8.

8. The key source on immigration is Susan Berglund and Humberto Hernández Calimán, *Los de afuera: Un estudio analítico del proceso migratorio en Venezuela, 1936–1985* (Caracas: Centro de Estudios de Pastoral y Assistencia Migratoria, 1985). Research on Venezuelan immigration is summarized in Daniel Hellinger "Venezuelan Immigration Policy and Politics," in *The Gatekeepers,*

Comparative Immigration Policy, ed. Michael LeMay (New York: Praeger, 1989), pp. 155–184.

9. On use of chemicals, see data cited in Rodríguez Campos, *Venezuela, 1948–1958,* p. 132. On construction and its impact on the social structure, see Clemy Machado de Acedo, Elena Plaza, and Emilio Pacheco, *Estado y grupos económicos en Venezuela* (Caracas: Editorial Ateneo de Caracas, 1981). On housing, see *América Latina en cifras,* (New York: CEPAL, 1973) and Rodríguez Campos, p. 53.

10. Acedo et al., *Estado y groupos económicos,* p. 160.

11. The extent of insecurity experienced by capitalists in the latter days of the regime is indicated by various testimonies that appeared in newspapers in 1958, quoted in Rodríguez Campos, *Venezuela, 1948–1958,* pp. 233–236.

12. Ibid., p. 53. All data cited from this source are originally from Central Bank annual reports.

13. Ibid., pp. 49–55.

14. Ibid., pp. 46–51.

15. See analysis and data cited by M. Ignacio Purroy, *Estado e industrialización en Venezuela* (Valencia: Vadell Hermanos, 1982), pp. 162–179.

16. Rodríguez Campos, *Venezuela, 1948–1958,* pp. 72 and 166.

17. Ibid., pp. 57–64.

18. Ibid., p. 230.

19. Domingo Alberto Rangel, *La oligarquía del dinero* (Valencia: Vadell Hermanos, 1971).

20. Except where noted, the account of the fall of Pérez Jiménez draws upon Rodríguez Campos, *Venezuela, 1948–1958* and Stambouli, *Crisis política.*

21. Betancourt denied that Mendoza was a part of the political negotiations, but Terry Karl has confirmed his role. See Terry Karl, "Petroleum and Political Pacts: The Transition to Democracy in Venezuela," *Latin American Research Review,* 22 (No. 1, 1987):79.

22. Robert Alexander, *Rómulo Betancourt and the Transformation of Venezuela* (New Brunswick, N.J.: Transaction Books, 1982), p. 335.

23. Karl, "Petroleum and Political Pacts," p. 81.

24. See Karl, "Petroleum and Political Pacts," and Jennifer McCoy, "Labor and the State in a Party-Mediated Democracy: Institutional Change in Venezuela," *Latin American Research Review,* 24 (No. 2, 1989):39–44.

25. Quoted and cited in Luigi Valsalice, *La guerrilla castrista en Venezuela y sus protagonistas, 1962–1969* (Caracas: Ediciones Centauro, 1979), pp. 27–28, 59.

26. The clearest exposition is Robert Alexander, *Rómulo Betancourt,* pp. 465–501, a chapter entitled "Constitutonal President: Preventing and Suppressing Subversion."

27. Quoted in Pedro España, "30 años de 'vida nacional'," *Revista SIC 50* (December 1987):564.

28. Betancourt, *Venezuela, Oil and Politics,* p. 260.

29. Ibid., p. 382.

30. On the break with Cuba, see Betancourt, *Venezuela, Oil and Politics,* p. 396, and Alexander, *Rómulo Betancourt,* pp. 400–501, both unfriendly to the

Cuban view. Friendly to Cuba is Manuel Caballero, *Rómulo Betancourt* (Caracas: Ediciones Centauro, 1979), pp. 110–120. More balanced are Valsalice's valuable *La guerrilla castrista en Venezuela*; Carlos A. Romero, *Política exterior de Venezuela* (Caracas: Centro Gumilla, Curso de Formación Sociopolítica 24, 1984); and Elena Plaza, *Historia de la lucha armada en Venezuela, 1960–1969* (Caracas: Centro Gumilla, Curso de Formación Sociopolítica 16, n.d., probably 1976).

31. Angel Márquez, ed., *El imperialismo petrolero y la revolución venezolana, tomo 2, las ganancias extraordinarias* (Caracas: Editorial Ruptura, 1977), pp. 288–292.

32. Ibid., pp. 299–317.

33. See Bernard Mommer, *La cuestión petrolera* (Caracas: Editorial Tropykos, 1988), pp. 137–148.

34. Ibid. Márquez, *Las ganancias extraordinarias*, p. 311.

35. A review and analysis of these developments can be found in Mommer, *La cuestión petrolera*, pp. 114–199.

36. Dorothea Mommer, *El estado venezolano y la industria petrolera* (Caracas: Universidad Central de Venezuela, 1974), pp. 30 and 34.

37. Rodríguez Campos, *Venezuela, 1948–1958*, pp. 40–43. Pérez Jiménez did create a state steel corporation, Siderúrgico de Orinoco (SIDOR), but it also developed links of dependence with foreign capital. (See Chapters 5 and 6.)

38. Sergio Aranda, *La economía venezolana*, 2nd edition (Caracas: Editorial Pomaire, 1984), pp. 190–198.

39. Luis Ugalde, *Análisis económico de Venezuela, II* (Caracas: Centro Gumilla, Curso de Formación Sociopolítica 9), pp. 6–7.

40. This data and analysis are found in M. Ignacio Purroy, *Estado e industrialización*, pp. 161–254. See also Ugalde, *Análisis económico*, passim, and Aranda, *La economía venezolana*, pp. 181–230.

41. Purroy, *Estado e industrialización*, pp. 187–203. Ugalde, *Análisis económico*, pp. 7–8.

42. Ugalde, *Análisis económico de Venezuela, II*, pp. 7–8.

43. Aranda, *La economía venezolana*, pp. 220–224.

44. Ugalde, *Análisis económico*, pp. 9–10.

45. Purroy, *Estado e industrialización*, pp. 163 and 173. Ugalde, ibid., pp. 8–10. The government report was reprinted as "Informe Merhav" in *Resumen*, (Caracas), Sept. 21, 1980. The author of the report was Israeli economist Meir Merhav.

46. Aranda, *La economía venezolana*, ibid., pp. 221–222. Alexander, *Rómulo Betancourt*, pp. 502–505.

47. John Duncan Powell, *Political Mobilization of the Venezuelan Peasant* (Cambridge: Harvard University Press, 1971), p. 109.

48. Ibid., p. 113.

49. Ibid.

50. Alberto Micheo, *La agricultura en Venezuela* (Caracas: Centro Gumilla, Curso de Formación Sociopolítica 12, 1987), pp. 14–18.

51. Calculated from Central Bank data presented by Aranda in *La economía venezolana*, p. 209.

52. Ibid. Also, Micheo and J. A. Ciriza, *La existencia campesina* (Caracas: Centro Gumilla, Curso de Formación Sociopolítica 22, 1978), p. 9.

53. Micheo, *La agricultura en Venezuela*, pp. 18–19.

54. On shares of income and social conditions, see Aranda, *La economía venezolana*, p. 220, and Alberto Micheo, *La producción agrícola* (Caracas: Centro Gumilla, Curso de Formación Sociopolítica 13, 1985), p. 7. On land distribution and urban migration, see "Reforma agraria, sirve para incrementar el exodo campesino," *Frontera* (Mérida), June 11, 1981, report on a speech by Dr. Ramón Vicente Casanova, agronomist at the University of the Andes.

55. Powell, *Political Mobilization*, pp. 212–228.

56. On the guerrilla era, I have relied on two relatively disinterested studies: Plaza, *Historia de la lucha armada* and Valsalice, *La guerrilla castrista en Venezuela*. Valsalice is an Italian diplomat writing under a pseudonym, and Plaza's study was sponsored by Jesuit Centro Gumilla.

57. Plaza, *Historia de la lucha armada*, p. 18.

58. Gloria M. Lacava, "Neighborhood Associations in Caracas, 1960–1984" (Paper presented at the Congress of the Latin American Studies Association, Albuquerque, New Mexico, April 18–20, 1985).

59. Ibid., p. 23.

60. Enrique Baloyra and John D. Martz, *Political Attitudes in Venezuela: Societal Cleavages and Political Opinion* (Austin: University of Texas Press, 1975), pp. 185, 211, 213.

61. The letter is reprinted in Alexander, *Rómulo Betancourt*, pp. 601–603.

62. Stuart I. Fagan, "Unionism and Democracy," in *Venezuela: The Democratic Experience*, ed. John Martz and David Myers (New York: Praeger, 1977), pp. 180–181.

63. Betancourt, *Venezuela, Oil and Politics*, pp. 601–603.

64. Asdrúbal Baptista, "Gasto público, ingreso petrolero y distribución de ingreso," (Mérida: Universidad de los Andes, Department of Economics, 1978, mimeo). Data reproduced in Luis Ugalde, *Análisis socio económico*, p. 10.

65. On the consolidation of the party system, see David Blank, *Politics in Venezuela* (Boston: Little, Brown, 1973), pp. 125–183.

CHAPTER 5

1. Sanin (pseud. for Alfredo Torre Murzi), *Venezuela Saudita* (Valencia: Vadell Hermanos, 1978).

2. See Bernard Mommer, *La cuestión petrolera* (Caracas: Fondo Editorial Tropykos, 1988), pp. 219–254. Ramón Rivero (pseud.), *El imperialismo petrolero y la revolución venezolana, tomo 3, La OPEP y las nacionalizaciones: La renta absoluta* (Caracas: Fondo Editorial Salvador de la Plaza, 1979), pp. 276–334. Ricardo Hausmann, *State Landed Property, Oil Rent and Accumulation in Venezuela: An Analysis in Terms of Social Relations* (University of Michigan, Ph.D. dissertation, 1981), pp. 329–426; Luis Pedro Espafna, *Democracia y renta petrolera* (Caracas: Universidad Católica Andrés Bello, 1989).

3. Mommer, *La cuestión petrolera*, pp. 251–154. Rivero, *El imperialismo petrolero*, pp. 343–368. Equipo Proceso Político, *CAP 5 años, un juicio crítico* (Caracas: Editorial Ateneo, 1985), pp. 145–200.

4. In 1979 the real rate of interest on a six-month certificate of deposit was 11 percent in New York but only 7.25 percent in Venezuela. *Latin America Economic Report* (January 12, 1979).

5. See Jennifer McCoy, "The Politics of Adjustment: Labor and the Venezuelan Debt Crisis," *Journal of Interamerican Studies and World Affairs* 4 (Winter 1986–1987):109–111.

6. Inter-American Development Bank (IDB), *Economic and Social Progress in Latin America, 1987 Report* (New York, 1987), pp. 117–126, 406–408.

7. Ramón Espinasa, "El déstino de la renta petrolera, 1974–1986," *Revista SIC*, 50 (February 1987):53–54. *Latin America Weekly Report* (London), March 22, 1990.

8. Leftist politician and former presidential candidate José Vicente Rangel estimated in 1989 that 70 percent of all debt was contracted illegally. See "Un paquete inmoral," *Revista SIC*, 52 (May 1989):188.

9. IDB, *Economic and Social Progress*, p. 463. McCoy, "Politics of Adjustment," pp. 109–111.

10. Ibid. The deterioration of its member nations' bargaining position led to the decision by the Andean Pact nations to lift all restrictions on foreign credit in 1986.

11. On the collapse of reserves, see Eduardo Ortiz, "1986: El año del derrumbe petrolero," *Revista SIC*, 51 (January 1988):8.

12. Miguel Ignacio Purroy, "Bonanza real y crisis financiera," *Revista SIC*, 51 (December 1988):445–447. The economic data for 1988 are provisional estimates in "Vida nacional," *Revista SIC*, 52 (January–February 1989):45. On capital flight, see Hector Valecillos T., "Deuda externa, dolarización y empobrecimiento," *Revista SIC*, 51 (December 1988):448–450.

13. José Ignazcio Cabrujas, *El día que bajaron los cerros* (Caracas: Editorial Ateneo, 1989), p. 12.

14. John Lombardi, *Venezuela, the Search for Order, the Dream of Progress* (New York: Oxford University Press, 1982).

15. Guillermo O'Donnell, "Reflections on the Patterns of Change in the Bureaucratic State," *Latin American Research Review*, 13 (No. 1, 1978):3–38.

16. See Daniel Hellinger, "Populism and Nationalism in Venezuela: New Perspectives on Acción Democrática," *Latin American Perspectives*, 11 (Fall 1984):33–59.

17. Robert Alexander, *Rómulo Betancourt and the Transformation of Venezuela* (New Brunswick, N.J.: Transaction Books, 1982), pp. 511–512. A detailed examination of this process is Miguel Ignacio Purroy, *Estado e industrialización en Venezuela* (Valencia: Vadell Hermanos, 1982), pp. 179–255.

18. Cited in Purroy, *Estado e industrialización*, p. 262.

19. Ibid., p. 292.

20. Ibid., p. 260.

21. Ibid., p. 264. See also Terry Karl, *The Political Economy of Petrodollars*, vols. 1 and 2 (Ph.D. dissertation, Stanford University, 1982). Pedro Duño, *Los*

doce apóstoles (Valencia: Vadell Hermanos, 1975). Equipo Proceso Político, *CAP 5 años: Un juicio crítico*. Fernando Coronil and Julie Skurski, "Reproducing Dependency: Auto Industry Policy and Petrodollar Circulation in Venezuela," *International Organization*, 36 (Winter 1982):61–94.

22. This analysis, unless otherwise indicated, draws heavily upon Karl, *The Political Economy of Petrodollars*, for political developments and upon Purroy, *Estado e industrialización*, pp. 256–304, for economic trends. On labor, see Jennifer McCoy, "Democratic Dependent Development and State-Labor Relations in Venezuela," (University of Minnesota, Ph.D. dissertation, 1985).

23. For a comparison of Plans IV and V, see Purroy, *Estado e industrialización*, pp. 276–284.

24. *El Universal* (Caracas), June 3, 1985.

25. Central Bank data cited in Sergio Bitar and Eduardo Tronconso, *El desafío industrial de Venezuela* (Caracas: Editorial Pomaire, 1983), pp. 257, 259.

26. Virtually all trade union officials and journalists interviewed by me in Ciudad Guayana in the summers of 1985 and 1988 expressed this view, and several named specific individuals and cases. It was repeated by the Rector of the Central University in Caracas, a representative of the Archdiocese of Caracas, the labor correspondent for *Revista SIC*, and other participants at a labor forum in Caracas, July 26, 1988, called to discuss a conflict at HEVENSA in Guayana. (See Chapter 6.)

27. Economic Commission on Latin America, *La distribución del ingreso en América Latina* (New York: United Nations, 1970), Graph IV.

28. On infant mortality, see a report by Venezuelan pediatricians, "Epidemiología y Estadística Vital," cited in Michel Chossudovsky, *La miseria en Venezuela* (Valencia: Vadell Hermanos, 1977), p. 125. Chossudovsky's book details extensively the inequalities in Venezuela in the early 1970s. For later years, see Norelis Betancourt and Arturo Sosa A., *Realidad Social de Venezuela* (Caracas: Centro Gumilla, Curso de Formación Sociopolítica 6, 1985).

29. On taxes, see "International Series: Venezuela" (New York: Ernst and Whinney, Inc., March 1984).

30. Alan Riding, *New York Times*, December 10, 1978, IV, p. 2, and Everett G. Martin, *Wall Street Journal*, February 3, 1981, p. 3, respectively.

31. Census data reported in Betancourt and Sosa, *Realidad social*, p. 21. A partisan but well-documented study of unemployment, wages, and prices was published by COPEI's Centro de Documentación y Análisis para los Trabajadores (CENDA). See "Indicadores para el análisis de la realidad nacional, perspectiva de los trabajadores" (Caracas: Mimeo, January 1988).

32. Miguel Ignacio Purroy, "Medio siglo de industrialización," *Revista SIC*, 50 (November–December 1987):484.

33. Banco Central, *Informe económico*, (1977, 1978, 1980, respectively).

34. John Sweeney, "Aluminum Update: CVG Group Announces Two New Smelters," *VenEconomy Monthly* (March 1988):14–16.

35. Miguel Ignacio Purroy, "Interrogantes sobre la expansión del aluminio," *Revista SIC*, 52 (November 1989):395.

36. Charles Ameringer, "The Foreign Policy of Venezuelan Democracy," pp. 336–348 in *Venezuela, the Democratic Experience*, ed. John Martz and David Myers, (New York: Praeger, 1977).

37. In February 1977, the Venezuelan press carried reports that the U.S. Senate Select Committee on Intelligence Activities had identified Andrés Pérez, who was Betancourt's Minister of the Interior, as a recipient of payments from the CIA. España, "30 años de 'Vida Nacional'," *Revista SIC*, 50 (December 1987):568.

38. Judith Ewell, "Debt and Politics in Venezuela," *Current History*, 88 (March 1988):123. The bombing is described in Edward S. Herman, *The Real Terror Network* (Boston: South End Press, 1982), pp. 68–69.

39. "Venezuelan President Asked to Pressure Nicaraguan Government by U.S." and "Former Presidents Carter and Ford to Head Committee to Monitor May 7 Panamanian Presidential Elections," *Central America Update* (Latin American Institute, University of Minnesota, March 31 and April 5, 1989). On military exercises, see Lars Shoultz, *National Security and United States Policy* (Princeton: Princeton University Press, 1987), p. 182.

40. The basic outlines of these disputes are described by Carlos A. Romero, *Política exterior de Venezuela* (Caracas: Centro Gumilla, Curso de Formación Sociopolítica, 24, 1984). See also Jacqueline Anne Braveboy-Wagner, *The Venezuelan Guyana Border Dispute: Britain's Colonial Legacy in Latin America* (Boulder, Colo.: Westview Press, 1984).

41. Coronil and Skurski, "Reproducing Dependency," pp. 61–94.

42. See the summary of the scandal in *Revista SIC*, 51 (November 1988):390.

43. Karl, *The Petroleum Economy*, pp. 444–496.

44. *Latin America Economic Report* (December 15, 1978); *El Nacional* (Caracas), June 4 and 10, 1978.

45. Ada Urribarri, "Gonzalo Barrios siempre creyó que Ciliberto se entregaría," *El Nacional*, Caracas (July 16, 1990), D1.

46. Direct expenditures by the central government as a percentage of all public expenditures (including those by state and local governments, state enterprises, foundations, etc.) fell from 70 percent in 1960 to 48 percent in 1970, and then to 28 percent by 1975. Purroy, *Estado e industrialización*, pp. 274–280; Banco Central de Venezuela, *Anuario de cuentas nacionales, 1984* (Caracas), p. 84.

47. Janet Kelly de Escobar, "Las empresas del estado: Del lugar común al sentido común," pp. 124–125, 131–143 in *El caso Venezuela, una ilusión de armonía*, ed. Moisés Naím and Ramón Piñango (Caracas: Ediciones IESA, 1985).

48. Kelly de Escobar, "Las empresas del estado," p. 125.

49. Moisés Naím, "La empresa privada en Venezuela: ¿Qué pasa cuando se crece en medio de la riqueza y la confusión?" pp. 152–182 in *El caso venezolano*. ed. Naím and Pinango.

50. Ibid.

51. Héctor Valecillos T., "Crisis económica y responsabilidad social del empresario," *Revista SIC*, 47 (May 1984):199.

52. Typical of this genre is Aníbal Romero, *La miseria del populismo: Mitos y realidades de la democracia en Venezuela* (Caracas: Ediciones Centauro, 1987).

Marcel Granier, closely associated with *Grupo Roraima* and the Cisneros family, is a television journalist and author who has done much to popularize this perspective.

53. Bernard Mommer and Ramón Espinasa, "Política petrolera: Una polémica necesaria," *Revista SIC*, 53 (August 1990): 292–294.

54. Interview with Bernard Mommer, Caracas, July 27, 1990.

55. Jennifer McCoy, "Labor and the State in a Party-Mediated Democracy," *Latin American Research Review*, 24 (No. 2, 1985):35–68. On wages, see Betancourt and Sosa, *Realidad social*, p. 18. Real wages were relatively stable in 1985.

56. Carlos Andrés Pérez, *Manos a la Obra* (Caracas: Textos de Mensajes, Discursos y Declaraciones del Presidente de la República, Ediciones de la Presidencia de la República, Tomo I, vol. 2, 1977), p. 14.

57. Héctor Valecillos, "La dinámica de la población y del empleo in la Venezuela del siglo XX," p. 54 in *El caso Venezuela*, ed. Naím and Piñango.

58. World Bank, *World Development Report 1984* (New York: Oxford University Press), Tables 19 and 20.

59. Ibid., Table 20.

60. Valecillos, "La dinámica de la población," passim.

61. Carolina Oteyza, "La mujer del barrio," *Revista SIC*, 52 (June 1989):218–219.

62. On food prices, see *El Nacional* (Caracas), July 9, 1988. Information on *buhoneros* was obtained from dozens of informal interviews in June and July 1988 and from a formal interview with two leaders of independent *buhonero* organizations in Ciudad Guayana on June 29, 1988. On the problems of organizing women in the *barrios*, see Oteyza, "La mujer del barrio," pp. 218–219, and María Fernanda Mujica R., "El trabajo las une y las independiza," *Revista SIC*, 52 (March 1989):104–106.

63. Inocencia Orellana y Diana Vegas, "La mujer y la democracia," *Revista SIC*, 52 (March 1989):100–103.

64. Ibid.

65. Based on list of elected senators and deputies in *El Universal* (Caracas), December 10, 1988.

66. *Daily Journal* (Caracas), October 31, 1988.

67. See the summary of various studies in Daniel Hellinger, "Venezuelan Immigration Policy and Politics," in *The Gatekeepers, Comparative Immigration Policy*, ed. Michael C. LeMay (New York: Praeger, 1989), pp. 177–183.

68. Ibid. A. Pinto, "Undocumented and Illegally Resident Migrant Women in Venezuela," *International Migration*, 19 (Nos. 1 and 2, 1981):241–262. Gabriel Gidegain Greising and Anitza Freitez Landaeta, "Los colombianos en Venezuela," *Revista SIC*, 52 (June 1989):212–215.

69. The study and the quotation are cited in Marcelino Bisbal, "Venevisión: Twenty five years, more and better television," *Revista SIC*, 49 (May 1986):214–215.

70. Ibid.

71. Paul Henley, *The Panare, Tradition and Change on the Amazonian Frontier* (New Haven, Conn.: Yale University Press, 1982).

72. Ibid., p. 231.

CHAPTER 6

1. For example, see Arturo Sosa A., "De ésta a otra democracia," *Revista SIC*, 50 (November 1987):504–509 and "Autoritarismo o democracia: Dilema de Sistema político venezolano," *Revista SIC*, 52 (July 1989):246–248.

2. For example, see Aníbal Romero, *La miseria del populismo* (Caracas: Ediciones Centauro, 1987).

3. In 1988, the Supreme Electoral Council nearly separated the presidential and congressional ballots, but at the last moment AD and COPEI gained the additional vote needed to defeat the measure.

4. Diego Bautista Urbaneja, "El sistema político, o cómo funciona la máquina de procesar decisiones," in *El caso Venezuela, una ilusión del harmonía*, ed. Moíses Naím and Ramón Piñango, (Caracas: IESA, 1985), p. 235.

5. These operations are often assigned colorful names. For example, one AD effort in a district was called "Operation Fly," so COPEI countered with "Operation DDT." See José Virtuoso y Gustavo Albarran, "Observando el proceso electoral," *Revista SIC*, 52 (January–December 1989):16–17.

6. D. A. Rangel, *Los mercadores del voto* (Valencia: Vadell Hermanos, 1978), pp. 120–121.

7. Ibid.

8. In one survey carried out in that year, 50 percent of respondents indicated that they would not vote were they not obligated by law to do so. See Enrique Baloyra and John Martz, *Political Attitudes in Venezuela* (Austin: University of Texas Press, 1979), p. 215.

9. For various analyses of abstentionism, see *El Nacional* (Caracas), December 13; *Revista SIC*, 52 (January–February 1989) and 53 (January–February 1990).

10. *The Daily Journal* (Caracas), October 31, 1988.

11. Tomás Eloy Martínez, "Radio, prensa, y televisión: Entre el equilibrio y el estancamiento," p. 315, in *El caso Venezolano*, ed. Naím and Piñango.

12. Specifically, there were allegations that votes were shifted to ensure that one or another important person on the list of a *plancha* achieved election but without changing the overall distribution of seats among the parties. See Arturo Sosa A., "Las elecciones de 1988," *Revista SIC*, 52 (January–February 1989):9–10. An example from one district is published in "Vida Nacional" *Revista SIC*, 53 (January–February 1990):25.

13. For example, Simón Sáez Mérida, former secretary general of the MIR, claims that he resigned from the party because it accepted contributions from COPEI, which hoped that the left would drain votes away from AD. See Asociación Venezolano de Derecho Tributario, *La corrupción en Venezuela* (Valencia: Vadell Hermanos, 1983), pp. 97–98.

14. The high figure is from Sosa, "Las elecciones de 1988," pp. 9–10. The lower estimate is from Leopoldo Linares, "¿Vale la pena votar en diciembre?" *Revista SIC*, 51 (November 1988):389.

15. For a favorable view of MAS, see Steven Ellner, *Venezuela's Movimiento al Socialismo: From Guerrilla Defeat to Innovative Politics* (Durham, N.C.: Duke University Press, 1988).

16. Based on interviews in Ciudad Guayana, Caracas, Mérida, and Barquisimeto, summers of 1985, 1988, and 1990.

17. *Revista SIC*, 51 (May 1988):194.

18. *Revista SIC*, 51 (December 1988):457.

19. For accounts of Amparo, see "Massacre of Venezuelan Fishermen," a report by the Justice and Peace Commision of the Venezuelan Conference of Religious Congregations, the Support Network for Peace and Justice, the Maryknoll Missioners of Venezuela, the Federation of Families of the Disappeared, and the Latin American Foundation for Human Rights, December 29, 1988. Foreign Broadcast Information Service, reports from October 30 to November 5, 1988. *Revista SIC*, 51 (December 1988), with follow-ups in subsequent issues through June 1989. On the investigation of MAS Deputy Walter Márquez, see Alba Sánchez, "Márquez: El Amparo hubo homicidio intencional," *El Nacional* (Caracas), December 10, 1988. Two other highly suspicious incidents in which security forces wiped out alleged guerrilla forces without taking casualties and under other suspicious circumstances (e.g., "captured" weapons laden with rust) took place on October 4 in Cantaura and in May 1986 in the state of Yaracuy. Four other alleged battles in Apure in 1988 produced thirteen dead "guerrillas" and no admitted military casualties.

20. See, for example, "Ordenan desalojo de 200 familias en región apureña," *El Nacional* (Caracas), July 1, 1988.

21. In June 1987, nine Venezuelan soldiers were killed by drug smugglers in Perija, an incident that many suspect was related to military involvement in drug smuggling. The government refused to permit an independent investigation. See *Revista SIC*, 50 (July–August 1987):309. On Brazilian miners, see *Revista SIC*, 52 (June 1989):127. On the guerrilla *foco* in Anzoátegui, see "Resurgen las guerrillas en Anzoátegui," an eye witness report by the highly respected reporter Roberto Giusti, *El Nacional* (Caracas), July 6, 1989, which includes a photo of a guerrilla training camp.

22. José Vicente Rangel, *Los 'perros de la guerra' y el 'secreto militar' en Venezuela* (Caracas: Ediciones Centauro, 1988).

23. Military expenditures in Venezuela have jumped while falling elsewhere. "América latina redujó los gastos militares," (Central America Resource Network, August 23, 1989). On discontent over the promotion process, see *El Nacional*, (Caracas) July 2 and 3, 1988; Alfredo Alvarez, "General de Brigada (AV) Gaviria Valero, La política y la corrupción amenazan institucionalidad de las FAN," *El Nacional*, July 3, 1988.

24. See Arturo Sosa A., "¿Qué fue lo que pasó?" *Revista SIC*, 52 (April 1989):104.

25. *Amnesty International Report, 1987* (London), p. 142.

26. Ibid.

27. In contrast, Amnesty International's 1987 report asserted that at least 600 people were imprisoned in Cuba for political reasons, of which twelve were

considered "prisoners of conscience." See also *Human Rights in Cuba, The Need to Sustain the Pressure* (New York: Americas Watch, 1989). Americas Watch has not issued a recent report on Venezuela.

28. On Amparo, see *Revista SIC*, 52 (May 1989):181–182. On the Amnesty International telegram, see the Reuters report in *The New York Times*, March 12, 1989. The other developments are reviewed by Judith Ewell, "Debt and Politics," *Current History*, 88 (March 1988):123–148.

29. Reprinted in *Revista SIC*, 51 (January 1988).

30. This account of the struggle in El Carmen is based on interviews conducted in 1981 and 1989 with students and residents.

31. See Gloria Lacava, "Neighborhood Associations in Caracas, 1960–1984," (Paper delivered at the Meeting of the Latin American Studies Association, Albuquerque, New Mexico, April 1985).

32. Ibid.

33. Bautista Urbaneja, "El sistema político," p. 245.

34. José Virtuoso, "Desafíos pastorales," pp. 80–81.

35. *Revista SIC*, 52 (June 1989):217. Interviews with Luis Miguel Abad, a leader in the *Movimiento Vecinal del Estado Lara* (MOVEL), Barquisimeto, July 1985 and June 1988.

36. See Alberto Micheo, "El Negro Miguel," *Revista SIC*, 52 (May 1989):32–34; Julio Mora Contreras, "¿Quién se beneficia? Los desconocidos 'logros' del 'milagro agricola'," *Revista SIC*, 51 (May 1988):201–203.

37. See *El Nacional*, May 30, 1985. On the economic background to the dispute, see Alberto Micheo, "FONCAFE: La mejor defensa, el ataque," *Revista SIC*, 50 (February 1987):61–62.

38. Alberto Micheo, "La lucha está en el puente," *Revista SIC*, 51 (April 1988):156–159.

39. *La Frontera* (Mérida), July 4, 1988.

40. Alberto Micheo, "La Corte que no es Suprema," *Revista SIC*, 52 (March 1989):75–77.

41. In 1985 and 1986 alone, there were 94,464 applications for 42,015 places. See Ingrid Catellanos, "La prueba de aptitud esta en el banquillo de los acusados," *El Diario de Caracas*, June 24, 1988. On percentage graduating, see Javier Dupla, *La educación en Venezuela* (Caracas: Curso de Formación Sociopolítica 25, 1983), p. 425. Student organizations claim that there are 200,000 fewer places than needed to meet the demand.

42. On the professors' strike of 1986, see the "Vida Nacional" column in *Revista SIC*, 49 (July–August and September–October 1986).

43. The account of events in Mérida is derived from "El mercado principal de Mérida," *Reportaje* (Mérida, Fall 1987); from accounts in *El Nacional* and *El Diario* (Caracas) and in *Frontera* (Mérida), July 1 through 14, 1988; from interviews with several merchants, students, members of ERA Agricula (an alternative technology research co-operative), and an activist of CESAP (the church-affiliated Centers of Education and Service for Popular Action).

44. Bernard Lestienne, *El sindicalismo Venezolano* (Caracas: Centro Gumilla, Curso de Formación Sociopolítica 26, 1981), pp. 12–14.

45. *El Nacional,* June 19, 1985.

46. "La prepotente democracia sindical," *Revista SIC,* 45 (March 1982):107.

47. Kenneth Coleman, "La politización de la clase obrera: Datos comparativos y el caso venezolano," *Revista Relaciones de Trabajo,* 6 (September 1985):145–167, and Coleman and Charles L. Davis, "Labor and the State: Union Incorporation and Working-Class Politicization in Latin America," *Comparative Political Studies,* 18 (January 1986):395–417.

48. See José Arrieta, "Análisis del conflicto textil" and the round table discussion of labor leaders, "Textiles: Oportunismo, politiquería y demogogia," both in *Revista SIC,* 43 (September–October 1980):340–343. Also Ernesto Herrera and Santa Durand, "Toma de la catedral: Los obreros textiles responden," *Esfuerzo,* 9 (February–March 1980):4–7. Daniel Hellinger, "Venezuela and the Challenge of Nuevo Sindicalismo" (Paper for the Meeting of the Latin American Studies Association, Boston, Mass., October 23–25, 1987). The studies by Coleman and by Coleman and Davis (see Note 47) indicate that "classist" leaders often operated in a style little different from the AD and COPEI leaders.

49. Census figures reported in Rosanna Jiménez, "Hablan los Matanceros," *Cuadernos de la letra R,* (No. 1, April 1979).

50. *Revista SIC,* 52 (March 1989):72.

51. Jiménez, "Hablan los matanceros." José Arrieta, "¿Por qué intervinieron a SUTISS?" *Revista SIC,* 44 (December 1981):458–460 and "La prepotente democracia sindical," *Revista SIC,* 45 (March 1982), and Orlando Villalobos, "¿La zona del hierro: Un nuevo movimiento sindical?" *Esfuerzo,* 4 (February–March, 1980):16–18. For a more complete account of labor struggles in Guayana, see Daniel Hellinger, "Venezuelan Democracy and the Challenge of the *Nuevo Sindicalismo.*"

52. José Arrieta, "Elecciones en SIDOR: La reconquista de SUTISS," *Revista SIC,* 50 (October 1987):455–456. Carmen Carrillo, "La Causa R ganó elecciones en SUTISS," *El Diario de Caracas,* August 28, 1987.

53. Charles Bergquist, *Labor in Latin America* (Stanford, Calif.: Stanford University Press, 1986), pp. 191–273.

54. Jennifer McCoy, "Labor and the State in Venezuela," *Latin American Research Review,* 24 (No. 2, 1989):59–61.

55. Interview, Toto Rodríguez, labor correspondent, *El Pueblo de Guayana,* June 1988. The METALCREDITO operation was denounced by the National Executive Committee of AD on March 11, 1985.

56. According to three CORALUM workers interviewed by the author in June 1988 during the course of the dispute. One of the three workers suddenly dropped out of the struggle the day after my first interview. His companions informed me that he had accepted an offer from AD to be flown to Caracas for labor education.

57. Carlos Eduardo Febres, "¿El movimiento sindical, actor social o gestor institucional?" pp. 306–307, in *El caso Venezuela,* ed. Naím and Piñango.

58. For a summary of the dispute, see José Arrieta, "Hevensa: Siete meses en defensa de la legalidad," *Revista SIC,* 48 (February 1985):78 and Hellinger, "Venezuelan Democracy and the Challenge of the *Nuevo Sindicalismo.*"

59. *El Nacional*, June 13, 1985.

60. See José Arrieta, "La CTV toma el paso: Congreso y Paro," *Revista SIC*, 52 (June 1989):196–199. Later in 1989, Delpino resigned; he was succeeded by Antonio Rios, head of AD's Labor Bureau.

61. Reports from *Excelsior* (Mexico City) summarized in *Monthly Foreign Press Digest, Latin American News Update*, (Chicago), March 1990. "Tasa de desempleo subió a 10.9 porciento," *El Nacional*, July 26, 1990, p. 1.

62. Rafael Nuñez, "CTV rechazó puntos de Ley del Trabajo," *El Nacional*, June 10, 1990. "Posición del Sindicato de Artes Graficos y de Sindicato de Trabajadores de La Prensa ante el projecto de Ley de Trabajo: Aquí estń las propuestas para mejores de Ley del Trabajo," advertisement, *El Nacional*, July 8, 1990. For a business view, see John Sweeney and Rita Funaro, "Labor Law: Common Sense vs. Populism," *VenEconomy Monthly*, 7 (No. 8, May 1990).

CHAPTER 7

1. Roberto Giusti, "El show debe concluir" in *El día que bajaron los cerros* (Caracas: Editorial Ateneo de Caracas, 1989), p. 19. My description of the inauguration is taken from this account by reporters for *El Nacional* (Caracas) of events between the election and February 27.

2. Ibid.

3. See, for example, the comments cited by Alan Riding, "Rumblings in Venezuela," *New York Times*, March 2, 1989.

4. For various accounts of the explosion, see *El día que bajaron los cerros*; *Revista SIC*, 52 (April and May, respectively, 1989); Miriam Kornblith, "Deuda y democracia en Venezuela: Los sucesos del 27 y 28 de febrero" (Paper presented at the Meeting of the Latin American Studies Association, Miami, Florida, December 1989). Ironically, Mérida escaped violence because a curfew had already been declared after protests earlier in the week.

5. The phases are described in Arturo Sosa A., "¿Que fue lo que paso?" *Revista SIC*, 52 (May 1989):101–106.

6. See accounts of witnesses in some neighborhoods most affected by the violence, "Testimonios," *Revista SIC*, 52 (April 1989):111–117.

7. Julie Skurski, "Bloody Riots Hit Caracas Price Hikes," *Guardian* (New York), March 15, 1989.

8. "Scandal Grows over Cheap-Rate Dollars," *Latin American Weekly Report*, June 15, 1989, p. 5.

9. "Inteligencia y concertación," *Revista SIC*, 52 (May 1989):168.

10. Kim Fuad, "All Eyes on the Latest Pérez Style," *Hemisphile* (May 1990), p. 3, claims that when Pérez took office, "his only option was a shock program."

11. "CAP Now Turns on Interest Rates," *Latin American Weekly Report* (London) June 22, 1989, p. 9.

12. "Scandal Grows," p. 5.

13. On milk, see John Sweeney, "Rising Tensions Fuel Coup Rumors," *VenEconomy*, 7 (No. 8, May 1990), p. 9. On gasoline and transport, see, for example, Elides Rojas, "Se radicaliza conflicto del transporte en Lara," and

"Saquean negocios en Maracaibo por segundo día de distyurbios," *El Nacional*, June 22 and July 27, 1990.

14. *Revista SIC*, 53 (July 1990):242–243.

15. Sweeney, "Rising Tensions Fuel Coup Rumors," p. 9.

16. "Oil Boom Fails to Balance the Books," *Latin America Weekly Report* (London) November 8, 1990, p. 9.

17. Address to conference, *"Si Hay Salida,"* Caracas, July 24, 1990.

About the Book and Author

In 1988 Venezuela marked the thirteenth anniversary of its first experiment with electoral democracy; few other Latin American countries could boast so long a period of stable, civilian rule. Then on February 27, 1989, the country was wracked by widespread rioting that caused hundreds of deaths in cities all over the country. Suddenly, the stability of oil-rich Venezuela could no longer be taken for granted.

Before 1958, Venezuela, birthplace of Simón Bolívar and the struggle for Latin American independence, had never witnessed the successful transfer of power from one elected president to another. The nation had experienced two of Latin America's most brutal military dictatorships in this century. But political change was inevitable, given the vast social and economic changes set in motion by the oil boom that commenced in 1922. The capital city of Caracas was at that time a quiet settlement of 92,000 people nestled in a lush, tropical valley where the Andes meet the Caribbean. Today it is a sprawling and polluted metropolis of four million, home to many Europeans and Latin Americans who immigrated after World War II. With the massive infusion of petrodollars came an invasion of North American consumer goods and culture, challenging the "creole" culture, a blend of Caribbean, *llanos* (plains), and Andean traditions. The collapse of oil prices and a staggering international debt have triggered disillusionment with the current political and economic model. This situation has triggered a debate, the author shows, between those who want to limit democracy and those who want to enhance and extend it.

Dr. Hellinger provides a balanced assessment of one of the region's most interesting countries. His economic and political history is supplemented by a lively commentary on Venezuela's rich cultural heritage and a broad overview of the emergence of new social movements and agendas in areas such as educational reform, labor, environmental protection, women's issues, and immigration policies. Finally, the author examines Venezuela's influence in hemispheric and world affairs, including its role as a founder of OPEC.

Daniel C. Hellinger is professor of political science at Webster University.

Index